Proceedings of the Boston Area Colloquium in Ancient Philosophy

Proceedings of the Boston Area Colloquium in Ancient Philosophy

VOLUME XXXV

Edited by

Gary M. Gurtler, S.J.
Daniel P. Maher

BRILL

LEIDEN | BOSTON

This hardback is also published in paperback under ISBN 978-90-04-43857-6.

Typeface for the Latin, Greek, and Cyrillic scripts: "Brill". See and download: brill.com/brill-typeface.

ISSN 1059-986X
ISBN 978-90-04-43858-3

Copyright 2020 by Koninklijke Brill NV, Leiden, The Netherlands.
Koninklijke Brill NV incorporates the imprints Brill, Brill Hes & De Graaf, Brill Nijhoff, Brill Rodopi, Brill Sense, Hotei Publishing, mentis Verlag, Verlag Ferdinand Schöningh and Wilhelm Fink Verlag.
All rights reserved. No part of this publication may be reproduced, translated, stored in a retrieval system, or transmitted in any form or by any means, electronic, mechanical, photocopying, recording or otherwise, without prior written permission from the publisher. Requests for re-use and/or translations must be addressed to Koninklijke Brill NV via brill.com or copyright.com.

This book is printed on acid-free paper and produced in a sustainable manner.

Contents

Preface VII

Notes on Contributors x

COLLOQUIUM 1

The Authorship of the Pseudo-Simplician Neoplatonic Commentary on the *De Anima* 1

   Gary Gabor

Commentary on Gabor 23

   Dana Miller

Gabor/Miller Bibliography 28

COLLOQUIUM 2

How to Argue about Aristotle about Practical Reason 31

   Giles Pearson

Commentary on Pearson 59

   Howard J. Curzer

Pearson/Curzer Bibliography 68

COLLOQUIUM 3

Questioning Aristotle's Radical Account of Σωφροσύνη 73

   Christopher Moore

Commentary on Moore 98

   Jesse Bailey

Moore/Bailey Bibliography 103

COLLOQUIUM 4

Mythological Sources of Oblivion and Memory 105

   Diego S. Garrocho

Commentary on Garrocho 121

   Santiago Ramos

Garrocho/Ramos Bibliography 130

COLLOQUIUM 5
Final Causality without Teleology in Aristotle's Ontology of Life 133
Francisco J. Gonzalez
Commentary on Gonzalez 173
Brian Julian
Gonzalez/Julian Bibliography 178

Index of Names 181

Preface

Volume 35 comprises five papers, each paired with a commentary, presented to the Boston Area Colloquium in Ancient Philosophy during academic year 2018–19. Three papers concentrate primarily on Aristotle, one addresses whether a Neoplatonic commentary on Aristotle's *De Anima* is properly attributed to Simplicius, and another explores the mythological themes of memory and oblivion in a range of classical sources.

Gary Gabor advances new arguments in favor of the traditional ascription of the Neoplatonic Commentary on *De Anima* to Simplicius, countering recent attribution to Priscian of Lydia. He appeals to the presence in the text of uniquely Simplician interpretive procedures, especially the mode of harmonizing differences between Plato and Aristotle. While Gabor seeks to secure the traditional attribution, the commentary by Dana Miller cautions against certainty in such matters, relying on the credibility of evidence in weighing such issues.

Giles Pearson examines Aristotle's thinking about practical reason with contemporary understandings of the so-called Humean theory of motivation, which involves both a cognitive dimension and an ineliminable non-cognitive dimension in desire. Although he reads Aristotle as defending at least an explanatory role for cognition at the basis of desires and thus as tending toward an anti-Humean theory, he regards the issue as unsettled. Howard J. Curzer supports Pearson's reading and argues more generally in favor of the claim that for Aristotle the goals of action are specified sometimes by reason, sometimes by desire, and sometimes by both.

Christopher Moore maintains that Aristotle's interpretation of σωφροσύνη in *NE* 3.10–12 as focused narrowly on the pleasures of touch and taste contrasts with the much broader range of meanings that appear in contemporaneous Greek literary and philosophical sources, especially Plato's *Charmides*. Jesse Bailey endorses the line of argument begun by Moore and urges its extension in light of the dialectical structure of the whole *Nicomachean Ethics*. Bailey claims this will reveal that Aristotle's account of the virtues in *NE* 3 is incomplete, especially in terms of his discussion in *NE* 6.

Diego S. Garrocho explores the essential interconnections between the several forms of memory and forgetting in the literary, philosophical, and mythological sources of ancient Greece and, consequently, in our cultural life to the present day. Naturally, the tradition emphasizes the association of memory with knowledge, but it is crucial to recognize that oblivion too is sometimes necessary and justified. Santiago Ramos wonders whether Garrocho has presupposed too much historical continuity between the mythical and the philosophical conceptions of memory and oblivion.

Francisco J. Gonzalez aims first to clarify Aristotle's account of final causality by distinguishing it from the teleology rejected by modern natural science and second to propose that the ontology of living organisms provides the proper context for understanding Aristotle's sense of final causality. Brian Julian argues in the opposite direction that Aristotle's account of final causes sheds scant light on contemporary concerns because, even if we grant that living organisms have ends, those ends are not genuine causes and they do not explain what we observe in living things.

The order of publication in this volume follows the order in which the several colloquia occurred at the participating schools in the Boston Area Colloquium in Ancient Philosophy: Boston College, the College of the Holy Cross, St. Anselm College, and Assumption University. By publishing the paper together with the commentary, we hope to preserve an essential element of the dialogical character of the colloquia. The primary authors had feedback from the commentators, the audience, and outside reviewers in revising their papers for publication, and the commentators had similar feedback and a look at the revised papers to adjust their commentaries. The editors are grateful to the following scholars for their generous and careful review of the manuscripts: Erica Holberg, Monte Johnson, Kathryn Lindeman, Jan Opsomer, and Anne-Marie Schultz.

At the end of the volume, together with the section 'About our Contributors,' readers will find a general index of names collated by our editorial assistant, Lydia Winn.

In conclusion, I would like to thank my co-editor, Gary M. Gurtler, S.J., who invited me to share in the work of editing these proceedings beginning with last year's volume. At many points along the way, his judgment and guidance have led to significant improvements, for which he will not get the credit he deserves. As all the contributors to this volume know, we are greatly indebted to our editorial assistant, Lydia Winn, whose careful eye improved every page of this volume and who is unfailingly professional, prompt, meticulous, and cheerful.

This year I am pleased to write this preface and express my appreciation for the privilege of being directly involved in the publication process, which brings many months of work by many people to satisfying completion. Our colleagues on the BACAP committee, directed by May Sim, have invited and evaluated proposals, selected contributors and commentators, and managed the logistical details of campus visits. Without their work and cooperative labors, the colloquia and this volume would not come to pass. I also thank the speakers and commentators whose visits enlivened our campuses and whose contributions to this volume preserve and deepen the rich tradition of the Boston Area Colloquium in Ancient Philosophy. Finally, the administrations of the four participating schools have provided financial support that makes the campus colloquia possible, and we draw special attention to the administration of Boston College for generously sponsoring the publication of this volume and thereby expanding the footprint of BACAP and enabling many others to participate in these colloquia.

Daniel P. Maher
Assumption University

Notes on Contributors

Jesse Bailey

got his Ph.D. in Philosophy from Penn State University after getting his MA from St. John's College Santa Fe and his B.A. at UT Austin. His recent book, *Logos and Psyche in the Phaedo*, offers an original interpretation of Plato's *Phaedo*. The focus of the book is an exploration of the relation between *logos* and the soul. The goal is to understand the ethical and political dimensions of philosophy as "care of the soul." In addition to ancient Greek philosophy, he has also published widely, including work on Heidegger, Emerson, Augustine, and Plotinus.

Howard J. Curzer

received his Ph.D. from the University of Texas at Austin and his M.A. and B.A. in Mathematics from Wesleyan. He is a Professor of Philosophy at Texas Tech University. His publications include a book entitled *Aristotle and the Virtues* (Oxford, 2012), a textbook/anthology entitled *Ethical Theory and Moral Problems* (Wadsworth, 1999), and articles on ancient philosophy, contemporary virtue ethics, the Confucian tradition, moral development, research ethics, biomedical ethics, the ethics of care, and the Hebrew Bible. He co-edited a special issue of the ILAR Journal (2013) (a journal of the National Academy of Sciences), and has written Bible commentary for the Huffington Post.

Gary Gabor

received his Ph.D. in Philosophy from Fordham University in 2011. He received a Fulbright Fellowship to the University of Leuven, Belgium, for 2009–2010. He is a member of the Board of Directors for the International Society for Neoplatonic Studies. From 20012–2018, he was Assistant then Associate Professor of Philosophy at Hamline University in St. Paul, MN. He is currently a financial advisor at Ameriprise Financial.

Diego S. Garrocho

teaches ethics and political philosophy at Universidad Autónoma de Madrid. He has been a visiting researcher at Boston College, Massachusetts Institute of Technology, and Johns Hopkins University. He has published *Aristóteles. Una ética de las pasiones* (Avarigani, 2015) and *Sobre la Nostalgia* (Alianza Editorial, 2019). His work is mainly focused on the contemporary treatment of ancient thought.

Francisco J. Gonzalez

is Professor of Philosophy at the University of Ottawa. He received his M.A. and Ph.D. from the University of Toronto. He has published in the areas of ancient philosophy and contemporary continental philosophy. Publications include *Dialectic and Dialogue: Plato's Practice of Philosophical Inquiry* (Northwestern, 1998) and *Plato and Heidegger: A Question of Dialogue* (Penn State, 2009). He is currently working on Heidegger's reading of Aristotle in published and unpublished seminars as well as on Aristotle's metaphysics and biology.

Brian Julian

teaches philosophy at Boston College and Boston University. He received his B.A. from Gutenberg College and his Ph.D. from Boston University. He has published an article discussing Aristotle's argument in the *De Anima* for the definition of soul. His research focuses on Aristotle's account of soul and its relationship to his biology.

Dana Miller

is Associate Professor of Philosophy at Fordham University. He received his Ph.D. in Classical Philosophy at Harvard University. He has published on Plato's cosmology, metaphysics, and theory of rhetoric as well as on Aristotle's theory of productive reasoning. He is now working on parallels in Aristotle's *De Sensu* with contemporary debates in the philosophy of perception.

Christopher Moore

is Associate Professor of Philosophy and Classics at Penn State, having previously taught at Skidmore College and the University of Texas at Austin. His degrees are from Dartmouth College and University of Minnesota. In addition to many articles and chapters, he has written *Socrates and Self-Knowledge* (Cambridge, 2015) and *Calling Philosophers Names: on the Origin of a Discipline* (Princeton, 2019), edited *Brill's Companion to the Reception of Socrates* (Brill, 2019), co-edited *Socrates and the Socratic Dialogue* (Brill, 2018), and co-written and co-translated *Plato's* Charmides: *A Translation with Introduction, Notes, and Analysis* (Hackett, 2019).

Giles Pearson

is Senior Lecturer in Philosophy at the University of Bristol. His published work thus far has primarily focused on Aristotle's moral philosophy and philosophical psychology, although he has also published on Plato and on contemporary metaethics. He has published two books: a monograph, *Aristotle on*

Desire (Cambridge University Press, 2012) and an edited book, co-edited with Michael Pakaluk, *Moral Psychology and Human Action in Aristotle* (Oxford University Press, 2011). He is currently at work on a third book on Aristotle on the emotions.

Santiago Ramos

teaches philosophy at Boston College. He has published articles on Plato, Kant, and the philosophy of tragedy and beauty. He studied at Boston College, Georgetown, and Rockhurst University. He is currently working on topics in aesthetics and Greek philosophy.

COLLOQUIUM 1

The Authorship of the Pseudo-Simplician Neoplatonic Commentary on the *De Anima*

Gary Gabor
Hamline University

Abstract

The traditional ascription of the Neoplatonic commentary on the *De Anima* to Simplicius has prominently been disputed by Carlos Steel and Fernand Bossier, along with J.O. Urmson and Francesco Piccolomini, among others. Citing problems with terminology, diction, cross-references, doctrine, and other features, these authors have argued that the commentary cannot have been composed by Simplicius and that Priscian of Lydia is a favored alternative. In this paper, I present some new arguments for why the traditional attribution to Simplicius is, in fact, the correct one. In particular, while addressing some of the terminological facts that have also been discussed by Christina Luna, Peter Lautner, Patricia Huby, and Philippe Vallat,[1] among others, I offer a more secure basis for identifying the author of the *De Anima* commentary with Simplicius than has so far been proposed. In place of the disputes regarding terminology, which the debate has largely centered upon, I argue that certain unique and characteristic interpretive procedures, which one only finds in the undisputed Simplician works, allow us to identify the authorship of the *De Anima* commentary with Simplicius securely. Further, comparison of these methodological features with the extant works of Priscian rules out the possibility of his authorship of the commentary. I also provide some suggestions for resolving a few remaining issues of cross-reference between the *De Anima* commentary and the rest of Simplicius's work. Finally, I conclude with some words on how that particular form of harmonization pursued by Simplicius's contemporaries differs from both that of the *De Anima* commentary as well as his other works.

---

1 Vallat's contributions are incorporated in Hadot (2014). For Luna, see the introduction to Luna (2001). For Lautner's skepticism on the Bossier-Steel hypothesis, see his notes to Steel (1997). For Huby on apparent differences between Priscian and the pseudo-Simplician author of the *De Anima* commentary, as well as a potential mutual reliance on Iamblichus, see Steel (1997, 105; 55n123; 54n94; and 64n313).

© KONINKLIJKE BRILL NV, LEIDEN, 2020 | DOI:10.1163/22134417-00351P02

Keywords

Simplicius – Priscian – *De Anima* – commentary – authorship

1 Introduction

One significant issue in contemporary scholarship on the late antique philosophy is the disputed authorship of the Neoplatonic commentary on the *De Anima*. The manuscript tradition attributes the commentary to Simplicius of Cilia, student of the last Athenian Platonic scholarch Damascius as well as Ammonius Hermiae. But Francesco Piccolomini in 1602, then Carlos Steel and Fernand Bossier in 1972, followed by J.O. Urmson in 1995, have raised doubts about the traditional ascription. The style differs too much from Simplicius's other Aristotelian commentaries, the argument goes. Such authors further indicate differences in technical vocabulary, philosophical content, and more mundane grammatical constructions, suggesting the commentary is not, in fact, by Simplicius. Further, there are internal references in the *De Anima* commentary to other works that have been difficult to identify in any extant writings of Simplicius. Based on one of these references, along with some other similarities in diction and philosophical terminology, Simplicius's fellow late-Platonist, Priscian of Lydia, has been proposed as a possibility for the real author of the text.

Despite the doubts raised by Piccolomini, Bossier-Steel, and Urmson, however, not all have been convinced. After tentatively accepting Bossier-Steel's argument against Simplicius's authorship, Ilsetraut Hadot quickly reversed her position and has increasingly strengthened a counter-argument in favor of the traditional attribution over the course of three decades. Christina Luna, Peter Lautner, and Patricia Huby have all also identified mistakes in Bossier-Steel's original argument, for instance finding examples of the use of technical terms and turns of phrase that Bossier and Steel had originally thought to be missing from Simplicius's others writings. Because of the difficulty and complexity of the issue, some scholars have offered compromise positions. Perhaps, Henry Blumenthal argued, both early in the controversy and towards the end of his life, what one has here is a text that cannot be easily attributed to *either* Simplicius or Priscian, but is rather a kind of composite, perhaps lecture notes of Simplicius's exposition of Aristotle's *De Anima* taken by Priscian, supplemented in turn by Priscian's own additions. This was, indeed, a very common procedure in late antique philosophical culture where much of the work proceeded by the commentary on texts. John Dillon, John Finamore, Frans De Haas,[2] and others, have alternately weighed in on the controversy, modifying their views based on the latest available evidence, given the inherent complexity of the matter.

What I intend to do in this contribution is to offer several arguments—a few probable, but not, I believe, fully certain, along with one extremely strong case, in my mind, for why the traditional attribution to Simplicius is, in fact, the correct one. In doing so, I will be building upon and supplementing some of Ilsetraut Hadot's recent restatement of the case for attribution to Simplicius in her 2014 co-authored study of Simplicius with Philippe Vallat, but also adding what I believe is a more secure basis for identification of Simplicius's interpretive procedure, which is less disputable than the identification or lack of identification of single technical terminology, upon which the debate, up until this point, has largely proceeded. The new evidence that I will be presenting derives from certain characteristic features of the authentic Simplician commentaries on Aristotle. Such features will become extremely important, given the relatively subjective nature of the claims about what is "characteristic" of Simplicius's authentic commentaries.

II   The Arguments against Simplician Authorship

Let us begin with a restatement of the main lines of the argument against Simplicius's authorship of the *De Anima* commentary. Given the opportunity to update his position in the introduction to his 1997 translation of *In De Anima* 2.5–12, Carlos Steel writes the following: "Our argument has always been: just start reading and 'after a couple of pages' you will be convinced" (1997, 105). It is too dependent on Iamblichus, Steel thinks, too forceful and uncareful of an interpretation of Aristotle to have come from Simplicius, and it is missing some of the characteristic features of Simplicius's other commentaries on Aristotle. Steel continues:

---

2   For Dillon and Finamore in favor of Priscian's authorship, see Finamore and Dillon (2002, 18–24). For a recent reassessment by Finamore, see Finamore (2014, 290): "the contradictory position of the two philosophers on the two intellects ... indicate that the author of the de Anima commentary is not Priscianus. I. Hadot's (2002) stance that the similarities between Simplicius and Priscianus are caused in part by the two authors' reliance on the same commentary of Iamblichus is enticing. This reliance would also explain the commentator's differences in style from other works of Simplicius[.]" For De Haas, see his argument against the possibility of a definitive attribution in De Haas (2010).

> Simplicius always approaches the Aristotelian text with the primary intention of explaining it to his readers as faithfully as possible. ... His commentaries also contain a rich historical and doxographical documentation, which has considerably enlarged our knowledge of the antecedents of Aristotle's philosophy and of the later development of the Peripatetic school. In fact, in order better to understand Aristotle's text, ... Simplicius makes an effort to bring us in direct contact with the philosophers who preceded Aristotle and against whom he reacted (the Presocratics and Plato), quoting long extracts from their works. ... This is an important question, because the commentator knew from experience that stupid or malign readers (such as John Philoponus) liked to use these critical remarks to ridicule the whole endeavour of philosophy by pointing to the insoluble disagreements between the philosophers. (1997, 108)

In contrast to this general method of Simplicius elsewhere, Steel finds the *De Anima* commentary wildly different. "The commentary on the [*De Anima*]," Steel writes, while "a genuine 'commentary,'" nevertheless, is "'totally untrustworthy' as an exposition of Aristotle's work. ... Instead of clarifying Aristotle's text, the author approaches the text from a preconceived view of the soul which he absolutely wants to find within the Aristotelian text itself" (Steel 1997, 110).

One of the basic flaws, Steel thinks, in the commentary, due to which it cannot come from the hand of Simplicius, is because of its general hermeneutical principle. It does not extensively compare the works of Aristotle to those with whom he is engaging, nor does it address the different critical interpretations that have been raised in the centuries after Aristotle's death by those commentators seeking to understand his text. The commentary on the *De Anima* does not do any of these things sufficiently to have been by Simplicius, in Steel's view. Urmson has also added a few other minor points. First, the lemmata are composed differently in the *De Anima* commentary than in the other Aristotelian commentaries of Simplicius. And the commentary poses a particular problem for Urmson regarding the psychological interpretation of Aristotle by not viewing the text, as it generally is viewed today, as holding the view "that the soul is the actuality (*entelecheia*) of the living body, with the exception of the contemplative intellect (*theōrētikos nous*), which he regards as an independent substance." But instead it rather "ascribes to him the view that there is a soul that is the actuality of the living body, giving it its form (*eidopoiousa*), and another soul that initiates the changes (*kinētikē*) of the animate body, like the

PSEUDO-SIMPLICIAN NEOPLATONIC COMMENTARY ON THE *DE ANIMA*   5

sailor in his boat."[3] This 'untrustworthy' doctrinal difference that "is repeated over and over again in the commentary,"[4] along with the stylistic and methodological differences from the other Aristotelian commentaries by Simplicius, in the view of Steel and Urmson, allows one to conclude the commentary is not by Simplicius, despite the universal attribution of the manuscripts.[5]

Now, Blumenthal already noted the problems in using purely stylistic features as a means for dis-attributing works for ancient philosophical authors. Further, there are problems with the 'inauthentic' interpretation of Aristotle that Urmson and Steel find so irresponsible as not to have possibly been the result of Simplicius's caution. Those writing on Simplicius's extant commentaries on both Aristotle and the Stoic Epictetus frequently complain that, despite his care, many of the specific points that Simplicius makes in interpreting Aristotle can be disputed. This possible disputation arises because of Simplicius's potential excessive Neoplatonic influence, as well as his tendency to go beyond the original text and attempt both to identify the underlying truth of any given point or issue under consideration and to extend the original analysis to later doubts and problems raised by subsequent authors. So, for instance, one small point: in his commentary on the *Categories*, Simplicius raises the question, only hinted at by Aristotle, of whether there is a proper order or derivation of the ten categories from each other, with some categories being more primary than others. Porphyry also raised this question in his commentaries on the *Categories*, but, at the end of the day, it is Iamblichus's proposals in his

---

3 Urmson 1995, 3.

4 Urmson 1995, 3.

5 For a summary of the doctrine of soul in the *Metaphrasis*, see De Haas (2010, 761–762). Some pertinent details from De Haas's account: "In commentaries on *De caelo* and *Physics*, Simplicius paraphrases Aristotle in such a way that only the irrational parts of the soul are inseparable as the *entelecheia* of the body, whereas the rational part is truly separable (cf. Simpl. *In Cael.* 279.16–20, 380.16–19; *In Phys.* 268.6–269.4 against Alexander). The *De Anima* commentary, however, accepts the claim that the soul is the *entelecheia* of the body, and develops it in a different way. In its role of formal i.e., defining cause (*kath' ho*) the soul actualizes the potentialities of the body, which is constituted by nature, by making it a living body. Next, the soul utilizes the living body thus constituted and fulfills its potentialities in order to be able to operate in the sensible world. This is presented as a different aspect of the formal causation of soul by which it actualizes the potentiality for motion in the living body (*huph' ho*). On this view, the two aspects of the soul's formal actualization of the body are present on all levels of the soul, and concern all its parts or functions, including thought. If, for instance, strong impressions harm the sense organ, this is to be regarded as the organ losing its 'defining life.' However, there is something stronger than any of these soul powers in us, which exists in us without *entelecheia*. This is the Peripatetic *nous poietikos* of *De An.* 3.5, which is truly separate (cf. Simpl. *In An.* 109.2–11). Despite the convergences between the texts noted above, the *Metaphrasis* does not seem to contain any of the terminology of the double *entelecheia*" (De Haas 2010, 762).

(lost) *Categories* commentary that Simplicius ends up endorsing and extending in his comments. This clearly is a case of 'going beyond' the original Aristotelian text in a way that many would consider 'totally untrustworthy' today, at least when it comes to elucidating Aristotle's text alone. And yet, it is something that Simplicius regularly does in *all* of his extant commentaries. Notice also the dependence, in this case, upon Iamblichus, which similarly pervades Simplicius's approach, even though he is also often ready and willing to criticize Iamblichus on particular points and even general interpretive approaches, as noted by both Hadot and Steel.

Further, while it is true that, in the *De Anima* commentary, there are not extensively long quotations from non-Aristotelian authors, it is simply not true that the author, as Steel claims, rarely engages substantially with any thinkers besides Aristotle, excepting, perhaps, the Pythagoreans. In fact, there is regular and extremely frequent engagement not only with Presocratic thinkers mentioned by Aristotle, but also Plato, referring both to specific dialogues and passages in extreme detail, on a level comparable to a great many of the frequent references to Plato that one finds in the other commentaries on Aristotle by Simplicius. The commentary also engages with Alexander of Aphrodisias, whom we know from Simplicius's other commentaries, Simplicius very much respected as an interpreter of Aristotle, even if he frequently disagreed with him.

This provides the first, not conclusive, I admit, but still extremely telling, comparison between the approach of an author like Simplicius and another contender for the commentary like Priscian. In the *De Anima* commentary, as well as the other commentaries of Simplicius, on the one hand, there is always regular and extensive engagement with the dialogues of Plato (and with generally the same dialogues cited in this commentary), other works of Aristotle (again, along the same lines as Simplicius's comments elsewhere, although in the case of the *De Anima* commentary with a certain precedence to the lost Aristotelian dialogue *Eudemus*, which purportedly also examined the nature of the soul), Presocratics, and the commentary tradition after Aristotle's writing. In the extant works of Priscian, on the other hand, there are no specific references to any dialogue or work of Plato's, no explicit mention or reference to any work of Aristotle's other than the *De Anima* (the context of Priscian's main relevant extant work is a summary or 'Metaphrasis' of Theophrastus's *On the Soul*—and not Theophrastus's *Physics*, it should be noted), nor references to any commentator other than Theophrastus himself. The relevant contrast, then, is between an author who regularly and frequently engages with the thought of others besides Aristotle in commenting on him, and one who does not. It is Simplicius's other extant commentaries that display this tendency.[6] Priscian's commentary, short as it is (approximately fifty pages in the Berlin edition), does not furnish a single example. Within any text of Simplicius's, one will usually find at least a dozen such references in the course of fifty pages.

This is also the case in the *De Anima* commentary.[7] For while it is true that the *De Anima* commentary does not quote from these authors in depth like Simplicius's other Aristotelian commentaries do, it still references and sum marizes the views of Iamblichus, Porphyry, Alexander, and more. In this, as I. Hadot points out, it is also like Simplicius's commentary on Epictetus's *Enchiridion*. Further, the apparent references in the *De Anima* commentary 'from memory,' as it were, versus closely textual, are entirely in keeping with the style of Simplicius's references 'from memory' in the *Categories*, *De Caelo*, and *Physics* commentaries. Simplicius has an incredible memory, and his knowledge of the Platonic and Aristotelian corpus, and many other authors, is simply exemplary and rivals that of the best interpreters of these authors today (as, for instance, Lloyd Gerson and Han Baltussen both point out). Rather, the simple explanation necessary for the difference in extent of quotation is one theory that has already been offered—either Simplicius was in a bit of a rush and did not have the time (or the later opportunity to revisit) to add such extensive quotations, or he simply may have temporarily been in a location where his access to published materials was more restricted than when composing the other Aristotelian commentaries.[8] Alternatively, his methods may

---

6 From the other commentaries by Simplicius, we know he was familiar enough to speak with intelligence on: *Apology, Crito, Euthydemus, Alicibiades 1, Protagoras, Gorgias, Phaedo, Symposium, Phaedrus, Theaetetus, Republic, Timaeus, Statesman, Sophist, Philebus,* and *Laws.* For a general account of Simplicius's interpretation of Plato, see Gabor (2018).

7 Priscian's sources, mentioned at least, in the *Answers to Chosroes* is more impressive, yet still does not match the breadth of Platonic and Aristotelian texts referenced in the *De Anima* commentary. De Haas gives the following list: "Priscian names Plato's *Timaeus, Phaedo, Phaedrus* and *Politeia*; Aristotle's *Physics, De caelo, De generatione et corruptione, Meteorologica, De somno et insomniis,* along with *De philosophia* and the probably spurious *De mundo*; various works or passages from Theophrastus; Hippocrates' *De aere aquis et locis*; Strabo *Geographia*; Albinus and Gaius on Plato; Geminus on Posidonius' *De meteora*; Ptolemaeus *Geographia* and *Astronomica*; Marcianus *Periegesis*; Arrian *Meteora*; Didymus, Dorotheus, Alexander of Aphrodisias and Themistius on Aristotle; Theodotus from the *Collectio Ammonii scholarum*; Porphyry *Commixtae Quaestiones*; Iamblichus's *De anima*; Plotinus *Enneads*; and finally Proclus's *Tres sermones* on the immortality of the soul" (De Haas 2010, 757). One further argument in favor of Priscian's authorship, and against my thesis here, is that many of the topics examined in the *Answers to Chosroes* are focused on the soul, suggesting perhaps some expertise on Priscian's part on the topic. See De Haas 2010, 757–758.

8 I thank Michael Griffin for discussion on this topic.

have changed over time, for instance, in favor of the more extensive quotations and tracts as one finds in the *Categories* and physical commentaries.

More importantly, the specific way in which the author of the *De Anima* commentary approaches the interpretation of Plato and Aristotle is extremely telling, and once again extremely in favor of Simplicius's authorship. First, whereas Priscian is ready and willing, when he does briefly and generally allude to 'Plato' or 'Platonic views,' to find a sharp contrast and difference of approach between Plato and Aristotle, Simplicius pursues not only a very extreme, but also a very specific form of harmonization between the two. Simplicius is aware, first, that Plato often employs the dramatic voice of the characters of his dialogues, in ways that may, but also may not necessarily, represent the views of Plato himself. Thus, like an interpreter of Plato today, he distinguishes between the 'Platonic Socrates' and the historical Socrates,[9] between the Pythagorean views expressed by a character like Timaeus, and the differing views of Plato, Aristotle, and Simplicius. Indeed, because of this problem, Simplicius goes to some good lengths to show that, in fact, most of the things Timaeus says are things that Plato himself agrees with too, while still distinguishing them on important points when it comes to harmonizing Plato with Aristotle.[10] None of this finesse is found in Priscian, but it is regularly employed by the author of the *De Anima* commentary.

III   Simplicius's Harmonization of Plato and Aristotle

Even more precisely, in his other commentaries, when Simplicius does turn to the question, as, for instance, was raised by earlier commentators like John Philoponus or Alexander Aphrodisias, of whether Plato and Aristotle disagree on any particular points, Simplicius develops a brand of harmonization that is entirely unique to him. Namely, rather than the general method of Porphyrian harmonization, which attributes to Aristotle a concern with 'terrestrial matters' and to Plato 'theological matters,' or to the 'analogical' interpretation of Platonic (and Pythagorean) doctrines in Iamblichean harmonization, Simplicius prefers a much more subtle interpretation, and, I suggest, one particularly necessary, given the forceful textual arguments for incompatibility raised in general by Alexander, but, in particular, by John Philoponus. Philoponus, in his extensive commentaries on Aristotle, as well as, especially, his later treatises

---

9   Cf. Simplicius, *In Ench.* 3.3–19.

10   Cf. *In An.* 40.4–26.

dedicated to critiquing the 'harmonization thesis' generally prevalent in pre-
ceding Platonism, provides very precise, grammatical (hence befitting his epi-
thet as the "Grammarian") arguments that Plato and Aristotle, in fact, use the
same terms in the same ways. Thus, all previous attempts to harmonize by providing different ontological referents for their terms are bound to fail. And so,
one finds that the previous attempt to harmonize in the manner of a Porphyry
or Iamblichus is not pursued by Simplicius. It is not, as it was previously
thought, that Aristotle was "the obscure" who preferred to hide the true course
of his thought from the unintelligent masses. But rather, for Simplicius, Plato
and Aristotle use terms in the same way. However, Aristotle understands the
common, crude interpretation that most people will give to Plato's terms, and,
hence, when it appears that Aristotle is criticizing Plato, in fact, he is criticizing
those who interpret Plato's language in an inappropriate way. So, when Aristotle, in providing another usage for the terms, appears to conflict with Plato, he,
in fact, does not.

In the *De Caelo* and *Physics* commentaries, Simplicius attends to the various
ways in which 'generation,' and, so, also the generation of the world, can be
understood. He relies on how Plato and Aristotle use and define the terms differently.

So for instance, in a way that is representative of Simplicius's approach in
general, consider his comments on the *De Caelo*:

> [L]et us see next in what sense of generation Aristotle denies that the
> heaven is generated, seeking to demonstrate that it was ungenerated, and
> in what sense Plato says that both the heaven and the entire cosmos were
> generated. That Aristotle means by 'generation' only the temporal change
> from non-being to being, and which invariably admits of destruction, on
> the basis of which he will demonstrate the heaven to be not only un-
> generated but also indestructible as well, is clear; ... For it is clear that he
> treats generation and destruction as things which occur at particular
> times and which apply to sublunary things, having for this reason dem-
> onstrated that there is another fifth substance besides the sublunary
> ones, namely that of the heavenly body, which is naturally prior to and
> more complete than them. ...
>
> Plato certainly knew of this kind of generation, which applies to sublu-
> nary things and is the opposite of destruction, when he wrote the follow-
> ing in the tenth book of the *Laws*:

and what sort of affection is it which is such as to bring about the generation of all things? Clearly whenever a first principle, having grown, comes to the second change, and from this to the next, and having come to the third allows perception to the things which perceive. So everything is generated by changing and being altered in this way. Something is really real whenever it persists; but when it is changed into some other state it is completely destroyed. (*Laws* 10, 894a)

But he also knew of another sort [of generation], according to which what comes into a corporeal extension, not being capable of producing itself, but which is said to be generated only [in the sense that] something else produces its existence as its cause, in contrast with what is really real, which is its own principal cause. ... [And so] that Plato thought the cosmos was neither created at a particular time nor destroyed at a particular time is clear from what he wrote in the *Timaeus*. (Simplicius, *In De Caelo* 103.1–105.8, Hankinson, tr. 2002)

Thus, Simplicius continues:

But since the whole argument depends on these two things: first that if something is going to be generated and destroyed there must at all events be both a substrate and a contrary out of which it is generated and into which it is destroyed, and second that there is no motion contrary to circular motion, of which he [Aristotle] will proceed a little later to offer a demonstration in many ways, while the former he now assumes without demonstration as having been proved in the *Physics*, we must now recall what was said there, having first distinguished the various senses of 'generated' to clarify which one it is in respect of which Aristotle constructs his argument and what sort of generated thing he denies the heaven to be, so that we may also understand how, while Plato said that the totality was generated and Aristotle [said that it was] ungenerated, they did not contradict one another. (Simplicius *In De Caelo* 92,22–31, Hankinson, tr. 2002)

Now, let us compare the *De Anima* commentary. On the interpretation of Aristotle in general, our author in question states that "Aristotle was always accustomed to recount and examine the superficial meaning, and to understand words in their colloquial sense. But he did not destroy the truth itself by his thoroughgoing examination" (*In An.* 28,12–15, Urmson, tr. 1995). Some further examples of the employment of this interpretation in the *De Anima* commentary:

> The Pythagoreans were accustomed to philosophise symbolically via mathematics about the supernatural, the soul and natural phenomena. Plato makes Timaeus play the part of a Pythagorean, and so, as he assigns the five straight-sided solids to the simple bodies, so he depicts the being of the soul of the universe by straight lines and lines curved in a circle, in order to display at the same time its mean place between the undivided and the substance divided amongst bodies, just as the line is a mean between the point and solids, and, at the same time, a descent most close to intellect. ... [But] even if intellect also moves the heavens, it is with the soul as well which, through its own developing life as intermediate, leads the indivisible kinetic energy of the intellect into the continuous and divisible activity of the heavens. It is this alone that this philosopher [Aristotle] calls motion, and he contradicts Timaeus about his ascription of a divided extension and activity to the soul, lest we, following the customary usage of words, should so understand Plato, or think it to be a magnitude or motion in a bodily manner. (*In An.* 40.4–26)

Or again:

> It has already been mentioned how Plato says that the soul is in motion through its descent from the prime mover. ... For the term *auto* shows for Plato that the unitary substance and the perfect activity are the same thing, just as 'being moved' is indicative of the divided. ... But Aristotle applies the term 'motion' only to the activity that is altogether fragmented and has its being in becoming. (*In An.* 26.22–32)

Also:

> Plato uses the word 'change' also of the life of the soul as it unfolds, neither being totally fragmented nor remaining purely unitary. He calls this change because of the total descent from unity, and makes self-change the essence of the soul, as living essentially such a life. (...) But Aristotle is accustomed to call change only the divisible and the continuously numerable, in accordance with the common use of the word, so that he not only denies change to the psychic substance but declares that the soul is in no way in motion as such. (*In An.* 34,8–19)

Finally, there is *In De Anima* 49.19–50.17. The context here is the 'motion' of the soul and its possible relation, or not, to cosmic motion, as well as Aristotle's refutation of the idea that the motion of the soul is in some way circular, which is one interpretation, for instance, of *Timaeus* 36e[11]:

> Such a hypothesis as that the soul's rotation is the cause of the heavenly rotation having been disproved [by Aristotle], its cause remains fully unclear. 'For neither is the essence of the soul the cause of the rotation,' as those who think that motion is its essence and that its rotation is essential propose as thus causing it. For the soul does not move in a circle nor in any way whatsoever. So it will not be the cause by its motion, for it does not move of itself but incidentally, while the body is not the cause either of its proper motion or of the incidental motion of the soul.

Continuing after the statement of the next lemma:

> [T]he origin of change is superior to the principle according to which things change. For that is how nature is a principle, as being that in accordance with which, not that by agency of which. Perhaps that which is also Iamblichus's opinion is suggested, namely, that the celestial body has also life through itself, and derivatively as our bodies do. ... This, then, is all correct, but how is it truly said that even for Plato the cause of the heaven's travelling in a circle is obscure, since it has been proved that the soul does not rotate or move at all? For bodily and natural motion has been disproved in this case, and this is also not Plato's meaning as in the case of the soul. For if we understand the motion of the soul as does Plato, as being a form of life that has descended from intellect and slackened its indivisible bond, but is not yet divided up nor has departed from itself, but is turned on itself in a secondary way, which is what he hinted at mathematically by rotation, then the cause of the heavenly rotation is obvious. For the immediate cause of the celestial motion which is continuous and divisible but always perfect, from and to the same place, and always the same, is the aforementioned life, which by its descent from the undivided, activates division but does not suffer it, and, by its reversion upon itself, remains in a secondary way in itself, bringing about a

---

11 "The Soul, being woven throughout the Heaven every way from the center to the extremity, and enveloping it in a circle from without, and herself revolving within herself, began a divine beginning of unceasing and intelligent life lasting throughout all time. And whereas the body of the Heaven is visible, the Soul is herself invisible but partakes in reasoning and in harmony."

motion that is always continuous, from and to the same place and always the same. But, as we keep on saying, Aristotle understands it [motion] *according to the popular use of words*, examines it, and says that *so understood* the cause is obscure. (*In An.* 49.19–50.17)

Indeed, there are over a dozen of other instances where the *De Anima* commentator leans upon this particular distinction, just as Simplicius does in the *Categories*, *Physics*, *De Caelo*, and *Enchiridion* commentaries.[12] Thus, while Steel and Urmson do not spy the 'authentic voice' of Simplicius in the *De Anima* commentary, these methodological passages, I suggest, provide a far more sure and secure means for identifying the continuity of authorial hermeneutical style and approach than (again, very much disputed) arguments based on the presence or absence of certain bits of technical terminology or the frequency of use of certain prepositions. This is methodological, precise, and pursued with this regularity and frequency by only one person: Simplicius (more on why only him below). And, in fact, the 'authorial voice,' which I very much became familiar with in examining his approach to an outside source, such as Plato in his Aristotelian commentaries, very much came 'screaming back to me,' as Steel might otherwise say, in reading the *De Anima* commentary. Indeed, even the author of *In De Anima*, just as Simplicius does elsewhere, both somewhat complains about and comments upon this hermeneutical device as a particularly frequent and repeated hallmark of his reading of Plato and Aristotle.

Now, other reasons that Steel gives against Simplicius's argument also fail. For instance, he notes that there is a 'wholly different' theory of the soul developed in the *De Anima* commentary and Simplicius's other works. Steel appeals to his hypothetical reconstruction[13] of Iamblichus's view of the soul as a 'changing substance,' which, straddled along the limits of eternity and becoming, *substantially changes* in nature from one to the other. This, on Steel's telling, is against the more orthodox position of Plotinus, Porphyry, Proclus, and other Neoplatonists for whom the soul's nature always remains among the class of eternal intelligibles, like, for instance, the gods or the Forms. That the *De Anima* commentary appears to endorse Iamblichus's theory, while Simplicius's other writings do not, Steel thinks, provides a doctrinal reason to reject Simplicius's authorship.

---

12   In addition to the passages cited above, cf. also *In An.* 25.18; 34.8; 39.5; 49.12; 76, 32–77.8; 89.24–31; 98.6–14 (indeed, there are even more).

13   See Steel 1978.

It is not possible to go into depth on this topic here, but a few words. First, there are issues with Steel's reconstruction of Iamblichus's position, which, even he notes, is highly speculative at points. There certainly are new considerations about the soul, and thinking about substantial kind membership, that Iamblichus introduced in his writings, for instance, in the first book of the *Letter to Anebo* on categorization of the 'higher classes' of gods, *daimons*, and heroes. But, briefly, Steel's notion of a radical rejection of Iamblichus's ideas in Simplicius's other writings and his account of the degree of the 'substantial change' in Iamblichus's own thought on the nature of the soul, is misleading and distorted at times. So, for instance, in his 1978 *Changing Self*, where Steel elaborates his argument at length, some of the language that he attributes to Iamblichus as endorsing radical change is exaggerated and, unfortunately, goes beyond what the text allows. This would require a more extended defense than is allowable here, but, in general, Steel's argument for the radicalness of Iamblichus's position on the soul requires tempering. The analyses provided by Finamore and Dillon (2002), for instance, provide for a more nuanced reconstruction, which is more in line with the main strands of Neoplatonic interpretation, even if there are many important variations and innovations introduced by Iamblichus.

Now, the more moderate contemporary interpretation of Iamblichus's view on the soul is reconcilable with Simplicius's other statements on the soul. These views are, then, not unique to Priscian, as Steel holds, but rather a comparatively common feature held from Iamblichus to Simplicius as one preferred resolution of the problem of the eternality of the soul. We also see that Iamblichus uses technical terminology in his account of the soul—for instance, some kinds may be predicated μονοειδῶς—but Steel does not account for this.

For example, Steel argues that Iamblichus and the author of the *De Anima* commentary hold a radical view on the changeability of the soul in their desire to describe how the soul may perfect its nature. To indicate a position where the soul was previously imperfect and is now perfected, Steel suggests,[14] is to hold a view on the soul where its substance literally changes from a thing that was not perfect to a new thing that is. But there is a compelling alternative here, which is that, for Iamblichus, to say that the soul goes from the imperfect to the perfect is not to suggest a change of substance on its part, but rather that that is the unique differentiating characteristic of the unique and predicatively

---

14   Steel 1978, 54–55. In fact, throughout his account of Iamblichus (Steel 1978, 52–69), the material presented as evidence for his interpretation is much more tentative than his assertive declarative statements suggest.

PSEUDO-SIMPLICIAN NEOPLATONIC COMMENTARY ON THE *DE ANIMA* 15

μονοειδῶς nature of the soul itself. Thus, every one of the characteristics that Iamblichus, as well as Simplicius later, attributes to the soul can be understood, not as a *substantial change* within the soul, but rather as demonstrating that the substantial nature of the soul is itself to change from its potential, as a substance that inhabits and is affected by the sensible world, to its actualization, which is a full habitation within the immaterial, intelligible realm. So, while the soul changes, this is part of its essential nature, and not a substantial change from one kind of substance to another. Steel would not be willing to accept this, however, since it goes against one of his most distinctive theses.

But that this is what is going on in the *De Anima* commentary can be seen when Simplicius states that "in every case of coming to be the advance is from the incomplete to the complete" and that "both the incomplete and the complete are observed in a single thing when, even in a case of coming to be, another complete thing must pre-exist, from which comes what is incomplete in another case" (*In An.* 89.14ff). In fact, we get another example of Simplicius's distinctive hermeneutical method here:

> He does not, indeed, like Plato, use the expression 'coming to be' of existing at a time, since our soul also is shown by him to be ungenerated and indestructible... . But Aristotle uses the word 'generated' of things existing at some time. But if not in its substance, still in activity and completeness, coming to be and perishing are clear in the case of the human soul, which is both harmed and hindered at times. (*In An.* 89.26–33)

This, in fact, *agrees* with what Simplicius says about generation in the passage from his commentary on the *Physics* quoted above.

Similarly, many of Steel's terminological arguments, while requiring consideration, break down upon further examination. For instance, in response to I. Hadot, who has shown resonances of the view of the soul in the *De Anima* commentary in Simplicius's other works, Steel has responded that this only shows "Damascius's influence on Simplicius."[15] This response is strange, however, since, in his own view,[16] Damascius also espouses the notion of the substantial change of the soul just as strongly as Iamblichus-Priscian. Continuing, Steel then notes that, "On the other hand, the author of the *In An.* never uses the typical vocabulary of Damascius as εἶδος τῆς ὑπάρξεως and οὐσιώδης μέθεξις to talk about the substantial change in the soul."[17] Yet, their absence in the

---

15   Steel 1997, 118.
16   Steel 1978, 95–96
17   Steel 1997, 118.

De Anima commentary is no argument against Simplicius's authorship, as Steel suggests, since they are also completely absent in his other writings. Steel's argument regards other distinctive terminology about the soul, for instance that "[t]he doctrine of the προβολή or projection outwards of the soul is one of the most original contributions of this commentary *In An.* to the Neoplatonic doctrine of the soul. This doctrine, again, is entirely absent from Simplicius's genuine work, together with the vocabulary of προβάλλω, προβολή, προβλητικός that is so typical of the *In An.*"[18] Yet, as a simple *Thesaurus Linguae Graecae* search shows, this is not true at all; several times Simplicius uses the same language in association with the activities of the soul in his commentaries on the *Physics*, *De Caelo*, and *Categories*. For all these reasons, the doctrinal and terminological arguments offered by Steel are much weaker than they first appear, and looking at the methodology of Simplicius's approach to the commentaries, along with comparing them to the methodology of the *De Anima* commentary, provides a much clearer way of settling the debate. With regard to the supposed stylistic differences spied by Urmson and Steel on the *De Anima* commentary, as well as its more frequent use of Iamblichus and willingness to either 'stray from' or, to put it in another way, 'complete' Aristotle's account of the soul, there is another important precedent. In his commentary on Epictetus's *Enchiridion*, Simplicius makes a similar point that, when it comes to the theory of the soul, certain aspects that are incompatible with the (Neoplatonic) truth about its nature require supplementation and correction. These considerations also come into play in the *De Anima* commentary, since Simplicius is aware of the more materialistic Peripatetic interpretation of the soul offered by predecessors like Alexander Aphrodisias. So that none of his readers are led astray, and also to show that Aristotle is more in line with the views of later Platonists, Simplicius is compelled, I suggest, to supplement his account with the considerations of Iamblichus, Plotinus, and others, since there is a different interpretive issue at stake than in his commentaries on the *Categories*, *Physics*, *De Caelo*, *Meteorologica*, and so forth. Indeed, looking at the latter three works, we see that Simplicius has interpretive goals throughout his work and allows his commentary to address them, especially, for instance, his dispute with Philoponus on the eternity of the world and the agreement of Plato and Aristotle.

---

18   Steel 1997, 118.

IV   Simplicius's Authorship and Rival Alternatives

Now, if we see this is a characteristic and uniform methodology for Simplicius throughout his commentaries, where does this method come from? It is true that there are a few scattered similar sorts of readings of Plato and Aristotle before him as well as a limited number of interpretations contemporary to him that might seem to come close to his own. Ammonius, for instance, once or twice, employs a similar lexical harmonization reading, as does Themistius long before both of them.

For instance, in *Oration* 34, Themistius states:

> Now does Aristotle differ from Plato in all this? He has a greater curiosity (πολυπραγμοσύνη) and love of detail (λεπτουργία) than Plato, but still there is no part of his philosophical project (πραγματεία) and his cycle that neglects the question of the human good. (*Oration* 34.5, Panella, tr. 2000)

Meanwhile, in his own treatise on the *De Anima*, Themistius argues:

> If they dispute that what we name "activity" they call "movement," then we shall not dissent over the name. For one it is permitted to use names as one wishes, and particularly species in place of genera. For movement is a kind of activity, and so if something is a movement, it is also an activity; but if something is an activity, it is not always a movement, a [distinction] which it is clear that in many places Plato actually adopts in the same form. That is why there is no need to have a dispute over a name, but it must be realized that the references (τὰ πράγματα) [of the names] are vastly different—an imperfect versus a perfected entelechy. (Themistius, *In De An.* 18.30–36, Todd, tr. 1996)

In Philoponus's lecture notes from Ammonius's lectures on the *De Anima*, we see the following idea unpacked:

> These are the things that serve to show that even according to Aristotle himself the soul is subject to movement and that Plato was not wrong in assigning self-movement to it. And for an intelligent arbitrator (εὐγνώμονι διαιτητῇ) of these arguments no contradiction (μάχη) will be found to inhere in these, except in the words alone (πλὴν μόναις ταῖς φωναῖς). As [Aristotle] is used to do in many places when he is refuting the apparent [meaning] (τὸ φαινόμενον) he does so here, too. Since the real movements,

which we have recognized, too, are only the natural ones and since the soul is not subject to any of these [types of] movement (for the soul does not grow or get smaller or change quality or place), therefore, lest anyone would think that since Plato says that the soul is always in motion, he means that it is subject to any of the natural [types of] movement we recognize, he himself [Aristotle] demonstrates that it is wholly unmoved in respect of any of these movements. And this account is true, and it is the opinion of Plato, since Plato, too, thinks it is incorporeal, but according to Plato it can be subject to certain other types of movement, the intellectual and in particular the vital ones, in respect of which, Plato says, it is most of all always in motion; ... Now since Plato says that all actuality without further qualification is movement, whereas Aristotle says that only the natural movements are such, it seems that the account is right that says that according to Plato [the soul] is subject to movement whereas according to Aristotle it is not subject to movement, but the disagreement (διαφωνία) is found to lie only in the verbal formulation (ἐν μονοῖς ῥήμασιν)." (*In De An.* 95.7–26, Van der Eijk, tr. 2006)

It seems, then, that Ammonius himself likely became familiar with the idea by reading from Themistius himself, and he himself employed the notion once or twice. But it is not the only or regular hermeneutical interpretation given by him on the relation between Plato and Aristotle, and, indeed, many times he shows a clear preference for Platonic versus Aristotelian philosophy and dialectic (as, for instance, in the early pages of the *In Isagogen* lectures).[19] Thus, while a general harmony between Plato and Aristotle remains dogma among all the later Platonists, the particular lexical-grammatical version of the thesis is not maintained except by Simplicius. And, indeed, in his polemics with Philoponus, Simplicius significantly expanded on it, as we saw above.

More characteristic of the Platonists besides Simplicius are the methods and views of Olympiodorus, Damascius, and so forth. For instance, Olympiodorus, at *In Alcibiades* 62.2, suggests that Aristotle is an 'onerous,' eristic questioner; not necessarily a 'true' philosopher. Politically, Olympiodorus notes, Aristotle is also inferior to someone like Alcibiades, at least when the latter was under the guidance of Socrates (*In Alc.* 193.22–194.3). Olympiodorus, however, is happy and easily able to find accommodations between and harmonize apparently conflicting Platonic passages, for instance, reconciling Socrates' apparent claim that men and women have different tasks in the *Alcibiades I* with

---

19 For more on the clear superiority of Plato over Aristotle on logic and other philosophical matters in Ammonius's school, see Gertz (2018, 9).

PSEUDO-SIMPLICIAN NEOPLATONIC COMMENTARY ON THE *DE ANIMA*   19

the gender egalitarianism of the *Republic* by the fact that Socrates' discussion with Alcibiades occurs and is only valid in a non-ideal political community. Further, when discussing physical doctrines explored by Simplicius above, for instance, the 'generated' versus 'ungenerated' distinction from the *De Caelo*, the grammatical nuances of Simplicius's interpretation are entirely missing (*In Alc.* 118.11ff).[20] In Priscian, meanwhile, there is a general accommodational account of all the pagan philosophers,[21] but not between Plato and Aristotle specifically, and not on lexical grounds (while throughout his *Metaphrasis* on Theophrastus, contrasts between Plato and Aristotle are often drawn).

As a result, I have to disagree with Griffin when he states, "It is highly characteristic of Olympiodorus to suggest that superficial disagreement on the level of 'names' overlies deeper and genuine agreement on the level of reality" and that "whereas genuine philosophers drill down to the real, psychological meaning of myth and doctrine, and therefore rarely disagree" (2015a, 5). While Olympiodorus typically seeks to harmonize *true* philosophers, he does not, so far as I can tell, grammatically or lexically harmonize Plato with Aristotle, perhaps at least partly because Aristotle does not quite seem at the level of 'philosopher' in the way that he clearly is for Simplicius, for example. Now, Olympiodorus *does* employ something like the grammatical move once or twice, but in very different contexts, for very different purposes, and to a very different extent. One example is Olympiodorus on Plato, although harmonizing, notably, not with Aristotle, but with Homer:

> Plato is difficult to grasp since it is possible to interpret his words on the level of natural philosophy, ethics, or theology—in short, in many different senses—as is also the case with the [words] of Homer. For these two souls are said to have embraced every mode, which is why it is possible to take the words of both of them in all manner of ways. (*Vita Plato* 161–164, Griffin, tr. 2015)

---

20 Other examples, which again show a Porphyrian 'differing domains' version of the harmonization thesis as opposed to the Themistius-Ammonius-Simplicius grammatical one, include Olympiodorus's claims that, ethically, Aristotle adopts a "more human perspective" than Plato, desiring as he does external goods for well-being (*In Alc.* 230.13–14); metaphysically, that "Aristotle wants Intellect to be the first principle, [while] Plato wants the Good [to be]" (*In Alc.* 145.6–7; see also *In Alc.* 122.12–14); and that the traditional description of Aristotle as 'daimonic,' since at least Iamblichus's time, means for Olympiodorus (see his comments at *in Alc.* 218.13) merely that the Stagirite is quick and clever ("the ancients call everything speedy 'supernatural' [δαιμόνιος], on account of daimons' high level of activity, which is also the reason that they call Aristotle 'supernatural' because he is exceptionally quick," *In Alc.* 218.12–14).

21 Cf. *Solutions*, 42.5–43.21.

More typical of Olympiodorus's method is this passage from the *Categories* commentary:

> And so in order that the whole of substance might be treated, he takes up the particular. But about these things the most prominent of the philosophers, that is Aristotle and Plato, they differ in their accounts (διαφωνοῦσιν). For Aristotle takes up (ἐπιφέρει) the 'this particular something' of divisible things (τὸ τοδὶ τι ἐπὶ μερικοῦ πράγματος), and the 'certain somewhat' of the universal (τὸ τοιόνδε ἐπί τοῦ καθόλου). For these are the two things illustrated (or illuminated) by him, vis. the particular thing and the 'this somewhat' (δύο γὰρ ταῦτά ἐστιν παρακείμενα τὸ τόδε καὶ τὸ τοιόνδε). But Plato does not bring forth (ἐπιφέρει) as Aristotle does the divisible particular (το τόδε μερικῶς) or the universal such-and-such (τὸ τοιόνδε καθόλου). ... so it does not seem appropriate to us to comment on the disagreement of the chief philosophers and to dare to take a stand on these things of philosophy, which their proper treatment would require to take us. Instead one must see that neither of these two entirely go astray about the truth (ἰστέον οὖν ὅτι οὐδέτερος αὐτῶν διαμαρτάναει τῆς ἀληθείας). For it is possible to undertake an investigation about each kind of substance (*ousia*), that is both, the divisible particular and the universal. For we will show [later] that the [account of the] particular somewhat (τὸ τόδε τί) and the such-and-such a kind (τὸ τοιόνδε) of divisible substance (ἡ μερική ουσία) fits together with (ἁρμόζον) the 'this particular' (τὸ τόδε τί) and the such-and-such a kind (τὸ τοιόνδε) in the universal, and it is clear that [on this] the two agree (συμφωνοῦσιν)." (*In Cat* 68.34–69.5, my translation)

There is a harmonization here, no doubt, but it is one of scope, not verbal sense. Thus, I also disagree with I. Hadot when she states that "nothing distinguishes Simplicius, the representative of the School of Athens, from his Alexandrian colleagues with regard to their harmonizing" (2015). While this is, in a sense, true, there are still differences between Simplicius and his contemporaries on the precise mode of harmonization pursued. The details of Olympiodorus's 'accommodationalism' of Plato to Aristotle differ from Simplicius, and elsewhere in his *Gorgias* commentary he also does explicitly admit that some real disagreement between the two can occur, as Ammonius and many others at the time also did. Thus, while Griffin (2015) notes that while Olympiodorus employs a 'verbal' harmonization thesis once or twice, he does it with Plato and other philosophers, not Plato and Aristotle. Instead, Olympiodorus

PSEUDO-SIMPLICIAN NEOPLATONIC COMMENTARY ON THE *DE ANIMA*   21

appears to follow a different direction of harmonizing the two, again suggested by Ammonius, which is more in line with the latter's usual procedure as well:

> Concerning Aristotle we must point out that in the first place he in no way disagrees with Plato, except in appearance. In the second place, even if he does disagree, that is because he has benefited from Plato. For [Plato] says in the *Alcibiades* 'Unless you hear yourself speaking, do not put your trust in the words of another.' And again in the *Phaedo* he says 'Care little for Socrates, but greatly for the truth.' So Plato himself urges us not to believe him indiscriminately, but to inquire [for ourselves]. That is surely why the philosopher Ammonius says 'Even if it were to commit a bad act, I will nevertheless answer someone saying and affirming "Plato said so" that he did not say it in that way, and even—may Plato forgive me!—if he had said it in that way, I would not follow him without proof.' (Olympiodorus, *In Gorg.* 214.13–25, Westerink, tr. 1976. This translation conforms near the end to that of R. Jackson, K. Lycos, and H. Tarrant 1998, 267)

Olympiodorus here is closer to Ammonius's own practice, which was to be ready to criticize Aristotle, or Plato for that matter, if they ever appear to contradict the philosophical truth that seems apparent to the lecturing individual. Ammonius, along with Olympiodorus, was also ready to abandon either of their views much more so than Simplicius was. This might help also to explain why Ammonius's instruction also gave rise to the sort of independent philosophical examinations that we find not only in Olympiodorus, but also in Philoponus. Even this passage is rather unusual for Olympiodorus, however. Most of the time, he seems to function like much more of a 'piggy-back' harmonizer, often noting in a relatively simplistic fashion that Plato 'agrees' with Aristotle on some point, or vice versa,[22] and not addressing the contentious points on the eternity of the world, immortality of the soul, or nature of the first principle and prime mover on which Philoponus and Simplicius contended.

So, for a later Platonist of Simplicius's generation, there were many methods available for a commentator to harmonize Plato with Aristotle, if he felt so inclined. Simplicius was very much so inclined, more so even than his other contemporaries, due to the particular ire he felt in response to the grammatical objections raised by Philoponus in the latter's polemics against Proclus and Aristotle. In Simplicius's writings, however, the grammatical objection

---

22   See, for example, *In Gorg.* 3.7, 6.10, 14.3, 15.1, and 30.3.

becomes the main and dominant one, and its distinctive, peculiar presence, not only in Simplicius's *Physics*, *De Caelo*, *Meterologica*, and *Categories* commentaries, but also in the *De Anima* commentary, is one strong reason to assign the latter to his hand.[23]

---

[23] I am thankful to audiences that have heard and provided feedback on earlier versions of this paper, including the 2016 International Society for Neoplatonic Studies, the 2016 Society for Ancient Greek Philosophy annual conference, and the 2017 Minnesota Workshop in Ancient Philosophy, as well as specific discussion with Danielle Layne, Michael Griffin, Sandra Peterson, Del Reed, D.M. Hutchinson, David Butorac, John Finamore, Michael Chase, and Sara Klitenic Wear.

COLLOQUIUM 1

Commentary on Gabor

Dana Miller
Fordham University

Abstract

This paper gives a brief discussion of the problem of ascribing authorship to ancient philosophical texts when there is evidence both for and against traditional ascription. The case in point is tradition's claim that Simplicius is the author of the *De Anima* commentary. It is argued here that, while Gabor provides new and important methodological evidence for Simplicius's authorship, we should not expect certainty. It is suggested that, in cases where historical fact may never be ascertained, we will be better served by the notion of credences.

Keywords

authenticity – Simplicius – *De Anima* – historical fact – credences

Questions about the authorship of written works arise when we lack details of a writer's biography. The problem seems to have been recognized by the scholars associated with the Library of Alexandria, who compiled the canonical works of writers such as Sophocles, followed by Thrasyllus, in the case of Plato, and then the lists of Diogenes Laertius. But even with such canons we ask, did Plato write the *First Alcibiades*, the *Hippias Minor*? Did Aristotle write the *Problems*? What about Gorgias's *On What Is Not*? There is debate. At various times in the last several centuries, criteria have been developed to back up the claims of "genuine," "spurious," "closely associated." These criteria have also been used in debates about the chronological order of the assumed genuine works of a single writer, Plato, in particular. Very roughly, the criteria are "argument content" and "style." In the 18th and early 19th centuries, the focus for chronological order for Plato, as well as for Aristotle, was on argument content, under the assumption that a philosopher's thinking develops over time. However, this approach did not provide a detailed chronology and its basic assumption was challenged by the 'unitarian thesis.' From the mid-19th century until recently, the preferred criterion has been various forms of style-measurement or

© KONINKLIJKE BRILL NV, LEIDEN, 2020 | DOI:10.1163/22134417-00351P03

"stylometry": subtle changes in style indicate distinct periods of authorship. However, a worry about stylometry emerged when the style of a number of different authors of the same period was statistically analyzed. It was assumed that the analysis would reveal large differences between distinct authors and general homogeneity in the writings of the same author. This did not consistently occur.[1] But if stylometry could not distinguish with certainty one writer from another, how can it be trusted to establish chronology in the harder case of writings by the same author?

Moving away from the chronology to the question of authenticity, we again see appeal to these two dominant criteria: argument content and style. To a reader of the Greek original, significant variance in style is an immediate signal that instills doubts of authenticity. Take, for example, Carlos Steel's comment quoted by Gary Gabor, "Our argument has always been: just start reading and 'after a couple of pages' you will be convinced."[2] Of course, first impressions are not a strong reason to doubt authenticity, but they do constitute a certain kind of evidence, namely, evidence that suggests that we might want to consider the question of authenticity. To back up their "first impression," Bossier and Steel provide what I will call a "list" of stylistic discrepancies, as well as discrepancies that fall under the "argument content" criterion, that are found between the *De Anima* commentary and Simplicius's other known commentaries on Aristotle.[3] What should we think about this list? As Gabor points out, a number of the articles on the list have been challenged or discredited, and, therefore, many experts on this period of late Platonist philosophy do not find the list to be sufficient to establish the claim of inauthenticity, while there remain a number who do. The experts who do not think the evidence is sufficient hold that the burden of proof lies on those who claim, against the manuscript tradition, that Simplicius did not write this commentary: the list does not carry this burden. Even so I think we have to accept that the list tells us something. There are, in fact, discrepancies. I will return to this point.

In view of the ongoing controversy, Gabor offers us new evidence that strongly supports the 'authenticity claim,' namely, the strategy employed in the *De anima* commentary to harmonize Aristotle's views about the soul with Plato's—a harmony not easy to establish—is identical to the harmonization strategy used in Simplicius's recognized commentaries, and, further, argues that this strategy is unique to Simplicius. Therefore, when the rubber hits the road,

---

1   See Brandwood 1992, 112.

2   Steel 1997, 105.

3   Bossier and Steel 1972. A summary list is found on 819–822. See also the list of Urmson in the introduction to his translation (1995, 2–4).

COMMENTARY ON GABOR

that is, in a matter of fundamental importance to Simplicius, his interpretive methodology, the *De anima* commentary has his identifying stamp. As Gabor says:

> These methodological passages, I suggest, provide a far more sure and secure means for identifying the continuity of authorial hermeneutical style and approach than (again, very much disputed) arguments based on the presence or absence of certain bits of technical terminology or the frequency of use of certain prepositions. This is methodological, and precise, and pursued with this regularity and frequency by only one person: Simplicius. (2020, 13)

Gabor also provides an explanation of the origin of Simplician methodology. It seems to me that his argument here is strong.

If we grant that this new evidence weights the appropriate scales of judgment to Simplicius, we might want to ask the following question: since we take the commentary to be by Simplicius, what explains the unaccounted for discrepancies identified on Bossier's and Steel's list? I think it is doubtful that non-speculative answers can be given to this question.[4] So let us attempt to speculate.

To speculate, we need articles from the list and also not from the list. Let me begin with one not on the list: references to Alexander of Aphrodisias. In Simplicius's undisputed commentaries, Alexander is a go-to commentator whom Simplicius quotes freely. But in all the cases I have examined, the *De Anima* commentary does not quote Alexander directly or, *a fortiori*, at length. Instead, there are a handful of very brief references to Alexander. For example, Simplicius simply says: "So [the term] 'memory' can be used rather than 'recollection': this is Alexander's explanation" (206.24–25). Or again, explaining Aristotle's statement that the intellect "can think itself" (*An.* III.4, 429b9), Simplicius says, "Not incidentally, by having the intelligibles and being in a way the same as the forms that are thought, as primarily thinking the forms and not

---

4   Cf. the speculation of Blumenthal in the introduction to his translation: "Perhaps one [possibility] that is easiest to reconcile with the unwavering attribution to Simplicius in the tradition is that it is an *apo phones* work, composed by a pupil with no great gift for writing clear Greek and who, like others in the same relation to the original lecturer, allowed himself to insert ideas of his own ..." (2000, 6–7). Bossier and Steel, on the other hand, write that "such divergence between *In De Anima* and the other commentaries [of Simplicius] cannot be explained by Simplicius' own evolution. Therefore the *In De Anima* is falsely attributed to him" (1972, 822). Since this conclusion leaves us nowhere, they rather implausibly suggest Priscian as the author.

itself, as Alexander would have it" (230.12–14). Blumenthal notes that Simplicius might be quoting from Alexander's lost commentary on *De Anima*,[5] since these references cannot be found in Alexander's treatise *On the Soul* (2000, 142). In other words, we cannot verify that Alexander actually said these things.

How can we explain the minimal presence of Alexander in the *De Anima* commentary? One speculative explanation might be that Alexander did not think Aristotle's treatment of the soul can be harmonized with Plato's. So, Simplicius just avoids him. But that seems somehow un-Simplician. Another, and, in my view, more plausible, speculative explanation might be that Simplicius did not have to hand the relevant works of Alexander, possibly because he was in exile in Harran in Syria (today in Turkey), and, therefore, cited from memory only a few recollected points, not wishing to treat Alexander's views in depth without the text in front of him.[6] Or, perhaps, if the commentary was composed at the other end of his career, while just emerging from the influence of his teacher Damascius, then Simplicius focused primarily on the Platonist tradition.

Bossier and Steel point to "tortured phrasing" in the *De Anima* commentary that is lacking in Simplicius's other commentaries (1972, 822). As we all know, clarity and precision in composition requires a great deal of time and effort. Our hurried literary efforts are not pretty. So, one might speculate that Simplicius wrote the *De Anima* commentary in pressed circumstances. A parallel might be Myles Burnyeat's speculation that the peculiar absence of verbs in Aristotle's *Metaphysics Lambda* is due to its being written after his hasty departure from Athens and increasing illness.[7]

It might be possible to devise speculative explanations of all reported divergences between the *De Anima* commentary and Simplicius's other commentaries. But even if this were done, would we be more certain that the commentary is by Simplicius? I think not. And, recognizing the force of Gabor's arguments and new evidence, can we claim certainty about the authorship of the commentary? I think not. Fact is hard to establish, past or present. It would be a mistake, I think, to demand certainty where no certainty is to be expected. We are better off when we recognize that probabilities represent our best case for many facts, historical as well as contemporary.

In epistemology these days, a distinction is made between beliefs and what are called "credences." It is argued that beliefs do not come in degrees, while

---

5 Notes 373, 374.

6 Blumenthal briefly considers such a possibility in the introduction to his translation (2000, 4).

7 Burnyeat 2001, 148–149.

COMMENTARY ON GABOR

credences are rationally assigned, proportional to determined probabilities. A clear statement of the distinction by Lara Buchak is as follows:

> When an agent believes *p*, she in some sense rules out worlds in which *not-p* holds. The truth of *not-p* is incompatible with the attitude she holds towards *p*. ... On the other hand, having a particular credence in *p*, at least if it is not 0 or 1, does not rule out either the *p*-worlds or the *not-p*-worlds. The truth of *not-p* is compatible with the attitude she holds towards *p*, even when she assigns a very high (not-1) credence to *p*. (Buchak 2014, 286)[8]

If we accept this distinction between belief and credence, as I think we should, then, applying it to the case at hand, we can rationally give a rather high credence to the proposition that Simplicius wrote the *De Anima* commentary and nevertheless assign a rather low credence as well to the proposition that Simplicius did not write the commentary, given the epistemic status of our data. These two positions are compatible. They do not, however, satisfy our instinctive desire for certainty and the consequent adoption of "belief." This is, however, a desire we should resist. We might remember Aristotle's advice: "We should not look for the same degree of precision in all cases, but the degree that fits the subject-matter in each case and is proper to the mode of investigation" (*Nicomachean Ethics* I.7, 1098a26–29), the relevant reference of "precision" here being to credence about historical fact.

---

8 See also Moon (2017). An ancient parallel to credences might be the "plausible impression" (ἡ πιθανὴ φαντασία) of Carneades. See the discussion in Sextus Empiricus, *Adversus Mathematicos* 7.166 ff.

COLLOQUIUM 1

Gabor/Miller Bibliography

Baltussen, H. 2010. Simplicius of Cilicia. In *The Cambridge History of Philosophy in Late Antiquity*, vol. 2, ed. L. Gerson, 711–732. Cambridge, UK: Cambridge University Press.

Baltussen, H. 2008. *Philosophy and Exegesis in Simplicius: The Methodology of a Commentator*. London: Duckworth.

Blumenthal, H. 1993. *Soul and Intellect: Studies in Plotinus and Later Platonism*. Aldershot: Variorum Collected Studies.

Blumenthal, H.J., tr. 2002. '*Simplicius,' On Aristotle On the Soul 3.1–5*. London: Duckworth.

Bossier, F., and C. Steel. 1972. Priscianus Lydus en de *In de anima* van Pseudo (?)-Simplicius. *Tijdschrift voor Filosofie* 34:761–822.

Brandwood, L. 1992. Stylometry and Chronology. In *The Cambridge Companion to Plato*, ed. R. Kraut, 90–120. Cambridge, UK: Cambridge University Press.

Buchak, L. 2014. Belief, Credence, and Norms. *Philosophical Studies* 169:285–311.

Burnyeat, M. 2001. A Map of Metaphysics Zeta. Pittsburgh, Mathesis.

Busse, A. 1891. *Ammonius in Porphyrii Isagogen sive v voces. Consilio et auctoritate Academiae litterarum regiae borussicae*, CAG 4.3. Berlin: Commentaria in Aristotelem Graeca.

De Haas, F.A.J. 2010. Priscian of Lydia and Pseudo-Simplicius on the soul. In *The Cambridge History of Philosophy in Late Antiquity*, vol. 2, ed. L. Gerson, 756–764. Cambridge, UK: Cambridge University Press.

Finamore, J.F., and J.M. Dillon, eds. 2002. *Iamblichus, De Anima: Text, Translation, and Commentary*. Leiden: Brill.

Finamore, J.F. 2014. Iamblichus on the Soul. In *The Routledge Handbook of Neoplatonism*, eds. S. Slaveva-Griffin and P. Remes, 280–292. London: Routledge.

Gabor, G. 2018. Simplicius of Cilicia: Plato's Last Interpreter. In *Brill's Companion to the Reception of Plato in Antiquity*, eds. H. Tarrant, F. Renauld, and D. Layne, 569–579. Leiden: Brill.

Gerson, L. 2005. *Aristotle and Other Platonists*. Ithaca: Cornell University Press.

Gerson, L., ed. 2010. *The Cambridge History of Philosophy in Late Antiquity, Vol. 2*, Cambridge: Cambridge University Press.

Gertz, S., tr. 2018. *Olympiodorus, Introduction to Logic*. London: Bloomsbury.

Griffin, M., tr. 2015. *Olympiodorus, Life of Plato and On Plato First Alcibiades 1–9*. London: Bloomsbury.

Griffin, M., tr. 2016. *Olympiodorus, On Plato First Alcibiades 10–28*. London: Bloomsbury.

Hadot, I. 1978. *Le Problème Du Néoplatonisme Alexandrin. Hiéroclès et Simplicius*. Paris: Etudes Augustiniennes.

© KONINKLIJKE BRILL NV, LEIDEN, 2020 | DOI:10.1163/22134417-00351P04

Hadot, I. 1987. La vie et l'œuvre de Simplicius d'après des sources grecques et arabes. In *Simplicius. Sa vie, son œuvre, sa survie. Actes du colloque international de Paris (28 Sept.-1er Oct. 1985)*, ed. I. Hadot, 3–39. Berlin: Walter de Gruyter.

Hadot, I. 2002. Simplicius or Priscianus? On the Author of the Commentary on Aristotle's *De Anima* (CAG XI): A Methodological Study. *Mnemosyne* 55:159–199.

Hadot, I. 2014. *Le néoplatonicien Simplicius à la lumière des recherches contemporaines. Un bilan critique. Avec deux contributions de Ph. Vallat.* Sankt Augustin: Academia-Verlag.

Hadot, I. 2015. *Athenian and Alexandrian Neoplatonism and the Harmonization of Aristotle and Plato.* Leiden: Brill.

Hankinson, R.J., tr. 2002. *Simplicius, On Aristotle On the Heavens 1.1–4.* London: Duckworth.

Hankinson, R.J., tr. 2004. *Simplicius, On Aristotle On the Heavens 1.5–9.* London: Duckworth.

Hankinson, R.J., tr. 2006. *Simplicius, On Aristotle On the Heavens 1.10–12.* London: Duckworth.

Jackson, R., K. Lycos, and H. Tarrant., trs. 1998. *Olympiodorus: Commentary on Plato's Gorgias.* Leiden: Brill.

Luna, C. 2001. *Simplicius Commentaire sur les Catégories d'Aristote, Chapîtres 2–4, traduction par Philippe Hoffman, avec la collaboration de I. Hadot et P. Hadot; commentaire par Concetta Luna.* Paris: Les Belles Lettres.

Militello, C. 2019. Self-knowledge and self-reversion of the irrational soul in 'Simplicius', Commentary on *On the Soul*. In *Platonism and its Legacy Selected Papers from the Fifteenth Annual Conference of the International Society for Neoplatonic Studies*, eds. J.F. Finamore and T. Nejeschleba, 121–140. Lydney: The Prometheus Trust.

Moon, A. 2017. Beliefs do not come in Degrees. *Canadian Journal of Philosophy* 47.6: 760–778.

Panella, R. 2000. *The Private Orations of Themistius. Translated, Annotated and Introduced. The Transformation of the Classical Heritage 29.* Berkeley: University of California Press.

Perkams, M. 2005. Priscian of Lydia, Commentator on the de Anima in the Tradition of Iamblichus. *Mnemosyne* 58:510–530.

Renauld, F., and H. Tarrant. 2015. *The Platonic Alcibiades I: The Dialogue and its Ancient Reception.* Cambridge, UK: Cambridge University Press.

Sorabji, R. 2016. Introduction. In *Priscian, Answers to King Khosroes of Persia*, eds. P. Huby, S. Ebbesen, D. Langslow, D. Russell, C. Steel, and M. Wilson, 1–10. London: Bloomsbury.

Steel, C. 1978. *The Changing Self. A Study of the Soul in Later Neoplatonism: Iamblichus, Damascius and Priscianus.* Brussels: Koninklijke Academie voor Wetenschappen, Letteren en Schone Kunsten van België.

Steel, C. 1997. The author of the Commentary *On the Soul.* In *Priscian, On Theophrastus, On Sense-perception, with Simplicius, On Aristotle, On the soul 2.5–12*, eds. P.M. Huby, C. Steel, J.O. Urmson, P. Lautner, 105–140. London: Duckworth.

Steel, C., tr. 2012. *'Simplicius', On Aristotle on the Soul 3.6–13*. London: Bloomsbury.

Todd, R.B., tr. 1996. *Themistius: On Aristotle's On the soul.* Ithaca: Cornell University Press.

Urmson, J.O., tr. 1995. *Simplicius, On Aristotle's On the Soul 1.1–2.4, Notes by Peter Lautner*. London: Duckworth.

van der Eijk, P., tr. 2005. *Philoponus, On Aristotle On the Soul 1.1–2*. London: Duckworth.

van der Eijk, P., tr. 2006. *Philoponus, On Aristotle On the Soul 1.3–5*. London: Duckworth.

COLLOQUIUM 2

How to Argue about Aristotle about Practical Reason

Giles Pearson
University of Bristol

Abstract

In this paper, I consider Aristotle's views in relation to the Humean theory of motivation (HTM). I distinguish three principles which HTM is committed to: the 'No Besires' principle, the 'Motivation Out—Desire In' principle, and the 'Desire Out—Desire In' principle. To reject HTM, one only needs to reject one of these principles. I argue that while it is plausible to think that Aristotle accepts the first two principles, there are some grounds for thinking that he might reject the third.

Keywords

Aristotle – motivation – desire – reason – metaethics

I Introduction and the Humean Theory of Motivation

The title of my paper is intended to put one in mind of R.J. Wallace's article 'How to argue about practical reason' in *Mind* in 1990, in which Wallace attempted to work out what was really at stake in competing Humean and anti-Humean (for the latter, in Wallace's mouth, read primarily 'Kantian') accounts of motivation. Ultimately, I want to work out whether Aristotle can sensibly be said to advance a Humean theory of motivation or not, as I think that getting clear on this will be instructive not only with respect to understanding his views but also potentially of interest for contemporary debates on the matter. But before we can begin to try to work this out, we first need to establish what would *count* as establishing it.

There has been a long-standing debate about whether or not Aristotle was a 'Humean' about practical reason. Unfortunately, all too often it has not been made precise what would count as establishing this one way or the other or,

© KONINKLIJKE BRILL NV, LEIDEN, 2020 | DOI:10.1163/22134417-00351P05

indeed, why it should matter. For instance, in a recent discussion, Jessica Moss asked, in her title: 'Was Aristotle a Humean?' Faced with such a question, one might not unreasonably reply: 'Was Aristotle a Humean *about what*?' or 'What do you mean by 'Humean'?' And the opening lines of her paper perhaps do not illuminate her question quite as much as one would like. She writes:

> How much power does Aristotle grant to practical reason? He seems to characterize it as purely instrumental: as on Hume's view, our passions and desires set our goals, and reason is relegated to working out how to achieve them. And yet the whole tenor of his discussion of practical reason, and in particular of its virtue, *phronesis*, seems distinctively un-Humean: practical reason has an authority and an ethical significance that no Humean would allow. What then is his view? (2014, 221)

There is a clear allusion here to the thought that the Humean reading would resonate with Hume's celebrated claim that reason is the 'slave' of the passions, and thereby assign reason a purely instrumental role, whereas an anti-Humean reading would, presumably, provide reason with a non-instrumental role, such that it can *set* our ends or goals. She later contrasts the Humean reading with a 'Kantian' view of practical reason, according to which "we reach our goals through reasoning, and the job of non-rational passion is simply to follow along" (2014, 222). Even so, there are still several Humean theories in the vicinity that are, I think, worth distinguishing.

In contemporary metaethics, there are (at least) two central, but importantly different, Humean theories about practical reason. The **Humean theory of motivation (HTM)** concerns the conditions that are required for an agent's being motivated. HTM can very generally be characterised as committed to the view that there are two fundamentally distinct kinds of state necessary for motivation: cognitions and explanatorily basic conations (desires). And so, HTM maintains that cognitions alone are unable to account for motivation. I shall specify HTM more precisely shortly. By contrast, **The Humean theory of normative reasons (HTN)**, or *The Humean theory of instrumental rationality*, as it is also sometimes called, concerns what constitutes an agent's normative reasons, that is, what makes it the case that an agent *has* a reason to do something, whether or not she is motivated to act that way. A Humean theory, in this sense, amounts to the view that an agent's normative reasons must be traceable via 'a deliberative route,' or perhaps 'a sound deliberative route' as Bernard Williams maintains,[1] to the agent's basic desiderative states or dispositions, the agent's 'subjective motivational set,' as Williams again puts it.[2]

HTM and HTN are evidently distinct. One could (perhaps a little peculiarly) hold an anti-Humean theory of motivation, such that beliefs are capable of motivating us on their own, but nonetheless think that normative reasons must be grounded in the agent's desires, and one could (perhaps less peculiarly) think that explanatorily basic conative states are required for motivation, and so endorse HTM, but nonetheless think that normative reasons can apply to us regardless of our desiderative states.[3]

Now, I suspect that many would think that the debate about Aristotle that is being alluded to in the quote from Moss above does not neatly fall into either of these views.[4] Instead, it will be said to concern what we might call the *Humean theory of practical rationality* (HTR), that is, a theory about the instrumental nature of practical reason and its ability (or lack thereof) to set the agent's ends. HTR can be generally contrasted with an anti-Humean theory insofar as Humeans insist that practical reason is restricted to working out means to pre-given ends (set, for example, by desire and character), whereas anti-Humeans that think reason is capable of setting ends in its own right.[5]

---

1 Williams 1995, 36. The two formulations are not straightforwardly equivalent, since the latter introduces a notion of normativity not in the former. Williams (1995, 36) will embrace this, but others see the normativity inherent in instrumental reason as something that cannot simply be had for nothing; see, e.g., Korsgaard (1997).

2 Williams 1981, 102. Although it should be noted that some Kantians have argued that their accounts can meet this 'internalist requirement' (as Korsgaard puts it) while remaining rationalist (esp., Korsgaard 1996).

3 The two would only coincide if one thought that we only have normative reason to do what we are in fact motivated to do. But, besides being a very odd view to advance—we could not say that the person who wants a gin and tonic, but mistakenly thinks the petrol in her gin bottle is gin, has a (prudential or at least instrumental) reason not to drink the stuff—the two theories would still be distinct, since one would be making a claim about what the agent has reason to do, and the other about what she is motivated to do. I should also flag that the distinction between normative and motivating reasons is not itself entirely uncontroversial; see e.g., Dancy (1995) and (2000).

4 For some references to the literature on this debate, see Moss (2014, 222 and n3).

5 Moss (2014) calls her own reading 'quasi-Humean.' She there claims that Aristotle thinks reason can grasp ends, but not *set* ends. In calling this 'quasi-Humean,' rather than 'strictly' or 'purely' Humean' (her expressions), she appears to be claiming that reason, on Hume's view, cannot even grasp the end that passion motivates the agent to pursue. That would be a peculiar view for Hume to advance since any sort of deliberation about how to achieve an end would appear to require reason to at least *recognise* the end in question as one that has been set by passion. In her 2011 article and 2012 book, Moss advocates a reading of Aristotle that is anti-Humean by my lights (and indeed by her own: 2011, 251); see, n34 below.

Is HTR distinct from both HTN and HTM? HTN and HTR do indeed seem independent. One could think that normative reasons hold of agents regardless of their desires, and so reject HTN, but still nonetheless think that the role of practical reason is to work out means to pre-given ends (regardless of whether those ends are in fact choiceworthy) and so embrace HTR. And one could think (perhaps a little peculiarly) that normative reasons must be grounded in the agent's desires, and so embrace HTN, even though one thought that practical reason could itself set an agent's ends. Such a view would maintain that reason can set our ends independently of our desires and character, but what we really have reason to do must be grounded in our desires.

What about HTM and HTR? If these were also entirely independent, one could coherently hold that (1a) beliefs are capable of motivating us independently of our explanatorily basic desires (thereby rejecting HTM), even though (1b) reason is restricted to working out means to our given ends (as those are set by desire and character) (thereby embracing HTR). One could also coherently think that (2a) explanatorily basic conative states are necessary, alongside cognitions, for motivation (thereby embracing HTM), but nonetheless think that (2b) reason can set our ends independently of our desires and so play a non-instrumental role (thereby rejecting HTR).

But it is not so clear that the above conjunctions (1a & 1b and 2a & 2b) are coherent. If belief is capable of motivating us all on its own (1a) then, contra (1b), it is hard to see how it can be restricted to working out means to ends set by desire or character. Such a restriction would undermine its claim to be able to motivate *all on its own*. And if reason can set our ends independently of desire/character (2a) then, contra (2b), it is hard to see how an explanatorily basic conative state is also necessary for motivation. Such a need would seem to undermine reason's ability to be truly independent in setting ends.

This suggests that HTM and HTR are not entirely independent from each other. Granted, they do have different nuances. HTR is explicitly couched in terms of the (non-)instrumentality of reason, whereas the instrumentality in HTM is only tacit—via explanatorily basic desires (see DO-DI and n10 below). And HTR speaks of ends (or 'goals') being set by reason or desire/character, whereas HTM speaks of being motivated.[6] But these nuances aside, one cannot, it seems, reject one of the theories without also rejecting the other.

---

6   HTN could also speak of *normative* ends being set, but this is not the sense in which HTR intends 'ends.' HTR is not concerned with what makes an end one we ought to pursue (and so about normative reasons), but about what sets the ends we are in fact motivated to pursue. Even the vicious are intended to have ends in the relevant sense (see e.g., Moss 2014, 239) and yet Aristotle would not accept that vicious agents ought to act viciously (e.g., *Nicomachean Ethics* IX.8, 1169a15–16). It has been argued that Aristotle's vicious agent must also have a desire

My approach in this paper will be to tackle head on the question of whether or not Aristotle embraces HTM. I hope this will prove interesting in its own right and, given HTM's connection to HTR, potentially help us with the latter as well. For focussing, as we shall, on HTM will cast a different light on many of the debates that have been addressed through the eyes of HTR. For example, the putative limitations on deliberation, and the alleged instrumental character of reason, which Moss and others spend much time discussing, are more prominent if we focus on HTR rather than HTM, since the latter makes a claim about the role of beliefs or cognitive states in motivation more generally, not deliberation as such (although of course deliberation may lead to beliefs, and so has found its way into the discussion of HTM). The overall hope is that my discussion will open a new way of arguing about Aristotle via explicit consideration of his view in relation to HTM.

To proceed, we first need to state more precisely what we take the Humean theory of motivation to be committed to. Most are agreed that this theory is not attempting to characterise *Hume's* theory of motivation, not least because that account is itself a matter significant dispute. Hence it makes sense for a number of scholars to raise the question whether Hume himself was a Humean about motivation.[7] But even liberated from textual analysis of Hume, the commitments of HTM are somewhat controversial in contemporary metaethics. On my view, as I mentioned, HTM can very generally be characterised as maintaining that there are two fundamentally distinct kinds of state necessary for motivation, cognitions and explanatorily basic conations (desires), and so maintaining that cognitions are unable to account for motivation alone. More specifically, we can see HTM as committed to at least the following three principles (I shall elaborate on them a bit more, and on what I think is really at stake in them, in due course):

> **No Besires principle (No B-Ds):** Beliefs and desires are essentially distinct kinds of state. There cannot be states ('besires' as they've been termed[8]) that are somehow at once essentially both beliefs and desires;

---

for her normative good (e.g., for what is in fact good for her overall) (see Grönroos 2015a, 2015b), but only by insisting that such an end is 'unarticulated' in her and insufficient to guide actions (2015a, 162). For what it is worth, I would reject this conception of Aristotle's vicious agent, but I cannot argue the point here.

7 See, e.g., Persson (1997) and, for many more references and extensive discussion, Radcliffe (2018, Ch. 2).

8 Originally by Altham (1986, 284).

states that could not, even in principle, be decomposed or resolved into distinct beliefs and desires. [9]

Motivation-Out Desire-In principle (MO-DI): Motivation is not possible without a desire; desires are necessary for motivation.

Desire-Out Desire-In principle (DO-DI): An agent's desires are either basic desiderative states or desiderative dispositions, and so not themselves ultimately explicable in terms of other non-desiderative states of the agent, or they are traceable back to such basic desiderative states or dispositions via other cognitive states and desires. [10]

In order to establish a cognitive basis for motivation and reject the idea that two fundamentally distinct states are necessary for motivation, we need only deny one of these principles. If there are singular states that are both beliefs and desires at the same time and not further dividable, then we will not need two fundamentally distinct states for motivation and, so long as one sees the world aright, one will be motivated. [11] Similarly, if desires are not required for motivation (that is, we reject MO-DI) or if any desire that is required for motivation is explanatorily 'downstream,' as I shall put it, of the cognition that in fact does the motivational work (that is, we reject DO-DI) then a cognitive basis for motivation is in the offing.

A key culprit for confusion about HTM in contemporary metaethics is Michael Smith, since in spite of calling his view 'The Humean Theory of Motivation' (1994, chapter 4), his whole solution to what he calls 'the moral problem' (roughly, a motivational puzzle about how beliefs can bring about motivation

---

9   The key for the besire theorist is that there are states that *are* both beliefs and desires. HTM does not deny that there can be states that essentially *involve* beliefs and desires— indeed, motivation itself would be just such a state. But HTM maintains that any such state is *composite*, that is, is made up of distinct beliefs and desires that could, at least in principle, come apart. Some philosophers think of besires as having two different contents, a belief-based content *that p* and desire-based content *to q* (see, e.g., Little 1997). The Humean would query whether such a state is not really decomposable into distinct beliefs and desires.

10   Cf. Wallace 1990, 370 and Sinhababu 2009, 465. I will return to their formulations of DO-DI later. It is in DO-DI that there is a tacit instrumentality to HTM, insofar as it appeals to explanatorily basic desires and to occurrent desires being *traceable back* to such desires.

11   Cf. McNaughton 1988, 109: "the awareness of a moral requirement is a state which must be thought of, Janus-like, as having directions of fit facing both ways. The agent's conception reveals to him both that the world is a certain way and that he must change it."

on their own in rational agents), hinges on his rejecting DO-DI.[12] R.J. Wallace, in his 'How to argue...' paper, saw that DO-DI was crucial for distinguishing rationalist views (like his own Kantian view) from Humean views about motivation. And I, like some others (for example, Sinhababu 2009, 465–466), agree that DO-DI is fundamental for HTM, since without it we could still have a cognitivist account of motivation that accepts the other two principles: desires that are distinct existences might be necessary for motivation but nonetheless themselves be generated by cognitions.

It is worthwhile to note briefly why defending an anti-Humean account has seemed so significant to some. One reason is that a cognitivist basis for motivation has been thought to be required (though not itself sufficient, of course) for prudential and moral realism. We have a chance, at least, of reasoning with you to change your *viewpoint*, whereas if there is an in-eliminable desiderative or non-cognitive element to motivation, one which cannot be explained in terms of a prior belief or cognitive state, then it may seem, as Nagel wrote, that "if one lacks the relevant desire, there is nothing more to be said" (1970, 28). Hence, if you pardon the irony of my putting it this way, there has been a strong desire for some to put motivation on a cognitive footing.[13] For what it is worth, I might say up front that I reject the idea that prudential and moral realism requires a cognitivist account of motivation.

II   Arguing about Aristotle

The suggestion is that considering Aristotle's views directly in terms of the above three principles of HTM might help to bring some order to the widely divergent accounts of Aristotle's account of motivation in the literature. I also think, as I shall indicate, that it might stimulate further thought about some of those principles themselves and so, potentially, contribute to contemporary discussions. I should perhaps emphasise in advance that I approach the

---

12   In his 1987 paper in *Mind*, "The Humean Theory of Motivation," Smith did appear to commit to DO-DI. He claimed that beliefs and desires have different 'directions of fit' (section 6), that teleological considerations suggest that desires have a direction of fit with which the world must match (section 7), and finally that for any putative cognitive state that would bring about a desire, the teleological argument would iterate: "the state that motivates the desire must itself be a desire" (59). But, significantly, this argument drops out of Smith's later presentation of his Humean theory in *The Moral Problem* (1994, ch. 4). And, in a later paper, he explicitly rejects DO-DI (1997, 100n18).

13   Reasoning with you to change your viewpoint will obviously be less significant for those who adopt quasi-perceptual cognitivist theories—on McDowell's view, for instance, one may have to seek to get the person *to see* the world differently (see, e.g., 1978, 21).

investigation into Aristotle's views with a genuinely open mind. Although I think I advocate HTM, I remain open to the idea that Aristotle does not.

A. Aristotle and MO-DI. MO-DI states that desires are required for motivation, that is, that one cannot be motivated to do something without a desire. The precise relation between the desire that is putatively required and the action that is motivated requires elaboration and specification, of course, but I shall not pursue that here. For the key point is fairly simple. MO-DI is intended to rule out the idea that beliefs, or cognitive states more generally, can motivate agents without a desire being involved at all. It does not, however, preclude the idea that the desire that is required for motivation could be derived from, or explanatorily downstream of, some other cognitive state,—that is the role of DO-DI in HTM—all it does is insist on the necessity of desire for motivation.

In contemporary metaethics, those who have argued against MO-DI have often appealed to phenomenology. Sometimes we seem to be moved by the thought that some action is required of us, or is our duty to perform, without desiring to perform it. Think, perhaps, of cleaning out an aged relative's bedpan or going to the dentist for a filling.[14]

In response, the advocate of MO-DI will generally try to provide a notion of 'desire' according to which all intentional actions count as desired. We might, for example, take 'desire' to signify any 'pro attitude' towards an action or state of affairs, and then suggest there are pro attitudes in the cases in question, such as wanting to help the aged relative or the benefit of alleviating the toothache.[15] Alternatively, we might take 'desire' to include both 'positive desire' and 'aversion' (Sinhababu, 2009), and suggest that, in the cases in question, we are motivated by an aversion to the consequences of failing to clean out the bedpan or going for the dental procedure.

If we turn to whether Aristotle accepts MO-DI, I think it fair to say that this principle is probably the least controversial of the three to ascribe to him, insofar as he evidently identifies the capacity of desire (the ὀρεκτικόν) as the capacity owing to which we are moved in *De Anima* III, 9–10.[16] Of course, Aristotle is

---

14   Platts (1979, 256) and Shafer-Landau (2003, 123) have rejected MO-DI. Scanlon (1998, 39–40) and Barry (2007 and 2010) can also be understood this way.

15   'Pro attitude' was first introduced by Nowell-Smith (1954, 112); see also, esp., Davidson (1980, 3–4) and Schueler (1995, ch. 1).

16   E.g., "it is a capacity of the soul of this kind, that which is called desire, that produces movement" (433a31–433b1); 'That which produces movement will be one in kind, the capacity of desire (ὀρεκτικόν) as such" (433b10–11); "insofar as the animal is capable of desire so far is it capable of moving itself" (433b27–28). Contra Richardson (1997), it is clear that Aristotle means to identify the ὀρεκτικόν, the capacity of desire, rather than the ὀρεκτόν, the object of desire, as the capacity responsible for animal locomotion. I do not

HOW TO ARGUE ABOUT ARISTOTLE ABOUT PRACTICAL REASON

considering locomotion here, not motivation as such, but even so, since he is (i) considering *voluntary* locomotion (*An.* III.9, 432b16–17) and (ii) maintaining that the capacity for desire, in direct contrast to cognition or thought, is ultimately responsible for locomotion (*An.* III.10, 433a21–26, 433a31–433b1), the text surely points in the direction of MO-DI (even without trying to work out how motivation relates to voluntary locomotion) since it suggests that he would be inclined to think that cognitions cannot motivate agents to move *without* a desire being involved.

I suppose *De Motu Animalium* 6 might be thought to provide counter-evidence. For here, again considering what moves animals, Aristotle lists various cognitive capacities (thought [διάνοια], construal/imagination [φαντασία], perception [αἴσθησις]) and conative capacities (wish [βούλησις], spirit [θύμος], appetite [ἐπιθυμία]) as movers of animals. He then reduces these to thought (νοῦς) and desire (ὄρεξις) on the ground that the former are discriminatory capacities (κριτικά) and the latter are species of desire (ὄρεξις). He also mentions preferential choice (προαίρεσις), which he thinks straddles both reason and desire. The fact that Aristotle here leaves thought as a distinct mover, might be taken to suggest that he thinks cognitions alone can motivate us, and so rejects MO-DI.

But I think we can resist this suggestion and take *De Motu Animalium* to be filled out by *De Anima* III.9–10 rather than to conflict with it. In *De Motu Animalium*, Aristotle claims that it is not any kind of thought that can move us, but only thoughts concerned with what can be done (700b24–25). In *De Anima* III.9–10, he makes the same claim (433a14) as part of his argument that ultimately concludes that desire alone is the mover, but there he explains that, even when we are moved in accordance with thought, we are moved in accordance with desire. At the end of *De Anima* III.9, he had provided a consideration that seemed to show that thought could move us even contrary to desire, namely, the notion that enkratic agents act in accordance with their thoughts against their appetites. But, in correcting this *phainomenon* in *De Anima* III.10, Aristotle points out that even the enkratic agent is moved in accordance with *some* desire (ὄρεξις):

> It is clear that thought (νοῦς) does not move without desire (ὄρεξις), for wish (βούλησις) is a desire and, when one is moved in accordance with thought, one is also moved in accordance with wish. (*An.* III.10, 433a22–25)

think that his doing so has the consequences that Richardson thinks, though. I discuss this in my MS "Aristotle on the Role of Desire in Locomotion."

Thought can be deemed capable of moving us, as *De Motu Animalium* maintains, but even when it does, we are still moved in accordance with one kind of desire (ὄρεξις), namely, a wish (βούλησις). Thus, the notion that thought can move us does not jeopardise Aristotle's view that desires are necessary for locomotion. The same idea, *mutatis mutandis*, evidently applies to *phantasia* too. As Aristotle explicitly notes: "And when *phantasia* produces movement, it does not do so without desire (ἄνευ ὀρέξεως)" (*An.* III.10, 433a20–21).[17]

Thus, the notion that cognitions can move us does not jeopardise Aristotle's thought that desires are necessary for locomotion. MO-DI is surely on the cards.

B. Aristotle and the No B-Ds principle. The No B-Ds principle rules out there being states that are somehow at once essentially both beliefs and desires; states that could not, even in principle, be decomposed or resolved into distinct beliefs and desires (see also n9 above). Jimmy Altham called such (putative) states 'besires' (1986, 284). In so doing, he was characterising John McDowell's position in his 'Are Moral Requirements Hypothetical Imperatives?' and McDowell's view in that paper can, I think, reasonably be thought of as denying the No-B-Ds principle. McDowell wants to deny that states of the will and cognitive states need be 'distinct existences,' and correspondingly reject the notion that the world is motivationally inert. Grasping an 'ert' world, on McDowell's view, simply *is* to be motivated accordingly. Besires thus do appear to be in play.[18]

A key *proponent* of the view that Aristotle advances besires (without using the terminology) and, interestingly, unitary states that are at once perceptions and desires—'persires' we might call them—is David Charles (especially 2006). Charles maintains that Aristotle thinks that 'perceiving A as pleasant,' which appears to be a cognitive state, is *identical* with 'sensually desiring A,' a conative state, and maintains there is really only 'one type of activity' in play in

---

17   The other cognitive state on Aristotle's list in *MA*, sc., perception, is a little trickier. In *De Anima* III.9, Aristotle rules out perception as the mover on the ground that there are many animals that possess perception, but which are stationary and unmoving throughout, and yet nature does nothing without reason and so would have given such animals the parts enabling them to move if perception were the mover (432b19–26). However, such a consideration (if valid) would not rule out perception playing a role in locomotion in animals that *do* have the parts that facilitate movement. And it could be this that *MA* is alluding to. Insofar as perception can play such a role, however, it seems clear that Aristotle would apply the same restriction to it in *De Anima* III.9–10 as he does to *phantasia* and thought: perception cannot move without desire.

18   See also McNaughton (1988, e.g., at 109), Little (1997) and, more recently, Swartzer (2013).

such a scenario, which can be described in different ways. That looks like a persire. Charles applies the same line of thought to beliefs, and so ascribes 'besires' to Aristotle as well.

A key piece of evidence Charles appeals to is a complicated passage in *De Anima* III.7. Although I find Charles's reading fascinating, I do not think the text demands it. However, as this text is compressed and difficult, and addressing it quickly becomes fairly thorny, I shall reserve discussion of it for an appendix.[19] Instead, let me provide a couple of considerations, drawn from elsewhere, that perhaps suggest that Aristotle would *reject* besires.

First, consider again the passage from *De Motu Animalium* 6 we have already looked at. Insofar as Aristotle here groups cognitive states together as discriminative capacities (κριτικά), and thereby suggests that the mark of the cognitive is discerning or distinguishing something (he makes a similar claim at the beginning of *De Anima* III.3 and III.9), and, insofar as he groups these states together as *distinct from* desires, that naturally suggests that he views the states as different *in kind*. This is not jeopardised by the notion we glossed from *De Anima* III.10 that when one is moved in accordance with thought one is also moved in accordance with desire, since that evidently does not entail the *identity* of the moving thought with the desire (contra Charles 2006, 31–32). Nor is it jeopardised by the fact, as we saw, that Aristotle claims that preferential choice (προαίρεσις) straddles both thought and desire. After all, even the advocate of HTM, who accepts the No B-Ds principle, thinks that some states essentially *involve* both beliefs and desires. Indeed, the advocate of HTM claims that *motivation* is just such a state: one cannot be motivated without both beliefs and desires, where these are different kinds of state. So long as the beliefs and desires that make up the state are distinct existences, such that one could in principle have one without the other—and we do not identify the beliefs and desires—they will not count as besires. Preferential choices can be made up or composed of beliefs and desires without being besires.

Here is a second consideration. In contemporary metaethics, some philosophers have tried to argue against the existence of besires by appealing to the notion that beliefs and desires essentially have different 'directions of fit.'[20] Beliefs aim to fit the world, such that it is a failing in a belief if it fails to match the

---

19   Tuozzo (1994, 525) also appeals to *De Anima* III.7 in his attempt to argue that desire, for Aristotle, "is a special sort of cognition."

20   For discussion, see e.g., Platts (1979, 279), Smith (1987, 54 and 1994, 111–115), Little (1997), and Tenenbaum (2006). Several philosophers have argued that the distinction does not hold up under scrutiny; see Humberstone (1992) and, esp., Frost (2014). The notion of directions of fit is usually traced back to Anscombe's discussion in *Intention* (1957, 56), although Frost argues Anscombe has been misunderstood.

world; whereas failing to fit the world is not a failure in a desire, instead desires aim to change the world to fit them. Since beliefs and desires have different directions of fit—the argument goes—there cannot be states that are both. Or, rather, any state that appears to be such—such as *being motivated* itself—can in principle be broken up into distinct beliefs and desires with different directions of fit.

Interestingly, while it does not quite match this, one passage in Aristotle makes a related point. In *Nicomachean Ethics* VI.2, he writes:

> What affirmation and negation are in thinking (ἐν διανοίᾳ), pursuit and avoidance are in desire (ἐν ὀρέξει); so that since ethical virtue is a state concerned with preferential choice, and preferential choice (προαίρεσις) is deliberate desire, therefore both the reasoning must be true and the desire right (δεῖ διὰ ταῦτα μὲν τόν τε λόγον ἀληθῆ εἶναι καὶ τὴν ὄρεξιν ὀρθήν), if the preferential choice is to be good, and the latter must pursue what the former asserts ... [and we get] truth in agreement with right desire (ἀλήθεια ὁμολόγως ἔχουσα τῇ ὀρέξει τῇ ὀρθῇ). (1139a21–26, 31)

Aristotle appears to be drawing a distinction between two types of state, thinking and desire, and their corresponding appraisal. Thinking (διάνοια) can be said to affirm or deny something (of something) (see also especially *De Interpretatione* 6, 17a25–26), and is, accordingly, appraisable in terms of truth or falsity, whereas desiderative states can be said to pursue or avoid something and are, accordingly, appraisable in terms of correctness or incorrectness. In fact, presumably correctness and incorrectness is the broader category of which truth and falsity is a sub-category (hence the commonplace that beliefs will be *correct* if they are true). Beliefs or chains of reasoning will be correct or incorrect insofar as they are true or false, but desires are not literally true or false, although they can be correct or incorrect depending on whether or not they direct the agent to pursue or avoid certain actions—'correct' insofar as they motivate agents to pursue what they really *ought* to pursue and 'incorrect' insofar as they fail to do so.[21]

---

21   As this suggests, Aristotle advocates some kind of ethical realism. He thinks that the good person not only has different motivations from the bad person, but that the good person *gets it right* ('the good man differs from others most by seeing the truth in each class of things, being as it were the norm and the measure of them' (*EN* III.4, 1113a32–33; cf. *Eudemian Ethics* VII.2, 1235b18–1236a10; *EE* III.1, 1228b17–19; *EN* X.5, 1176a15–19). Of course, this still leaves open how the 'truth' in question is to be constructed, and what it actually amounts to (and how the good man *is* the norm and measure of it). For an exploration of Aristotle's moral realism, see, e.g., Charles (1995).

It is worth noting that in terms of their ultimate *appraisal* this would mean that beliefs and desires have the *same* direction of fit: they are both correct insofar as they match the 'world,' which amounts to *being true* for beliefs and *being good* or *choiceworthy* for desires. But that similarity is grounded in a more basic *difference of fit*. Thought *affirms* or *denies*, whereas desire *pursues* or *avoids*, and if we are to form a (good) preferential choice the (right) desire must *pursue* what the (true) thought *asserts*. Beliefs and desires, then, seem to be fundamentally different states, on Aristotle's view: the former are concerned with affirmation or denial, the latter with pursuit or avoidance.

If so, this counts against the besire reading of his view. For even when referring to a state that combines beliefs/thoughts and desires, namely, preferential choice, Aristotle keeps a sharp distinction between their relative roles. Preferential choices, it seems, in line with what we proposed earlier, are *composed of* or *incorporate* distinct thoughts and desires—an asserting thought and a pursuing desire—rather than form some new *sui generis* state that simply *is* both a desire and a thought. Decomposability seems to be accepted.

C. Aristotle and DO-DI. DO-DI insists that explanatorily basic desires are required for motivation. The key for this principle is that at some stage in the explanation, a desire that is not itself brought about or explained by a cognition is required for motivation. I shall return to issues connected with the formulation of DO-DI below. Many of those who advance anti-Humean accounts of motivation accept both MO-DI and the No B-Ds principle, and instead reject DO-DI. In contemporary metaethics, there are several different ways philosophers have attempted to reject DO-DI. They have held: (1) that beliefs or cognitive states can *generate* desires and so generate motivation (at least in rational agents); (2) that any desire that is required for motivation is merely *consequentially ascribed*, owing to the fact of motivation; and (3) that desiring and being motivated *are the same state*.[22]

It is probably fair to say that insofar as we can place their discussions in my framework, most of those who reject the notion that Aristotle advocates HTM would maintain that he rejects DO-DI. In fact, though, one central disputed topic in this area seems to me to be somewhat of a red herring. I refer to the

---

22   (1) seems to be advocated by Kantians, such as Korsgaard (1996) and Wallace (2006). Smith (1994, esp., ch. 3 and ch. 5) also appears to advocate this view (he explicitly rejects DO-DI in his 1997 article (100n18)). See also Darwall (1983, 39–40) and Foot (1995, 13). (2) seems to be the view advocated by Nagel (1970, 29–30) and Schiffer (1976). McDowell (1978) could also perhaps be construed as holding this view, rather than the besire version above. (3) seems to be the view of Dancy (1993, 19–20 and 2000, 86–88) and Alvarez (2010, 119–120).

fact, suggested by the quotation from Moss I provided at the beginning, that *phronesis* has some important bearing on this question. As Moss notes (2011 and 2014), a number of commentators have appealed to various features about *phronesis* in support of the view that Aristotle thinks that practical reason can set ends (thereby supporting an anti-Humean reading, as Moss characterises that). For instance, it is noted that Aristotle distinguishes *phronesis* from mere cleverness (*EN* VI.12, 1144a23–29), where the latter is closer to efficiency in instrumental reasoning; it is emphasised that Aristotle "endows *phronesis* with enormous ethical import," as Moss puts it, insofar as "without it, one cannot have any of the character virtues, and with it one has them all" (2014, 222; citing *EN* VI.13). It is also noted that some passages appear to attribute to *phronesis* the capacity of setting the goal. Indeed, in one he appears to claim that *phronesis* is 'true supposition of the end' (*EN* VI.9, 1142b31–32). On the other side, Humean interpreters emphasise a number of passages in which Aristotle claims that virtue makes the ends right and *phronesis* makes the things that contribute to (πρός) the ends right (see, for example, *EN* VI.12, 1144a7–9; VI.13, 1145a4–6). Overall, the dispute has led to a large literature in which advocates from both camps attempt to accommodate the (apparently) conflicting texts.[23]

My problem with appealing to *phronesis* in this context is that, however we ultimately understand Aristotle's claim that virtue sets the ends and *phronesis* the things that contribute to ends, it is going to be hard to construe *phronesis* as an undiluted rational process (unmixed with elements of desire) in the way that seems required for it to be germane to establishing whether or not Aristotle advances DO-DI. For he is very explicit that, strictly speaking, *phronesis* cannot exist without character virtue. "It is clear," he writes, "that it is impossible to be practically wise without being good" (VI.12, 1144a36–1144b1), where in context it is evident that 'being good' means possessing the character virtues. But then it is not going to be easy to construe *phronesis* as an undiluted cognitive process that *brings about* a conative state, as the anti-Humean would maintain, nor as a purely rational process that is itself incapable of doing so, as the Humean wants. The suspicion is, indeed, that if Aristotle had to demarcate a purely rational process in this domain, it would be 'cleverness', not *phronesis* (see especially VI.12, 1144a23–29 and VII.10, 1152a10–14). But it is unlikely that cleverness will motivate anything on its own, since *it* in fact *does* seem close to instrumental reasoning. Cleverness, Aristotle claims, "is such as to be able to do the things that tend towards the mark *we have set before ourselves*, and to hit

---

23 See, e.g., Fortenbaugh 1964; Irwin 1975; Sorabji 1973–4; Smith 1996; Moss 2011, 2012, chs. 7–8, and 2014.

it" (VI.12, 1144a24–25, my emphasis). It therefore will not itself support an anti-Humean reading either.

If focussing on the *phronimos* to address DO-DI is a bit of a red herring, it has at least helped reveal what we *do* need to establish in order to reject DO-DI, namely, a state that is un-contentiously cognitive needs to be shown to generate a desire or motivation without it tapping into, as we might put it, or drawing on some other desiderative state or disposition to get its desiderative or motivational force. Here are some considerations anti-Humean interpreters might offer. They might appeal, and have appealed, to the fact that Aristotle recognises a distinctly rational type of desire, 'wish' (βούλησις), which non-rational creatures cannot possess. If the rationality of wish is to be accounted for by it being grounded in deliberation (deliberation that is not itself dependent on some further non-deliberated desire), then Aristotle would appear to reject DO-DI, along the lines Nagel did when he introduced the notion of "motivated desires," that is, "desires that are *arrived at* by decision and after deliberation" (1970, 29).[24] Again, anti-Humeans might point to the fact that Aristotle claims that the non-rational part of the soul is capable of "listening to and obeying" reason (*EN* I.13, *EN* III.12, and *EN* VII.6). Does this not suggest that reason can motivate? And once again, it might be argued that Aristotle thinks that we can set components of our overall good by deliberation and be motivated accordingly (Irwin 1975).

These points, though, are not conclusive. There might be other ways of explaining the rationality of wish (βούλησις) without supposing that components of our overall good are grounded in deliberation. Perhaps Aristotle thinks that it is something about the end that these desires aim at that makes them only available to creatures that have *nous* and *logismos*, and hence appropriately labelled 'rational.' If so, then, although one might need rational capacities to possess such desires, the desires themselves would not need to be construed as *generated* by a purely cognitive process.[25] This could undermine the point regarding the non-rational part obeying and listening to reason as well: Aristotle

---

24 Interestingly, Nagel cites Aristotle's discussion of deliberation in *EN* III.3 as being a place where it was "pointed out before" that such desires exist. Irwin (1975, 571) calls such desires "deliberated desires."

25 See Pearson (2012, Ch. 7), Grönroos (2015b). Strictly, even the notion that *some wishes* (βουλήσεις) were formed through deliberation might seem to support the anti-DO-DI reading. But this would require that there wasn't any other desiderative force involved prior to the deliberation (see my response to the third anti-Humean consideration below) and yet wish (βούλησις) seems to be what is setting the end that is being deliberated about in the first place (*EN* III.5, 1113b3–5; *EE* II.10, 1226a11–14; cf. *EE* II.11, 1227b36–37) and so it is hard to see the deliberation as undiluted with desire, even if it channels and helps form a new desire.

might mean to refer to commands stemming from motivational wishes, which count as rational in the sense of the end aimed at, without intending to deny DO-DI by maintaining that an undiluted process of reasoning can resist a non-rational impulse. Finally, even if Aristotle thinks that we can deliberate about components of our overall good and be motivated accordingly (and against this, see, for example, Moss 2014, 223–224), this still might not involve him rejecting DO-DI. For it may be that, in order for this deliberation to be motivationally efficacious, it needs to draw on existing desires and desiderative dispositions that the agent already possesses. The deliberation might not, that is, create *ex nihilo*, desiderative states, but instead channel, shape, and make determinate, existing ones. Alternatively put, the deliberation may have to be embedded in appropriate desiderative states in order to make a motivational difference. In this respect, we might note that, in *De Motu Animalium*, Aristotle characterises practical reasoning in terms of premises pertaining to the good and premises pertaining to the possible (7, 701a11–25), and he clearly thinks of the former as identifying a desired end (an ὀρεκτόν) (*MA* 6, 700b23–29).

From the other side, it is natural for the Humean interpreter to appeal to Aristotle's emphasis on *character*. In *Nicomachean Ethics* VI.2, he writes:

> The origin (ἀρχή) of action—its efficient, not its final cause—is preferential choice, and that of preferential choice is desire (ὄρεξις) and reasoning (λόγος) with a view to an end (ὁ ἕνεκά τινος). This is why preferential choice cannot exist either without intellect and thought or without an ethical state (διὸ οὔτ᾽ ἄνευ νοῦ καὶ διανοίας οὔτ᾽ ἄνευ ἠθικῆς ἐστιν ἕξεως ἡ προαίρεσις); for good action and its opposite cannot exist without a combination of thought and character (εὐπραξία γὰρ καὶ τὸ ἐναντίον ἐν πράξει ἄνευ διανοίας καὶ ἤθους οὐκ ἔστιν). (1139a31–34)

Preferential choice (προαίρεσις) requires both reasoning with a view to an end *and* a desire. It cannot, that is to say, exist without both intellect and thought, the reasoning side, and an ethical state, the desiderative side. And here Aristotle traces the desiderative side of this equation back to the agent's character. Just as reasoning with a view to an end stems from intellect and thought, so too the desires that in part explain our preferential choices (and so actions) can themselves be traced back to our characters. Occurrent desires, on this understanding of Aristotle's view, stem from more basic desiderative dispositions we formed earlier.[26] The Humean interpreter may take this to support the DO-DI reading. When pressed on why an occurrent desire has formed in a particular

---

26   Characters are dispositions to act and feel; see, e.g., *EN* II.5.

HOW TO ARGUE ABOUT ARISTOTLE ABOUT PRACTICAL REASON   47

circumstance, the advocate of DO-DI will typically appeal to more basic desiderative states and character traits the agent possesses.[27]

However, simply witnessing Aristotle tracing desires back to character is not going to be sufficient to secure the DO-DI reading, and for three reasons. First, given what we have just noted about the relation between character and *phronesis*, we will need to know whether or not, when Aristotle refers to character, he has in mind character virtue 'in the strict sense,' since, if he does, that notion of character virtue will not easily help us work out whether or not he accepts DO-DI. Since character virtue in the strict sense requires a full complement of rational capacities, it will not be obvious whether cognitions themselves brought about the desires implied by such a state or not.[28] Second, Aristotle evidently thinks that some people are motivated to act in a way that *does not* match their character dispositions. One can, as he puts it, act unjustly, without being unjust (*EN* V.6, 1553a17–23; applied to akratic agents at *EN* VII.8, 1151a10).[29] But then, if the support for the DO-DI reading is meant to be provided by appealing to Aristotle's emphasis on character, how are the motivations of such agents to be explained in a way that is compatible with that principle?[30] Third, and most simply, the appeal to character does not strictly entail the rejection of DO-DI in any event. Even if Aristotle traces motivation back to character, he could also maintain that those character states were *in turn* formed in response to beliefs or other cognitive states the agent possessed.

---

27   Hence the need for 'desiderative dispositions' in the formulation of DO-DI. The advocate of DO-DI will appeal to the rich habituation and development of one's desiderative dispositions through the processes of growing up (and continuing to live). The *EN* VI.2 passage is perhaps more suggestive than the *phronesis* passages, insofar as Aristotle specifically considers the roles of desire and thought in action and so would not naturally be construed as having 'character in the strict sense' (which entails *phronēsis*, see next note) in mind.

28   Just as *phronesis* requires character virtue, so too virtue in the strict sense requires *phronesis* (*EN* VI.12, 1144b30–32; VI.13, 1144b19–21; and VI.13, 1144b26–28).

29   For discussion of this idea, see Pearson (2006).

30   Moss says something puzzling at this point. In spite of generally defending the view that character sets the end, she suddenly allows that reason *can* set the goal for akratic and enkratic agents, but insists that this is not how we are meant to get our values 'by nature' (2014, 240n26). If this were true, Aristotle would *reject* HTM: reason *can* bring about motivation on its own. The irony would be that it could only do so in *conflicted* agents, not unconflicted ones. The advocate of the HTM reading of Aristotle would, I think, be better off maintaining that even these actions that are apparently out of character can be traced to aspects of the agent's character, *when suitably specified*. Granted the agent does not have the character of someone who is fully unjust, but still her character is *such that* she can succumb to temptation on occasion and be led astray (cf. Pearson 2012, 249–250).

In this respect, perhaps more suggestive for the advocate of the DO-DI reading is the following passage from *Nicomachean Ethics* VII.8:

> virtue and vice respectively preserve and destroy the first principle (ἀρχή), and in actions that-for-the-sake-of-which (τὸ οὗ ἕνεκα) is the first principle, as the hypotheses are in mathematics; neither in that case is it reason (λόγος) that teaches the first principles, nor is it so here—virtue either natural or produced by habituation is what teaches right opinion about the first principle (ἀρετὴ ἢ φυσικὴ ἢ ἐθιστὴ τοῦ ὀρθοδοξεῖν περὶ τὴν ἀρχήν). (1151a15–19)[31]

Natural virtue and vices are possessed by non-rational animals and children from birth. Equally, 'habituated virtue,' here, presumably does not mean 'virtue in the strict sense,' since it is said to *teach us* right belief (ὀρθοδοξεῖν) about the first principle. In any event, there is evidently space, on Aristotle's account, between the states we are born with, on the one hand, and the states that we acquire by habituation but before we acquire full rational capacities, on the other. If Aristotle traces motivation back to character states that are not belief-based, this would suggest that he accepts DO-DI. No doubt, when rational capacities emerge in humans, such capacities will 'shape' and 'mould' these desiderative states in significant ways, but it seems reasonable to think that Aristotle holds that the desiderative force, as we might say, that is then shaped and moulded by further reasoning is there already, and, so, reasoning capacities do not *generate* desires as such.

In fact, though, even the idea that Aristotle thinks that our motivations can ultimately be traced back to non-belief-based habituated virtues would not itself rule out some kind of broadly cognitivist reading of Aristotle's account of motivation. Indeed, this is a respect where reflection on Aristotle's views might help contribute to the contemporary debates. Just suppose, for the sake of argument, that he rejects the view that beliefs can generate desires *ex nihilo* and, instead, holds, as suggested by the above passage, that our goals are, at some level, set by natural or non-belief-based habituated virtue. Would that mean that he rejects DO-DI?

---

31   Moss (2011 and 2012, 157) also appeals to this. Also important is *EE* II.11, 1227b22–25, which claims that there is no *logos* or reasoning about the goal. These seem more effective than some of the other 'goal passages' (as Moss terms them) which involve a contrast with *phronesis* (*EN* VI.12, 1144a7–9 and VI.13, 1145a4–6) for the reasons I have given above. The *EN* VII.8 passage, and the *EE* II.11 passage just mentioned, need contrasting with the *Metaphysics* XII passage I discuss below.

In fact, it might depend on how we formulate that principle. In his original 'How to argue ...' paper, Wallace formulated DO-DI as follows:

> DO-DI (Wal): "[the] processes of thought that gives rise to a desire (as 'output') can always be traced back to a further desire (as 'input'), one which fixes the basic evaluative principles from which the rational explanation of motivation begins." (1990, 370)

Neil Sinhababu formulates the principle as follows:

> DO-DI (Sin): "Desires can be changed as the conclusion of reasoning only if a desire is among the premises of the reasoning." (2009, 465)

The emphasis in these formulations on the 'process of thought' and the 'conclusion of reasoning' suggests that these versions of DO-DI only apply to belief-based or reason-based thinking, such that, if a desire were set by a state that *was not* grounded in a belief or a process of thought or in reasoning, then it would automatically satisfy DO-DI. But this invites the question of what DO-DI was intended to rule out. It was certainly intended to rule out the idea that a process of undiluted reasoning or deliberation could on its own generate desires. But ruling that out does not rule out some more broadly cognitivist reading of motivation, according to which motivational states are explanatorily downstream of cognitions more generally. In fact, Aristotle helps us to see just this point. In *De Anima* III.10, he writes:

> that which produces movement ... is first of all the object of desire (ὀρεκτόν); for this produces movement without being moved, by being thought of or grasped through *phantasia* (τῷ νοηθῆναι ἢ φαντασθῆναι)... (*An.* 433b10–12)

In order for an agent to possess a desire, she must grasp some object of desire, and, so, some desirability feature, through either thought **or phantasia**. But the latter, which can roughly be thought of as a quasi-perceptual construal, is, in this context, cognitive. It is, we might say, cognitive, but not thought-based. It shares the same direction of fit as other cognitive states (belief, perception), and, hence, Aristotle groups all such states together as discriminative capacites (κριτικά) in *De Motu Animalium* 6, but it does not require reasoning. And its inclusion here as a cognitive state that can grasp (at least some) desirability features enables Aristotle to explain our perception-based desires, as well as animal desire, which is important for him in *De Anima* III.9–10, since his

50 PEARSON

account of locomotion is meant to apply to all animals, not just human beings.[32]

Now, suppose we take it that the crux of HTM is to insist that two fundamentally different types of mental state are required to explain motivation, cognitive and conative. If so, we shall want to formulate DO-DI in terms of *cognitions broadly construed*, rather than in terms of belief, reasoning, or deliberation—as, indeed, I did at the beginning of this paper. Of course, broadening DO-DI in this way will put a different slant on Nagel's worry about adopting HTM that we mentioned then as well. Recall, rejecting HTM was thought by some (mistakenly in my view) to be necessary for prudential and moral realism. For we have a chance, at least, of reasoning with you to change your *viewpoint*, whereas if there is an ineliminable desiderative element to motivation, it may seem, as Nagel wrote, that "if one lacks the relevant desire, there is nothing more to be said" (1970, 28). But note that, even if a broadly cognitivist account of motivation is correct, this would not now entail that we could, even in principle, *reason* you into changing your viewpoint (and so motivation). For, just as a snake phobic may not be able to stop *seeing* a snake as dangerous, in spite of accepting the argument that it is not, so too our *phantasia*-based construals may not be responsive to such reasoning. Nonetheless, motivation will be taken to be explanatorily downstream, if not of our evaluative *beliefs*, at the very least, of our perception-based construals, and even if we cannot *reason you* into a change of motivation, effecting a change in motivation would still be a matter of getting you to see things differently.[33] Just as a course of cognitive therapy might enable the snake phobic to stop seeing the snake as dangerous, so too with moral matters.

Relatedly, on the view we are considering by drawing from *Nicomachean Ethics* VII.6, all the desires we form prior to developing rational capacities would be explanatorily downstream of certain perceptual-based *phantasiai*.[34]

---

32   I explore Aristotle's notion of perception-based desire and contrast it with the contemporary account provided by Scanlon (1998) in my 2011a chapter.

33   Cf. McDowell 1978, 21.

34   This, in fact, is Moss's reading of Aristotle, as that is spelled out in her 2011 article and 2012 book (e.g., 158ff). Although she holds that Aristotle thinks that *reason* cannot set ends, nonetheless, she does allow that we desire ends because they 'quasi-perceptually' appear good to us (2011, 254). This makes her view squarely *anti*-Humean by my lights, not 'quasi-Humean' as she states in her 2014 chapter. Indeed, in her 2011 article, she refers to her reading as 'non-Humean non-Rationalism' (251). Her ground, though, for accepting this version of anti-Humeanism seems rather weak to me. She simply appeals to the fact that wish (βούλησις), "a special and distinctively human species of desire," is "for the good, or at least what appears to one to be good" (2011, 251). If we could establish anti-Humeanism simply by appealing to the fact that desires have objects or involve seeing things a certain

HOW TO ARGUE ABOUT ARISTOTLE ABOUT PRACTICAL REASON

And this, of course, would naturally invite questions about what part *we* play in habituating ourselves into such states, given that we are not fully rational at the time. But even if a large part of this goes down to our upbringing (hence Aristotle's emphasis on such) that would still be compatible with a broad cognitivist reading. Educators could, in effect, whether they realise it or not, be seeking to make us *see* things a certain way, such that the motivations would then ensue.

But what about natural virtues and vices? Aristotle thinks that we possess natural virtues *at birth*. Does this not provide a clear instance in which desiderative states (those embodied in such traits) are not explanatorily downstream of cognitions? In fact, even that is not clear-cut. It could be that Aristotle would ultimately explain natural virtues and vices in terms of tendencies to see things a certain way, such that motivation ensues. If so, they would again be compatible with a broad cognitivist reading (a reading that sees him as rejecting DO-DI).

Rather than pursue this, let us instead turn to look at things from the other side. Can the anti-Humean interpreter actually offer an argument *in favour* of her reading? This reader, recall, is looking for a clear indication that Aristotle thinks that a cognitive state can bring about a desire without tapping into a prior desiderative disposition. Here's an argument for that conclusion I'd like to try out. In the *De Anima* III.10 passage just quoted, Aristotle claims that what *first of all* (πρῶτον πάντων) moves us is the object of desire, since this moves us without being moved, by being thought of or grasped through *phantasia*. The fact that the motivating content here is cognitive doesn't *itself* entail the rejection of DO-DI (and so support an anti-Humean reading). For it could be that even though the content that the agent is motivated by is cognitive content, that content will not be able to motivate the agent unless she desires it, whereby it is the desiring that makes the cognitive content light up as motivating. But, in fact, matters are a bit more complicated, since the priority in question does seem to be explanatory. Aristotle goes on to write:

> that which produces movement is twofold, that which is unmoved and that which produces movement. That is which is unmoved is the practical good, and that which produces movement and is moved is the faculty

---

way, we could have saved ourselves a lot of trouble. But, of course, we cannot. The question is whether we desire because we cognise the thing as good, such that the cognition explains or brings about the desire, or whether the desire is explanatorily basic, such that, even if it essentially involves some cognition, it is not to be explained as derivative of that cognition or generated by it.

of desire (for that which is moved is moved in so far as it desires, and desire as actual is a form of movement). (*An.* III.10, 433b14–18)

Desire, it seems, is actualised by the agent grasping a practical good. The unmoved mover in the practical case is the object of desire. And yet, it seems, it is our *grasping that* object of desire through some cognitive capacity that actualises the desire. Of course, Aristotle thinks that we can't have a desire without grasping some object of desire, and perhaps he thinks that we can't grasp an object of desire without desiring it. But he does at least seem to recognise an *explanatory* priority here. The unmoved mover (the object of desire) 'first of all' moves us in the sense that this is where the explanation of movement reaches its terminus. The unmoved mover can be said to move the moved mover (the capacity of desire, the ὀρεκτικόν) and the moved mover can be said to be moved by the unmoved mover and, in turn, itself move something else (the animal). Since it is our *cognising* the unmoved mover that enables the latter to actualise the moved mover, it appears that cognitions of value have at least an *explanatory* priority for Aristotle over desire.[35]

Promising though it may seem, the argument is inconclusive. The passage only strictly asserts the explanatory priority of the *object of desire* over *desire*, not the explanatory priority of **cognising the object of desire** over *desire*, and so it leaves open the precise relation between the latter two. The anti-Humean reading, which embraces besires, could exploit this and say the passage is compatible with the claim that cognising the object of desire *simply is* desiring it. Equally, the Humean reading, which accepts all three principles, could exploit it and maintain that the passage is compatible with the claim that cognising the object of desire only in part makes up (but is not identical with) desiring, which DO-DI can accommodate.

However, all is not lost, since there is some indication elsewhere that Aristotle would flesh out the explanatory priority in a way that *would* involve him rejecting DO-DI. In *Metaphysics* XII.7 Aristotle again makes his claim about the object of desire being an unmoved mover:

since that which moves is intermediate, there is a mover which moves without being moved ... the object of desire and the object of thought move in this way, they move without being moved. (1072a24–27)

---

35   Shields (2016, 362) misreads 433b13–18. That 'by which' motion is initiated (433b14) is not, as Shields claims, the faculty of desire. It is instead the 'instrument through which desire produces movement,' namely, 'something bodily' (433b19). And, contra Shields, the passage does indeed divide 'that which produces movement' into two, viz., an unmoved mover—the practical good—and a moved mover, the faculty of desire.

But, a few lines later, Aristotle draws the conclusion that wasn't explicitly stated in *De Anima* III.10, at least for thought-based desire. He writes (in Ross's translation): desire is consequent on opinion rather than opinion on desire, for thinking is the starting-point (ὀρεγόμεθα δὲ διότι δοκεῖ μᾶλλον ἢ δοκεῖ διότι ὀρεγόμεθα: ἀρχὴ γὰρ ἡ νόησις) (1072a2–30). This passage suggests we *can*, after all, fill out *De Anima* III.10 as stating that *cognising* the object of desire is explanatorily prior to desiring. And that looks like an argument in favour of thinking that Aristotle rejects DO-DI. Desire is consequent upon (διότι) belief (belief here—but presumably the argument would apply to cognition more generally)[36] because the starting point (ἀρχή), the first point we trace everything back to in our explanation, is an unmoved mover. The unmoved mover in the practical case is the object of desire. And yet it is our *grasping that* through some cognitive capacity that actualises the desire. Of course, Aristotle thinks that we can't have a desire without grasping some object of desire, and, as noted, it may well be the case that he thinks that we can't grasp an object of desire without desiring it. But he does seem to recognise an *explanatory* priority here. The unmoved mover (the object of desire) is what 'first of all' moves us in so far as this is where the explanation of movement reaches its terminus. The unmoved mover moves the moved mover (the capacity of desire, the ὀρεκτικόν). The moved mover is moved by the unmoved mover and itself moves something else (the animal). Since it is our *cognising* the unmoved mover that enables the unmoved mover to actualise the moved mover, it seems that cognitions of value have at least an *explanatory* priority for Aristotle over desire. This seems the strongest argument yet that he would reject HTM, via rejecting DO-DI.

Doubtless, further considerations and passages would need to be adduced to support and bolster this, but those will have to wait for another occasion. My chief goal in this paper has been to investigate Aristotle's views with respect to HTM. In clearly setting out the commitments of HTM, we can see what might count as a germane consideration one way or the other. For Aristotle to reject HTM, he must reject at least one of three principles: MO-DI, No B-Ds, or DO-DI. The Humean interpreter needs to show that Aristotle is plausibly thought of as committed to all three of these principles. The anti-Humean interpreter needs to show us conclusively that he rejects at least one of them. The goal going forward will be to attempt to establish the answer conclusively one way or the other. The goal is worth pursuing too, since it will have a bearing on our most

---

36   Moss (2012, 4 and n4) seems to wish to translate δοκεῖν, here, in a way that would be consonant with her view, namely, as 'seems.' But that we have νόησις in the second clause unequivocally specifies δοκεῖν as reason-based. And the context of the passage dictates this too.

fundamental understanding of Aristotle's ethical enterprise, from his account of habituation and upbringing, through to his account of practical reasoning, through to his prudential and moral realism. It will also have a bearing on the debate Moss and others have been having concerning HTR (unsurprisingly, if HTM and HTR aren't truly independent of each other, as suggested in section I above). In particular, the considerations adduced in reflecting on DO-DI seem germane to that discussion and the final denial of DO-DI would look to provide a sense in which reason can 'set' ends for Aristotle. Finally, working out Aristotle's view in this area may also have a bearing on current philosophical debates as well, as we have also seen at various points (for example, in the introduction and consideration of 'persires' and in the formulation of DO-DI).

Appendix on *De Anima* III.7

In section II.B, I noted that in support of his besire/persire reading of Aristotle David Charles appeals to *De Anima* III.7. A full discussion of the relevant parts of *De Anima* III.7 would require a paper on its own, so in this appendix I shall of necessity have to be fairly schematic. My aim is simply to argue that Charles's reading is not required of us. If the considerations I advanced in II.B also prompt us to think that Aristotle accepts the No B-Ds principle, they would provide further indirect support for my reading (or any reading that doesn't commit Aristotle to besires/persires).

Here is a key passage from *De Anima* III.7 that should serve for our purposes:

> [A] ... to perceive is like bare expressing or understanding; but when the object is pleasant or painful, [the perceptual soul], as if affirming or denying, pursues or avoids [the object]. [B] To feel pleasure or pain is to be active with the perceptual mean towards what is good or bad as such. Aversion and desire, with respect to their actualisation (ἡ κατ' ἐνέργειαν), are the same [as this] (ταὐτό). [C] The capacity of desire and the capacity of aversion are not different, either from one another or from the faculty of sense-perception, but their being *is* different. (431a8–14).[37]

---

37   There is substantial discussion of the passage in Whiting (2002), Charles (2006) and Corcilius (2011). There are also shorter treatments in, e.g., Modrak (1987, 141) Wedin (1988, 110–113), Tuozzo (1994, 535–536), Lorenz (2006, 139–140), and Gregoric (2007, 114–115). Hicks (1907, 527–530), Ross (1961, 303–304), Hamlyn (1968, 145–146) and Polanksy (2007, 483–487) provide commentary. We also have ancient commentaries by Simplicius* and Philoponus, and the mediaeval commentary of Aquinas. *Editor's note: Simplicius's authorship of the commentary on the *De Anima* is the topic of the first paper in this volume.

Charles (2006, 21) claims that Aristotle here commits himself to the following identity claims:

(1) perceiving A as pleasant = being pleasurably affected by A.
(2) being pleasurably affected by A = sensually desiring A
(3) perceiving A as pleasant = sensually desiring A

On Charles's view, this means that for Aristotle:

> perceiving A as pleasant, being pleasurably affected by A and desiring A are not distinct types of activity, instances of one occurring after instances of the other. Rather, there is just one type of activity which can be described in three different ways. (2006, 21)

The relevant part of this, for my purposes, is the equation of perceiving A as pleasant with sensually desiring A. For this, in my terminology, is to commit Aristotle to persires.

Without addressing potential philosophical difficulties with this view, I simply want to offer an alternative reading.[38] [A] clearly doesn't commit us to persires, since Aristotle could mean that when the object is cognised as pleasant or painful a further state of desire arises in response. But what about [B]? Doesn't this assert that desire and aversion are the same as some kind of (pleasurable or painful) perceptual activity, as Charles suggests? The key to resisting Charles's reading, as I see it, is the ἡ κατ' ἐνέργειαν which Charles takes to refer to the activity of the desire (he translates it: 'as far as the activity itself goes'). This signification follows the model of the way seeing is related to sight: when the capacity to see is actualised, seeing takes place. But Aristotle provides another model, instanced by the art of building, or the medical art. In such cases, the actualisation can either be thought of as the exercise of the capacity (in which case it would be analogous to the way in which seeing is the actualisation of sight) or, alternatively, the end product of it, what the successful execution of the activity results in. As Aristotle puts it: 'from the art of building there results a house as well as the process of building' (*Metaph.* IX.8, 1050a26–27). So too, the successful actualisation of the medical art is either healing or health. My suggestion is that when Aristotle claims that desire (ἡ) κατ' ἐνέργειαν, is the same as sensory pleasure, he means the realised desire or aversion in the sense in which the actualisation of the capacity to build can be thought of as, for example, a house, and the actualisation of the medical art can be thought

---

38   See my 2011b, 168, for some discussion.

of as health. He is, that is, referring to the realisation or fulfilment of the desire or aversion, rather than the simple activity of the capacity. On this reading, Aristotle is only claiming that a fulfilled sensory desire is the same as pleasure or that a realised aversion is the same as pain. He hasn't equated certain kinds of cognitive state (perceptions as pleasant) with certain kinds of desiring (sensually desiring), he has simply noted that a fulfilled sensory desire *just is* a sensory pleasure. If I fulfil my desire for an ice-cream, the fulfilment is the pleasure of eating the ice-cream. But that leaves the distinction between cognitive and conative states intact.

Now turn to [C]. Doesn't Aristotle here assert the identities that Charles highlights? The key to this is to grasp what Aristotle might mean in this context by things being 'the same, but different in being.' Aristotle claims that two things are the same but different in being if they are the same in some respect but have different accounts. An example he provides in *Physics* III.3 is that the road from Thebes to Athens is the same as the road from Athens to Thebes, but not the same in being (202b14–16) (as an example of two things that are the same in account he suggests 'raiment' [λώπιον] and 'dress' [ἱμάτιον]). Clearly the roads are the same spatio-temporal entity (so that if you are on one, you are always also on the other), even though they have different accounts (one gets you to Thebes, the other to Athens). Here then is one case, but Aristotle also uses the phrase 'same but different in being' even if the items said to be the same are not co-extensive, but one is just a subset of the other. A clear case of this is with Aristotle's notion of general justice. This type of justice picks out a subset of complete virtue (τελεία ἀρετή), namely, those that concern our relations to another (πρὸς ἕτερον) (EN V.1, 1129b26–27). And yet Aristotle is still happy to assert that justice in this sense and complete virtue are 'the same, but different in being' (V.1, 1130a12). His explanation is that 'what, as a relation to others, is justice is, as a certain kind of state without qualification, virtue' (EN V.1, 1130a12–13). A still different type of example is provided in *De Anima* II.12. Aristotle claims that 'that which perceives (τὸ αἰσθανόμενον)' (that is, the sense organ) is the same as but different in being from the perceptual capacity (τὸ αἰσθητικόν) (424a25–26). These are not physically the same thing; indeed, Aristotle states that only one of them (the sense organ) is a physical magnitude (424a26–28), whereas the other is a certain *logos* and potentiality of that. Instead, they are 'the same,' it seems, only in the sense that each actualisation of one is also, by that very fact, an actualisation of the other, and non-accidentally so (to see, for example, one exercises one's perceptual capacity and in so doing employs one's eyes).

The first two notions of sameness-but-difference-in-being might appear to suggest Charles's reading of [C], since on those readings Aristotle would be

HOW TO ARGUE ABOUT ARISTOTLE ABOUT PRACTICAL REASON

saying that one and same activity can be described as desiring or perceiving (the difference between these two understandings of sameness-but-difference-in-being here would simply be that on the latter there could be an imperfect overlap, but nonetheless when they do overlap, they are one and the same, except in account). But what about the third understanding of same-but-different-in-being? On this reading, the capacity of (sensory) desire, the capacity of (sensory) aversion, and the capacity of perception are all 'the same', in the sense that manifestations of each of these capacities are manifestations of the capacity of perception. What would this amount to? [B] suggests that to feel pleasure or pain involves being active with the perceptual mean, but here the suggestion is not simply that *realised* desires and aversions can be considered manifestations of the capacity of perception (i.e., as being sensory pleasures and pains), but that desires and aversions *themselves* can be considered manifestations of the capacity of perception. Does that commit him to persires? I think not. All it requires is that *perceptual content* is involved in sensory desires. Insofar as sensory desires involve *sensing something as prospectively pleasant*, they will involve manifestations of the perceptual capacity (mostly likely, the contents of perceptual *phantasia*),[39] and non-accidentally so. And, if the notion of sameness-but-difference-in-being is along the lines of the third example we considered of this, this need not imply that the perceptual content and the desire are one-and-the-very-same thing. Desire and aversion will essentially *involve* or *invoke* some kind of perceptual state—we can't have one without the other—but that wouldn't make them simply different ways of describing the same activity. Desires might be something over and above perceptual activities (namely, some kind of psychic pursuit). Analogously, the perceptual capacity isn't just another way of describing the perceptual organ but is something over and above that even though it essentially invokes it (for one thing, the latter, but not the former, is a physical magnitude).

Aristotle also claims in [C] that the capacity of desire and the capacity of aversion are the same as 'each other,' but different in being. This need not mean that he thinks each desire can also sensibly be characterised as an aversion (that is, a desire for A as an aversion to not-A). It could simply mean that psychic pursuits (desires) and avoidances (aversions) should be considered manifestations of the same underlying capacity, namely, being conatively affected by our environment. Analogously, to run towards something and to run away from something are manifestations of the same physical capacity.

---

39   In *De Anima* III.10 Aristotle claims that the capacity of desire is not possible without *phantasia*, and 'all *phantasia* is either deliberative or perceptual (φαντασία δὲ πᾶσα ἢ λογιστικὴ ἢ αἰσθητική)' (433b28–30).

Finally, it might be worth noting that while the *De Anima* III.7 passage does not entail Charles's persire/besire reading of Aristotle, part [A] in that passage might naturally suggest the anti-Humean account I've tentatively advanced in this paper. While normal perception is like a simple expressing or intellectual grasping (φάναι μόνον καὶ νοεῖν), when the object is pleasant or painful, the perceptual soul,[40] as if making something akin to an assertion or denial, pursues or avoids the object in question. 'Pursuits' of the perceptual soul would look to be desires: at the level of the agent, to experience one's perceptual part 'pursuing' something will presumably amount to feeling a perception-based desiderative response. But note that Aristotle simply claims that *when* the object is pleasant, such a desire is formed. Presumably he means: when the object is grasped by the perceptual soul as one that is prospectively pleasant, the agent forms a desire for that object. If that is the right reading, a desiderative response would seem to be entailed simply by the agent cognising the object as pleasant.[41] And that would seem to amount to a denial of DO-DI (and hence a denial of HTM).[42]

---

40   Although the subject is not expressed in the Greek, we do have feminine participles, καταφᾶσα and ἀποφᾶσα, with which the implied subject must agree. This rules out, e.g., 'man' (ἄνθρωπος). 'Perception' (αἴσθησις) is a possibility (Hicks 1907, 527), so too is 'soul' (ψυχή) (Ross 1961, 303–304; Hamlyn 1968, 63; Tuozzo, 1994, 535; Whiting 2002, 154; Lorenz, 2006, 139). However, later on in *De Anima* III.7, Aristotle develops a directly parallel account to the one above for 'the thinking soul' (ἡ διανοητικὴ ψυχή) (431a14), which suggests that in our passage, where he is concerned with perception, he most likely has in mind 'the perceptual soul' (ἡ αἰσθητικὴ ψυχή) (so too Charles 2006, 19).

41   Cf. also *EN* VII.6, 1149a25–b3 and, for discussion, my 2011b.

42   I would like to thank the audiences at my seminar and talk at the College of the Holy Cross for their stimulating and instructive discussion of my ideas here, and Howard Curzer for his written commentary. I would also like to thank an anonymous reviewer for extremely helpful comments on the submitted version. A much earlier version of the paper was given at Oxford University. Again, I thank the audience for their questions and comments.

COLLOQUIUM 2

Commentary on Pearson

Howard J. Curzer
Texas Tech University

Abstract

The *Humean* interpretation of Aristotle takes him to say that the goals of action are ultimately specified by desire. The *Combo* interpretation takes Aristotle to say that the goals of action are ultimately specified, sometimes by reason, other times by desire, and yet other times by both. I agree with Pearson that there are passages supporting each side and that the passages Pearson introduces into the debate support the Combo interpretation. To further support the Combo interpretation, I identify four features that Humeans want in a moral theory, and then show that a Humean interpretation of the passages bearing directly on the debate blocks the attribution of these features to Aristotle. A Humean interpretation may produce an Aristotle who is technically Humean, but this Aristotle will not accept the doctrines that make a Humean theory of motivation attractive to Humeans in the first place.

Keywords

Aristotle – Humean – motivation – desire – action

I   Introduction

I find myself in the classic nightmare scenario for commentators; I agree with everything Pearson says. Thus, my comment will have to go in a different direction.

The issues Pearson explores are important because they bear on a crucial, currently hot topic: How are goals of action in each situation specified, according to Aristotle? Three answers have academic backers in the secondary literature.

© KONINKLIJKE BRILL NV, LEIDEN, 2020 | DOI:10.1163/22134417-00351P06

The *Humean* interpretation says that the goals of action are ultimately specified by desire.[1]

Conversely, the *Anti-Humean* interpretation says that the goals of action are ultimately specified by reason.[2] I am familiar with three versions of the Anti-Humean interpretation:

a. Means are components, so goals are specified by deliberation (Wiggins 1980, 224–225).

b. Ends are also means, so goals are specified by deliberation (Cooper 1975, 18).

c. Ethics is an Aristotelian science, so goals are specified by theoretical reason (DeMoss 1990, 63–79; Reeve 1992, 7–66; and Sorabji 1980, 206–207, 216).

The *Combo Picture* says that the goals of action are ultimately specified, sometimes by reason, other times by desire, and yet other times by both (Curzer 2015, 129–153).

I agree with Pearson's claims that Aristotle does not hold the *Humean Theory of Normative Reasons*, and does hold the *No Besires* principle and the *Motivation-Out Desire-In* principle, which rules out pathway (C), below. The *Desire-Out Desire-In principle* offers two possibilities. Desire may produce action with no involvement of reason, which may be designated as pathway (A). Alternatively, reason may produce a desire, which, in turn, motivates, but only when reason has already been sparked by a desire in the first place (pathway (B)). In both cases, desire sets the goal. Practical reason is solely instrumental. If Aristotle accepts all three principles, then he accepts the *Humean Theory of Motivation* (HTM). The *Humean interpretation* attributes HTM to Aristotle.

The alternative I favor is the *Combo interpretation*, which is similar in some ways to the Dual Process views currently in vogue in psychology (Kahneman 2011). The Combo interpretation agrees that agents sometimes use the two pathways initiated by desire allowed by HTM, but maintains that agents sometimes respond to situations along a third pathway, too. This pathway has reason responding directly to perception by setting goals (pathway (D)). Agents come to believe through reasoning that they *should* have certain desires. Then, they talk and train themselves into feeling and acting upon these desires.

---

1 Moss (2012) is the most visible proponent, although she describes her view as 'quasi-Humean.'

2 Pearson (50n34) and Moss (2012) agree that perception and *phantasia* are cognitive, though non-rational. They disagree about whether goal-setting by these activities counts as Humean or anti-Humean. I shall dodge this dispute, and talk only about reason.

11 How to Argue about Dead Philosophers

In the next part of the paper, Pearson lists various passages that Humean interpreters and their critics use to try to defeat each other. Then, Pearson shows that none of these passages is decisive; the other side has countermoves in each case. This should surprise no one. Generally speaking, there are three standard approaches to interpretive disputes:

Overwhelming, straightforward textual evidence would convince people. But in such cases, disputes usually do not get going in the first place. Thus, overwhelming, straightforward textual evidence seldom settles anything.

Underwhelming, convoluted textual evidence never settles anything either because, when confronted with an inconvenient passage, interpreters (a) reinterpret, (b) retranslate, (c) find manuscript transmission errors, or (d) declare that Aristotle had a bad day when he wrote the passage.

Charitable interpretation of textual evidence never convinces people because interpreters are willing to attribute contradictory and counterintuitive views to pre-twentieth-century philosophers. Interpreters confronted with a charitable interpretation that takes a crucial passage in an unwanted direction: (a) dismiss the interpretation as anachronistic, (b) deny that it is more charitable, (c) go mystical, or (d) again declare that Aristotle had a bad day when he wrote the passage. Thus, charitable interpretation does not persuade.

So, I agree with Pearson that the range of passages deployed so far in the debate between Humean and Combo readings will not settle the debate. But that is because I believe that passages *never* settle interpretive debates. Since Pearson's title began, "How to argue about Aristotle..." and since he recognized that all passages so far are inconclusive, I hoped that Pearson would offer a new, *rhetorically effective* approach to textual interpretation in his paper's last section. Alas, he offered yet another pair of convoluted passages (*De Anima* 433b10–18, *Metaphysics* 1072a24–30).

Sigh!

For what it is worth, I think Pearson is right about these passages, although as he, himself, points out, Humeans do have a reply.

III   A Different Sort of Argument

The usual approach would be to argue that the Combo interpretation fits Aristotle's text better than the Humean interpretation. Since I believe that passages will not settle the debate, my approach is different. I shall argue that even if Humeans could construct a Humean interpretation that fits Aristotle's text very well, it wouldn't be worth doing *for the Humeans*. The Humeans will not be satisfied unless they show that Aristotle holds an *attractive version* of HTM, but in order to advance a Humean interpretation of Aristotle, Humeans must give up the aspects of HTM that they find attractive. When HTM is pressed into service as an interpretation of Aristotle, it becomes either uncool or unAristotelian. Humeans must give up either the advantages of HTM, or the things that make Aristotle, Aristotle.[3]

To be clear, I am not going to critique HTM itself. My claim is not that Hume was wrong, or that contemporary Humeans are wrong. Nor will I restrict myself to what Humeans *say* is attractive about HTM. Instead, I shall try to uncover what is *really* motivating them—the features of HTM that provide its unconscious, powerful appeal. For example, Sinhababu argues for HTM on the grounds of simplicity (2009, 465–500). He maintains that HTM is preferable to the alternatives because HTM requires the postulation of fewer entities. But this cannot be his main motive. After all, HTM runs counter to our phenomenological experience,[4] and postulates hidden motives, so HTM is counterintuitive and functionally unfalsifiable. The advantages of simplicity do not straightforwardly outweigh these drawbacks. Of course, attributing unconscious motivations to Humeans is a speculative business, but it coheres with the spirit of HTM. Humeans themselves make liberal use of unconscious motives.

---

3   Showing that *no* attractive features are left to HTM is a project beyond the scope of this comment.

4   Sinhababu (2009) tries to explain away the ways in which HTM mis-describes the experience of conflict between one's duty and desires by offering an explanation of why motives of duty feel different from motives of desire. But moral motivation does not just feel different; it feels moral.

COMMENTARY ON PEARSON   63

I shall list four of HTM's attractions, and show that they are incompatible with bedrock Aristotelian positions.[5]

IV   Right Rules

A. HTM. Anyone who has peered past the reasons people give for their actions and asked, "Why did he, she, or they *really* do that?" will quickly discover that the reasons offered for actions are frequently not the actual motives. Of course, some reasoning is instrumental, but I am talking about ultimate reasons. (a) In numerous cases, action is automatic or habitual; there is no decision-making. (b) In many other cases, agents act on unconscious desires. (c) In yet other cases, agents are engaged in self-deception; they act on sorta-kinda conscious desires. In all of these cases, there is the appearance of goal-setting reasoning but it is an illusion or a rationalization. From the obvious fact that goal-setting reasoning is *often* an epi-phenomenon, it is a small step to the Humean thesis that goal-setting reasoning is *always* an epi-phenomenon. This thesis is one of the underlying appeals of HTM. To put it crudely, Humeans can feel superior to the rest of us. We are fooled, but they recognize what is really going on in the agent's head.

B. Combo Picture. The Combo Picture is less extreme. It acknowledges that goal-setting reasoning is *often* illusion or rationalization, but also allows that sometimes our own decisions and those of others stem from goal-setting reasoning.

C. Aristotle. Aristotle illustrates decision-making in several passages, particularly within his discussion of incontinence. Each illustration explicitly includes a bit of reasoning that sets the goal within a certain situation by starting from a general principle and moving to a particular application of that principle. Aristotle does not mention a desire lurking upstream of the general principle. For example, Aristotle gets to the goal in one situation as follows: "I need a covering, a coat is a covering: I need a coat" (*De Motu Animalium* 701a17–19).[6] Supporting the claim that Aristotelian goal-setting begins with rule/case reasoning, Aristotle gives various rules and instructions about how to apply them (Curzer, 2015 57–92). For example, Aristotle says, "If we can, we should return the equivalent of what we have received" (*Nicomachean Ethics* 1163a1–2). He goes on to detail the application of this rule at length (*EN* 1163a1–1165a35).

---

5   Of course, all interpretations use passages. To establish Aristotle's bedrock views, passages are crucial. But these fall into the category of overwhelming, straightforward textual evidence.

6   See also *EN* 1146b35–1147a8, *EN* 1147a25–1147b3, and *An.* 434a16–21.

D. Verdict. The Combo picture, but not HTM, matches our experience. Reason sometimes *seems* to set goals. Similarly, the Combo picture, but not HTM, accords with Aristotle's illustrations of goal-setting, and his use of rules. A Humean interpretation of Aristotle might allow that rule/case reasons do motivate, but still maintain that the general rules derive from a previous, unconscious desire to flourish. Alternatively, each rule/case syllogism might be reduced to a means/ends syllogism, an intermediate link in a chain of motivations anchored in postulated, unconscious, goal-setting desires. But both of these moves would require twisting the text of Aristotle's illustrations. The straightforward way of reading Aristotle's examples is that they begin with syllogisms rather than desires and these are rule/case syllogisms rather than means/ends syllogisms.

v Conditioning

A. HTM. When it comes to character improvement, Humeans are impressed by the power of positive and negative reinforcement, and the impotence of everything else. People may talk and talk, but if they want to change their preteens', partners', prisoners', patients', or even their own personalities, then they must offer incentives. Indeed, according to HTM, agents perceive and desire things under the guise of the pleasant. All character improvement is accomplished through habituation, understood as conditioning. Teaching is useful only in improving instrumental reasoning.

B. Combo Picture. The Combo Picture is again less extreme. It acknowledges that conditioning is *often* the most effective strategy of character improvement but also allows that sometimes people are ready to be improved by teaching.

C. Aristotle. Aristotle does say that habituation is how agents acquire character virtues and teaching is reserved for the acquisition of intellectual virtues, including practical wisdom (*EN* 1103a14–17). But he clarifies this by observing that agents do not possess character virtues until they possess practical wisdom (*EN* 1144b30–31). Thus, mere habituation is insufficient to produce character virtue; teaching is also required. It is a necessary second stage on the way to character virtue (*EN* 1179b23–31). Teaching does not merely aim at improving instrumental reasoning but also aims to instill values and, thus, change desires. Agents striving to become virtuous not only ask themselves, "WW-*phronimoi*D?" but also ask their teachers, "What should I want to want?"

D. Verdict. A selling point of HTM is its story of character improvement through conditioning. But Humean interpreters must abandon this story in order to incorporate Aristotle's insistence on the need for teaching.

COMMENTARY ON PEARSON

VI   Human Exceptionalism

A. HTM. According to Humeans, practical reason is overrated. True, it does important work. But it is only instrumental, after all, so it differs from the reasoning of animals only by degree. Practical reason is not what sets us apart from animals. Nor is it the core of a happy life.

B. Combo Picture. The Combo Picture, by contrast, says that humans are special because, alone among animals, humans can set ends rationally. And the happy life of morally virtuous activity centrally includes the end-setting activity of practical reason.

C. Aristotle. Aristotle considers reason to be *the* feature that distinguishes us from other animals and what makes us human (*EN* 1097b25–1098a17). Because it is distinctive and essential, reason (both theoretical and practical) must be the focus of the happy human lives (the contemplative life and the life of morally virtuous activity). Aristotle famously says, "we state the function of man to be a certain kind of life, and this to be an activity or actions of the soul implying a rational principle" (*EN* 1098a12–14). In Aristotle's view, therefore, reason is supremely important.

D. Verdict. Humean interpreters might try to hold onto the idea that practical reason does not make people special, and seek for something else which does so. (a) They might observe that human perception is the distinctive and essential feature of humans because it includes "ethical sensitivity." However, insofar as human perception differs from the perception of other animals, it does so because it involves reason. (b) They might observe that humans deliberate, while animals do not. So, deliberation is the distinctive and essential feature of humans. However, animals have cleverness. The difference between human deliberation and animal cleverness is reason. (c) They might observe that humans engage in theoretical reasoning, while animals do not. So theoretical reasoning is the distinctive and essential feature of humans. However, Aristotle says that the life of morally virtuous activity is one of the two happy human lives. Yet it does not centrally involve theoretical reason. Generalizing, it seems that a Humean interpretation of Aristotle must concede the importance of practical reason since Aristotle takes it to be essential to our humanity and, therefore, central to the happy life. But both of these concessions are anathema to Humeans.

VII   Paradigm People

A. HTM. An ideal that fascinates many people is the *moral sage*. The moral sage not only reacts perfectly to all situations, but also does so without indecision or hesitation. In particular, the moral sage sees clearly and immediately what goals to try to achieve. We all know, and stand in awe of, people who seem to approach this ideal, people who reliably and automatically strike just the right note. The ideal of the shoot-from-the-hip moral sage combines nicely with HTM because what slows decision-making down is the attempt to set goals rationally. According to HTM, this attempt can be abandoned without cost; it is futile.

B. Combo Picture. The Combo Picture's paradigm person is comparatively unexciting. Being thoughtful—considering options carefully, taking one's time, reasoning one's way to a decision in hard cases—is not as glamourous as moral sagehood. However, thoughtfulness is what we ourselves aim at and what we urge our children to learn. Shooting from the hip may be what the cool kids do, but taking careful aim is what actually works.

C. Aristotle. Aristotle does not praise, or even mention, the ideal of effortless, thought-free gliding through life. Aristotle does not indicate that setting an end quickly is desirable.[7] The moral sage is not found in his corpus. Indeed, Aristotle's exemplars are people of practical wisdom (*phronimoi*). Aristotle gives pride of place to practical reasoning rather than to desire.

D. Verdict. The Combo picture fits Aristotle's view, but a Humean interpretation of Aristotle would have to give up the attractive ideal of the moral sage. Aristotle is just not interested in this ideal.

VIII   Conclusion

I have identified four points at which HTM conflicts with bedrock Aristotelian positions, and used these points of conflict to argue against the Humean interpretation in a novel way. Rather than arguing that the Combo interpretation fits the text better than the Humean interpretation, I observed that a Humean interpretation of Aristotle must relinquish four attractive features of HTM. Naturally, Humeans cannot be persuaded by mere reason to abandon the

---

7   Aristotle does stress the importance of perception (*EN* 1126b2–4, *EN* 1109b20–23, *EN* 1112b34–1113a1), but that is quite different than saying that perception is the sole determinant of decision-making. Aristotle's point is that correct perception of the situation is necessary for decision-making. He does not claim that it is sufficient.

Humean interpretation of Aristotle. One must show them that they do not *desire* such an interpretation.[8]

---

8 Many thanks to May Sim for inviting me to comment, to Giles Pearson for his fine paper, and for several suggestions that enhanced this comment.

COLLOQUIUM 2

Pearson/Curzer Bibliography

Alvarez, M. 2010. *Kinds of Reasons: An Essay in the Philosophy of Action*. Oxford: Oxford University Press.

Anscombe, G.E.M. 1957. *Intention*. Cambridge, MA: Harvard University Press.

Barry, M. 2007. Realism, Rational Action, and the Humean Theory of Motivation. *Ethical Theory and Moral Practice* 10.3:231–242.

Barry, M. 2010. Humean Theories of Motivation. *Oxford Studies in Metaethics* 5:195–223.

Charles, D. 1995. Aristotle and modern realism. In *Aristotle and Moral Realism*, ed. R. Heinaman, 135–172. Boulder: Westview Press.

Charles, D. 2006. Aristotle's Desire. In *Mind and Modality: Studies in the History of Philosophy in Honour of Simo Knuuttila*, eds. v. Hirvonen, T. Holopainen, and M. Tuominen, 19–40. Leiden: Brill.

Cooper, J. 1975. *Reason and Human Good in Aristotle*. Cambridge, MA: Harvard University Press.

Corcilius, K. 2011. Aristotle's definition of non-rational pleasure and pain and desire. In *Aristotle's* Nicomachean Ethics, *A Critical Guide*, ed. J. Miller, 117–143. Cambridge: Cambridge University Press.

Curzer, H. 2015. Aristotle's Practical Syllogisms. *The Philosophical Forum* 46.2:129–153.

Curzer, H. 2015. Rules Lurking at the Heart of Aristotle's Virtue Ethics. *Apeiron* 49.1:57–92.

Dancy, J. 1993. *Moral Reasons*. Oxford: Blackwell.

Dancy, J. 1995. Why there really is no such thing as a theory of motivation. *Proceedings of the Aristotelian Society* 95:1–18.

Dancy, J. 2000. *Practical Reality*. Oxford: Oxford University Press.

Darwall, S. 1983. *Impartial Reason*. London: Cornell University Press.

Davidson, D. 1980. *Actions and Events*. Oxford: Oxford University Press.

DeMoss, D. 1990. Acquiring Ethical Ends. *Ancient Philosophy* 10:63–79.

Foot, P. 1995. Does Moral Subjectivism Rest on a Mistake? *Oxford Journal of Legal Studies* 15.1:1–14

Fortenbaugh, W.W. 1964. Aristotle's Conception of Moral Virtue and Its Prescriptive Role. *Transactions and Proceedings of the American Philological Association* 95: 77–87.

Frost, K. 2014. On the Very Idea of Direction of Fit. *Philosophical Review* 123.4:429–484.

Gregoric, P. 2007. *Aristotle on the Common Sense*. Oxford: Oxford University Press.

© KONINKLIJKE BRILL NV, LEIDEN, 2020 | DOI:10.1163/22134417-00351P07

PEARSON/CURZER BIBLIOGRAPHY

Grönroos, G. 2015. Why Is Aristotle's Vicious Person Miserable? In *The Quest for the Good Life: Ancient Philosophers on Happiness*, eds. Ø. Rabbås, E.K. Emilsson, H. Fossheim, and M. Tuominen, 146–163. Oxford: Oxford University Press.

Grönroos, G. 2015. Wish, Motivation and the Human Good in Aristotle. *Phronesis* 60:60–87.

Hamlyn, D.W. 1968. *Aristotle's* De Anima: *Books II and III*. Oxford: Clarendon Press.

Hicks, R.D. 1907. *Aristotle* De Anima, *with translation, introduction, and notes*. Cambridge: Cambridge University Press.

Humberstone I.L. 1992. Direction of fit. *Mind* 101.401:59–83.

Irwin, T. 1975. Aristotle on Reason, Desire, and Virtue. *The Journal of Philosophy* 72:567–578.

Kahneman, D. 2011. *Thinking Fast and Slow*. New York: Farrar, Straus and Giroux.

Korsgaard, C. 1996. Skepticism about Practical Reason. In her *Creating the Kingdom of Ends*. Cambridge: Cambridge University Press.

Korsgaard, C. 1997. The Normativity of Instrumental Reason. In *Ethics and Practical Reason*, eds. G. Cullity and B. Gaut, 215–254. Oxford: Clarendon Press.

Little, M.O. 1997. Virtue as Knowledge: Objections from the Philosophy of Mind. *Noūs* 31.1:59–79.

Lorenz, H. 2006. *The Brute Within: Appetitive Desire in Plato and Aristotle*. Oxford: Clarendon Press.

McDowell, J. 1978. Are Moral Requirements Hypothetical Imperatives? *Proceedings of the Aristotelian Society*. Suppl. vol. 52:13–29.

McNaughton, D. 1988. *Moral Vision: An Introduction to Ethics*. Oxford: Blackwell.

Modrak, D.W. 1987. *Aristotle: The Power of Perception*. Chicago: University of Chicago Press.

Moss, J. 2011. "Virtue Makes the Goal Right": Virtue and Phronesis in Aristotle's Ethics. *Phronesis* 56: 204–261.

Moss, J. 2012. *Aristotle on the Apparent Good*: Perception, Phantasia, *Thought, and* Desire. Oxford: Oxford University Press.

Moss, J. 2014. Was Aristotle a Humean? In *The Cambridge Companion to Aristotle's Nicomachean Ethics*, ed. R. Polansky, 221–241. Cambridge: Cambridge University Press.

Nagel, T. 1970. *The Possibility of Altruism*. Princeton: Princeton University Press.

Nowell-Smith, P.H. 1954. *Ethics*. London: Penguin.

Pearson, G. 2006. Aristotle on acting unjustly without being unjust. *Oxford Studies in Ancient Philosophy* 30: 211–233.

Pearson, G. 2011a. Aristotle and Scanlon on desire and motivation. In *Moral Psychology and Human Action in Aristotle*, eds. M. Pakaluk and G. Pearson, 95–117. Oxford: Oxford University Press.

Pearson, G. 2011b. Non-rational desire and Aristotle's moral psychology. In *Aristotle's Nicomachean Ethics, A Critical Guide*, ed. J. Miller, 144–169. Cambridge: Cambridge University Press.

Pearson, G. 2012. *Aristotle on Desire*. Cambridge: Cambridge University Press.

Persson, I. 1997. Hume—Not a "Humean" about Motivation. *History of Philosophy Quarterly* 14.2:189–206.

Platts, M. 1979. *Ways of Meaning: An Introduction to a Philosophy of Language*. London: Routledge.

Polansky, R. 2007. *Aristotle's* De Anima. Cambridge: Cambridge University Press.

Quinn, W. 1993. *Morality and Action*. Cambridge: Cambridge University Press.

Radcliffe, E. 2018. *Hume, Passion, and Action*. Oxford: Oxford University Press.

Reeve, C.D.C. 1992. *Practices of Reason*. Oxford: Oxford University Press.

Richardson, H.S. 1997. Desire and the good in *De Anima*. In *Essays on Aristotle's De Anima*, eds. M. Nussbaum and A. Rorty, 381–99. Oxford: Clarendon.

Ross, W.D. 1961. *Aristotle: De Anima*. Oxford: Clarendon Press.

Scanlon, T.M. 1998. *What We Owe To Each Other*. Cambridge, MA: Harvard University Press.

Schiffer, S. 1976. A paradox of desire. *American Philosophical Quarterly*. 13.3:195–203.

Schueler, G.F. 1995. *Desire: Its Role in Practical Reason and the Explanation of Action*. Cambridge, MA: MIT Press.

Shafer-Landau, R. 2003. *Moral Realism: A Defence*. Oxford: Clarendon Press.

Shields, C. 2016. *Aristotle: De Anima*. Oxford: Clarendon Press.

Sinhababu, N. 2009. The Humean Theory of Motivation Reformulated and Defended. *Philosophical Review* 118.4:465–500.

Sinhababu, N. 2017. *Humean Nature*. Oxford: Oxford University Press.

Smith, A.D. 1996. Character and Intellect in Aristotle's *Ethics*. *Phronesis* 41:56–74.

Smith, M. 1987. The Humean theory of motivation. *Mind* 96.381:36–61.

Smith, M. 1994. *The Moral Problem*. Oxford: Blackwell.

Smith, M. 1997. In Defence of The Moral Problem: A Reply to Brink, Copp, and Sayre-McCord. *Ethics, Symposium on Michael Smith's* The Moral Problem 108:84–119.

Sorabji, R. 1974. Aristotle on the Role of the Intellect in Virtue. *Proceedings of the Aristotelian Society* 74:107–129.

Sorabji, R. 1980. Aristotle on the Role of Intellect in Virtue. In *Essays on Aristotle's Ethics*, ed. A. Rorty, 201–219. Berkeley: University of California Press.

Swartzer, S. 2013. Appetitive besires and the fuss about fit. *Philosophical Studies* 165.3:975–988.

Tenenbaum, S. 2006. Direction of Fit and Motivational Cognitivism. *Oxford Studies in Metaethics* 1:235–64.

Tuozzo, T.M. 1994. Conceptualized and Unconceptualized Desire in Aristotle. *Journal of the History of Philosophy* 32.4:525–549.

van Roojen, M. 2002. Should Motivational Humeans be Humeans About Rationality? *Topoi* 21:209–215.

Wallace, R.J. 1990. How to Argue about Practical Reason. *Mind* 99:355–385.

Wallace, R.J. 2006. *Normativity and the Will. Selected Essays on Moral Psychology and Practical Reason.* Oxford: Clarendon Press.

Wedin, M.V. 1988. *Mind and Imagination in Aristotle.* New Haven: Yale University Press.

Whiting, J. 2002. Locomotive Soul: The Parts of Soul in Aristotle's Scientific Works, *Oxford Studies in Ancient Philosophy* 22:141–200.

Wiggins, D. 1980. Deliberation and Practical Reason. In *Essays on Aristotle's Ethics*, ed. A. Rorty, 221–240. Berkeley: University of California Press.

Williams, B. 1981. Internal and External Reasons. In his *Moral Luck*, 101–113. Cambridge: Cambridge University Press.

Williams, B. 1995. Internal Reasons and the Obscurity of Blame. In his *Making Sense of Humanity*. Cambridge: Cambridge University Press.

COLLOQUIUM 3

Questioning Aristotle's Radical Account of Σωφροσύνη

Christopher Moore
Pennsylvania State University

Abstract

This paper investigates Aristotle's canonical analysis of σωφροσύνη in *Nicomachean Ethics* 3.10–12 against the background of earlier and subsequent uses, and analyses of the virtue term. It argues that Aristotle's is an outlier, brilliant but factitious, created to fit a theoretical scheme rather than reflect Greek understanding. Aristotle obscures the creativity of his account, presenting it as an ordinary language conceptual clarification that it is not. Many contemporary readers accept Aristotle's narrow theory—that σωφροσύνη is moderation with respect to those pleasures of touch related to nutrition and reproduction—as true, which may indicate that they are insufficiently familiar with fifth- and fourth-century literary, intellectual, and philosophical uses of the term. An important problem with this acceptance is that it prevents readers from recognizing the equal plausibility of non-Aristotelian accounts of σωφροσύνη, for example those found in Plato's *Charmides* and other dialogues.

Keywords

Plato – discipline – temperance – pleasures of touch – virtue

I   Introduction

This paper concerns the nature of σωφροσύνη, the central Greek virtue, and maybe, by implication, what it means to understand any classical virtue. It would seem that σωφροσύνη is not now well understood. In this paper, I will focus on just one of many interesting reasons: Aristotle's analysis of the virtue and the virtue term across his oeuvre but especially in his most visible account in the *Nicomachean Ethics*. I find that his account is an outlier, even a radical

© KONINKLIJKE BRILL NV, LEIDEN, 2020 | DOI:10.1163/22134417-00351P08

one, relative to those from or implied by others in the fifth and fourth centuries, and for that reason, could be judged misleading to the extent that he presents himself as not being radical. But his account has long been taken as basically the right one. Σωφροσύνη has been seen as what Aristotle says it is—namely, moderation with respect to some of the pleasures of touch, those concerned specifically with drinking, eating, and sex. Other classical analyses or glosses are, then, either resolved to Aristotle's, or treated as derivative of it, or even dismissed as confused or mistaken. The virtue is, accordingly, not well understood because, as it turns out, it is difficult to resolve those non-Aristotelian views in that way, or to find them as plausibly derivative, or to impugn their authors as blinkered about their own moral language.

I want to argue that some of our own confusion about the virtue—one, significantly, often treated as untranslatable or uniquely Greek—comes from giving undue primacy to Aristotle's account. He does not successfully identify the meaning of σωφροσύνη. He instead posits a new meaning, even if that new meaning can be seen as generalizing a particular element of σωφροσύνη as theretofore understood. What Aristotle provides is a novel, naturalistic account of the boundaries between the virtues—not, what he presents himself as giving, an ordinary language conceptual analysis. So, it might be tidy and sensible for σωφροσύνη to concern the pleasures of touch, which Aristotle treats as the most bestial since they pertain to the lowest, or most universal, functions of soul, nutrition and reproduction. But nothing says that virtues must be individuated by biological structure. Now, they might be; but it would take moral and conceptual reflection to show that they are natural kinds of this sort. Aristotle does not provide that, at least, not directly and rigorously, and some of his virtues do not seem obviously so individuated. And it remains an open question what, for classical Greek speakers, the virtues *are*. One purpose of this paper is to open that question through the case of σωφροσύνη.

My interest in talking about σωφροσύνη has some biographical-scholarly context. First, I once wrote a book about self-knowledge in fifth- and fourth-century Greece[1] and dealt with a number of passages, including in Heraclitus, Plato's *Charmides*, and the Platonic *Alcibiades* and *Rival Lovers*, where σωφροσύνη is grouped or explicitly identified with self-knowledge. I wondered how that relationship could seem both plausible and a good insight. Second, I wrote two papers about the term προμήθεια, a noun usually translated "forethought" but actually emphasizing rational reflection on one's stable principles of action, especially when in ignorance about the future.[2] This study

---

1   Moore 2015a.

2   Moore 2015b and Moore 2019.

revealed a deep thread of thinking about agency and commitment to norms in the generations up to Plato. It also included the discovery, remarkable to me, that the term is absent from Aristotle. Third, I co-translated and co-wrote a commentary on Plato's *Charmides*.[3] Two tasks in doing so had top priority. My collaborator and I had to find and defend an English translation of σωφροσύνη that would capture its referential scope, contexts of use, connotations, and moral gravity. We were not convinced that σωφροσύνη was a uniquely Greek virtue, but we also thought that familiar translations were not quite right for the dialogue. We also had to make sense of the interlocutors' proffered definitions—"some state of tranquility" (ἡσυχιότης τις), "a sense of shame" (αἰδώς), and "doing one's own things" (τὸ τὰ ἑαυτοῦ πράττειν), and the transformations of that one, "doing good things" and "knowing oneself" and its varieties—as well as their *not* offering certain imaginable definitions, like control or moderation of bodily desires, or ἐγκράτεια and self-control. Taking Plato seriously includes taking the definitions seriously, not as mere evidence of the interlocutors' benightedness.

In any event, if we know Socrates to know anything, it is that a core philosophical task is to inquire into the virtues, especially those we esteem or pride ourselves as embodying. I hope to take him as a model in this paper.

I start by showing what some people thought about σωφροσύνη before Aristotle wrote. The uses may seem pretty heterogeneous. In my favor, that itself tells against Aristotle's narrow unitary account and that is their primary use in my argument today. But I also think—and this I cannot argue for in detail here—that they share a common denominator. It is the disposition to be norm-governed despite the inner urgings of desire of every sort, or, put another way, the capacity to stick to long-term plans in pursuit of an overall good despite the opposing urgings of short-term appearances that the good lies elsewhere. Maybe this sounds like virtue in general. But the distinctions between the virtues come through distinctions of emphasis. Whereas courage, for example, focuses on overcoming fear of pain or the loss of life; justice focuses on the acquisition and sharing of property, rights, and responsibilities; and reverence focuses on due consideration for the more than human; σωφροσύνη focuses on treating as properly motivating only those desires that one deems good on reflection and in accordance with principles to which one is committed. Still, this paper's point is mostly negative, not positive.

In the second half of the paper, I will flesh out Aristotle's account. It is a remarkably tight, even uncompromising, account. *Prima facie*, compared to the earlier evidence, it is implausible. Despite that, I try to give some arguments in

---

3   Moore and Raymond 2019.

its favor and I adumbrate some rejoinders. The philosophical interest of the paper might be in this section; it certainly opens more questions than it can answer. I close with a brief analysis of some thinking about σωφροσύνη by followers of Aristotle, both direct and indirect. The long and short of it is that they do not accept his account.

II   Before Aristotle

Σωφροσύνη and its adjectival form appear four times in Homer. Apollo says to Poseidon that he would not be σαόφρονα were he to contend with him—another god—over mere mortals (*Iliad* 21.462); he then turns away in shame (469). Telemachus manifests σωφροσύνη throughout his search for and recovery of his father: when visiting great Menelaus, he is σαόφρων and "feels ashamed" (νεμεσσᾶται δ' ἐνὶ θυμῷ) lest he speak in an untoward fashion (*Odyssey* 4.158); and though he recognizes his father on his return, his thoughts are tempered by σαοφροσύνῃσι, and so he keeps his discovery to himself, in order not to tip off the suitors (*Od.* 23.30). Only a few lines earlier, Penelope's nurse reports her own realization that Odysseus has returned; but Penelope disbelieves her, thinking the gods have made her crazy, as the gods can, given that they can even do the reverse, namely, instill the "weak-minded" (χαλιφρονέοντα) with σαοφροσύνης (*Od.* 23.13).[4]

In each Homeric case, σωφροσύνη counts as "good sense" or "prudence," either as an emotional-dispositional or intellectual-epistemic achievement, though which it is can hardly be decided. For Apollo to battle Poseidon over a triviality exhibits either too hot a temper or too dull a calculation. For Telemachus to speak rashly to Menelaus exhibits either a childish impetuosity or an inadequate appreciation for social distinctions. In any case, this ambivalent term has clear connections to shame, a recognition of propriety, and social comportment.[5]

---

4 Homer draws attention to the element of "mind" or "sense" (φρήν) in this passage; Penelope is "prudent" (περίφρων, 10); she says her nurse was once "allotted with mind" (φρένας αἰσίμη, 14); the gods can make "mindless" (ἄφρονα) those who are "mindful" (ἐπίφρονα) (12). This binary contrast between being mindless and σωφρῶν recurs in Theognis (429–38, 454, 665); and continues as a dominant contrast in *Dissoi Logoi* (5.14) centuries later.

5 The term does not appear in Hesiod, who probably wrote around the same time. The consequence is uncertain. On the one hand, Hesiod's 2,000 lines are only about 7% of Homer's; many words do not show up. On the other, much of *Works and Days* moralizes in a way that could occasion talk of σωφροσύνη, and the rather fewer verses by Theognis (below) include it often, but they may also be from a century later.

QUESTIONING ARISTOTLE'S RADICAL ACCOUNT OF ΣΩΦΡΟΣΥΝΗ 77

With Theognis, we first see σωφροσύνη connected to control of bodily and sexual appetite: over-drinkers lack both it and a sense of shame (αἰδεῖται, 482) (467–98), and it represents maturation out from youthful dalliances (1326). But more frequently it points to a general state of human goodness as aiming at justice (379, 754) and having good judgment (701), both of which involve feeling awe or shame (ἄζεται) before gods (1135–42).[6] Pindar soon links the traits of courage, σωφροσύνη, and discretion (πινυτοί) (*Isthmian* 8.26); connects σωφροσύνη to "good order" (εὐνομίας) and "moderation" (ἐπὶ μέτρα) (*Paean* 1 fr. 52a.10, 3); and associates it with justice (*Partheneion* 1 fr. 94b.62). Hipponax (fr. 182) and Semonides (fr. 7.108) treat σωφροσύνη as all-around goodness in the domestic realm. Epicharmus adduces a commonplace connection to Ἡσυχία, and by treating both as divinities, he valorizes them (fr. 101 *PCG*). Finally, Phocylides says that "many who walk with order (κόσμῳ) seem to be σαόφρονες, though actually they have hardly any thoughts at all (ἐλαφρόνοοι) (Stob. 2.15.8).[7] All these usages presage the later fifth-century and Platonic conceptions of σωφροσύνη.

Interestingly, some of this pre-classical usage proves the availability of a proto-Aristotelian "physiological" σωφροσύνη as control—avoidance, management, or elimination—of alcohol and erotic hormones. It does not, however, prove that the Aristotelian content had conceptual dominance or even centrality. It would beg the question to assume that control of bodily desires is the original idea from which other usages gained metaphorical or analogical use, such that prudence would be like avoiding drunkenness or lustful irrationality. The opposite has as much or more evidence. Excessive drinking or cavorting may have looked to cause behavior akin to that typical of people without σωφροσύνη, people who were in general imprudent or impulsive in their choices. The usages canvassed so far show that σωφροσύνη amounts to a responsiveness to domestic, social, political, and even cosmological norms—formulated as shame, discretion, moderation—and the judgment necessary for identifying the extent and force of those norms.

---

6   See Rademaker (2005, 75–88) for its ("ideological") deployment in reference to justice and peacefulness, the rhetorical analysis of which I do not take up here.

7   The adjective ἐλαφρόνοος obviously plays on and contrasts with σώφρων (closely recalling—or alluding to?—the contrast at *Od.* 23.13), but its meaning is uncertain. It appears only here in early Greek. In Nonnus's *Dionysiaca* 10.247, it describes, from jealous Dionysus's perspective, the quality of his beloved that would cause him to turn his attentions elsewhere (Rouse: "fickle"). In a poem by Gregory of Nazianzus (col. 1573.7 Migne vol. 37), the spewed-back bronze slipper from Empedocles' leap into Aetna reveals him as an ἐλαφρονόοιο θεοῖο—can one say he is a "mentally lightweight" god?

The early fifth century preserves a pair of usages that seem to me to stand out as a conscious reflection on the history of σωφροσύνη usage. Heraclitus writes that "for all people there is a share in γινώσκειν ἑωυτοὺς καὶ σωφρονεῖν" (fr. 116DK = Stob. 3.5.6).[8] Whatever the imputation of the "and" (καί), self-knowledge and σωφροσύνη presumably have related scopes. Maybe it is that whatever self-knowledge achieves—in the Heraclitean context, presumably the recognition that we should not rely on our private inclinations—σωφρονεῖν also achieves: a distancing of ourselves from our desires or prejudices, allowing attention to the universally authoritative norms of *logos* and τὸ σοφόν. In another fragment, Heraclitus calls σωφρονεῖν the "greatest virtue" (ἀρετὴ μεγίστη), and probably connects it with "wisdom (σοφίη), speaking and doing what is true in accordance with nature, understanding (ἐπαΐοντας) [it]" (fr. 112DK = Stob. 3.1.178).[9] Heraclitean wisdom seems to be or involve self-knowledge—a hypothesis suggested by his fragment 101DK, "I searched for myself"—and so again we have a linkage of σωφροσύνη and the discovery of the authoritative norms that govern oneself.[10]

Fortunately for our study, Heraclitus's idiosyncrasy means that his vaunting of a phronetic or gignostic σωφροσύνη cannot be thought responsible for diverting the next century's discussion of σωφροσύνη into an adventitiously epistemic account. His writing instead shows the availability and intuitiveness of an epistemic account; he appears simply to purify it. And we see continued conscious reflection on this kind of account through the later fifth century, if now with a stronger or more mundane practical flavor.

Some sophists explicitly cite σωφροσύνη as essential to civic stability. Thrasymachus distinguishes ἐσωφρονεῖν from στασιάζειν ("engaging in political contention") and ὑβρίζειν ("acting hubristically," probably by undermining another's class rights) (D16 LM). A Euripidean character says that σώφρων (and just) leaders eliminate feuds and factions (fr. 282.25–27 K). Protagoras similarly attributes to justice and σωφροσύνη the defensive unity of cities (Plato *Protagoras* 322b–323a). These three make σωφροσύνη a matter of recognizing and acknowledging the civic structures, differentiations, or coordinations necessary for community preservation. This does not mean subordinating one's private interests to the common interest, a kind of self-sacrifice, but appreciating the

---

8   I argue for the authenticity of this fragment in Moore 2018a.

9   Laks and Most 2016, 5.197, divide this fragment into two independent fragments, the first only three words, and the καί before σοφίη normally attributed to Heraclitus actually Stobaeus's interjection. They do not explain their reasoning.

10   Euripides fr. 969.2–4 K provides an echo: "I judge nothing more leading than σωφροσύνη, since it is always associated with good men" (οὐδὲν πρεσβύτερον νομί- / ζω τᾶς σωφροσύνας, ἐπεὶ / τοῖς ἀγαθοῖς ἀεὶ ξύνεστιν).

overlap between them or, more concretely, taking a city's constitutional arrangements as the ones that ought to govern one's own life, whether as a leader or citizen. Thucydides makes this really clear.[11] And nobody will miss this as the marked meaning of σωφροσύνη in Plato's *Republic*—itself potentially influenced by or responsive to Thrasymachus and Protagoras, as well as Critias,[12] an earlier theorizer of σωφροσύνη in the context of political constitutions—as the virtue of all the city's classes' or the soul's parts' shared acknowledgement of a structure of authority.[13]

Other sophists write about σωφροσύνη in terms of its advancement of considered self-interest. Here's Democritus: "σωφροσύνη increases delight and makes pleasures even better" (σωφροσύνη τὰ τερπνὰ ἀέξει καὶ ἡδονὴν ἐπιμείζονα ποιεῖ, Stob. 3.5.27). He aims to undermine vulgar assumptions about the virtue, maybe that it involves limiting one's desire-satisfaction or that it compromises the wholeheartedness or spontaneity of enjoyment. How? Maybe with σωφροσύνη one comes to desire or privilege things that are ultimately more satisfying, or things not accompanied by pain, as hangovers, regrets, and ill-health are, or multiple things the satisfaction of which is not mutually undermining. In any case, we have no reason to assume that the view of σωφροσύνη against which Democritus argues has a scope limited to the pleasures of touch, or even of perception more broadly. Three other fragments attributed to Democritus conform to this view. "Chance sets a lavish table, σωφροσύνη [sets a table of] self-sufficiency" (Stob. 3.5.26)—here σωφροσύνη means not going beyond one's capacities and having to make oneself dependent on or even enslaved to others. "The σωφροσύνη of a father is the best lesson for his children" (Stob. 3.5.24), and "Strength and looks are the goods of youth; σωφροσύνη is the flower of old age" (Stob. 3.50.20)—σωφροσύνη amounts to full maturity and self-possession. The σώφρων life, we might say, concerns all the desires that one might have. And desires of whatever sort—namely, our felt commitments to the good.

Antiphon similarly looks at σωφροσύνη in the life of an individual; he emphasizes the element of self-restraint. He takes σωφροσύνη as the ability to refuse to satisfy one's shameful or evil desires or, as he puts it, to "dominate" and

---

11   Thucydides 1.68.1 has the σωφροσύνη of the Spartans imply an inner stability and mutual recognition, by contrast to knowing about foreign affairs, "external matters" (τὰ ἔξω πράγματα); cf. 3.37.3, where that stability is praised above mental acuity. The term refers to stable and fair government at 3.84.1 and 8.64.5.

12   See Donovan 2003; Howland 2018.

13   See Demos (1957) for the position.

"defeat" oneself (D55 LM = Stob. 3.20.66).[14] This domination over one's worse inclinations—the example he gives is refraining from harming another person—is what is called being "well-ordered" (κόσμιον) (D56 LM = Stob. 3.5.57). In another fragment, Antiphon even lists σωφροσύνη as the sole virtue in his argument for the strain simply to make one's own life go well, much less that of his own plus his wife's: maintaining one's health, financial livelihood, reputation, σωφροσύνη, renown, and good name (D57 LM = Stob. 4.22.66). Other commentators think this simply means "reputation for σωφροσύνη," but that would make the last four goals identical.[15] It must rather be something distinct to strive for, to apply oneself despite difficulties toward, as the other five cited elements of the good life are. Given Antiphon's example, this, presumably, means something like forbearance and playing the long game, withholding from acting in case something better comes from waiting.[16]

So, Democritus and Antiphon bring out the general connections between σωφροσύνη and prudence or rationality, being personally well ordered and Thrasymachus and Protagoras bring out the general connections between σωφροσύνη and civic peace and mutual respect, being socially well ordered. This broad equivalence provides important background for the canonical late fifth-century texts. In Aristophanes, for example, the noun σωφροσύνη means—I list this by chronological date of the play—orderly behavior inflected naively as conservative austerity, formulated for young men as silence and avoidance of "joking around" (βωμολοχεύσαιτ'), walking softly in public, dressing plainly, limiting oneself to old-timey tunes, avoiding salacious and flirtatious bodily poses, and not overeating (*Clouds* 962–984); civic stability, as forming a trio with εὐβουλία and εὐνομία (*Birds* 1539–1540);[17] female silence and diffidence, letting citizen males make all political decisions (*Lysistrata* 508–514); and κοσμιότης ("orderliness"), lawfulness, and the absence of *hubris* (*Wealth* 563–564). We saw a version of the *Clouds*' "comportment" usage already in Epicharmus and Phocylides, though here inflected, as befitting an Athenian argument, with a Laconophilic hardiness and a tone of meager rations—it provides evidence of late fifth-century debate about the value of σωφροσύνη over against

---

14   The hesitation to hurt a person from fear of reprisal is "sort of σωφροσύνη," because it prevents the worse harms that the attack may bring on (Stob. 3.20.66), but the "sort of" qualification shows that "fear" is not the most genuine cause of σωφροσύνη (cf. Lys. 2.57.4), akin to what Plato's Socrates will later say in the *Phaedo*.

15   See Pendrick 2002.

16   A parallel is Andoc. 1.131.4: Hipponicus's evil son overturned his wealth, his σωφροσύνη, and his whole life.

17   Cf. Thucydides 1.32.4, opposed to ἀβουλία and ἀσθένεια.

QUESTIONING ARISTOTLE'S RADICAL ACCOUNT OF ΣΩΦΡΟΣΥΝΗ   81

quick-witted opportunism.[18] We have already seen the *Birds'* "constitutional" usage in Pindar; the *Lysistrata's* "feminine" usage in the iambic poets; and the *Wealth's* "orderliness" usage from the time of Theognis. These are different faces, or contexts, of σωφροσύνη: the young person fitting his impulses, tastes, and passions to a socially acceptable pattern; the citizenry organizing itself thoughtfully and obediently; women playing their proper role in the household, governing only what they are granted to govern; and the proper orientation of neighbors or fellows to one another. These are diverse ways of treating oneself as generally norm-governed.

Euripides nicely reveals the way σωφροσύνη can be treated under one of its narrow guises. In *Hippolytus*, σωφροσύνη frequently means being sexually restrained, especially for women.[19] But chastity comes to seem especially important, in part, just because it can be alluded to as a specific realization of the overall virtue, σωφροσύνη.[20] Similarly, Hippolytus himself, who is proudly abstinent, seems to himself on that basis to embody σωφροσύνη overall.[21] Only once does he try to give a fuller account of his superlative σωφροσύνη: he reveres the gods, associates only with good friends (who command no evil and repay no disgraceful deeds in kind), and respects his companions whether they are around or not.[22] And elsewhere in the play, σωφροσύνη means women's quietness (704) and being reasonable and without a deranged mind (1013). So Euripides knows that σωφροσύνη is all the following: the recognition of one's superiors and the avoidance of harmful actions; bodily and verbal comportment; and intellectual clear-headedness.[23] This means that σωφροσύνη does not only mean sexual restraint, even for women. (I note parenthetically that contemporary epitaphic evidence shows that σωφροσύνη is neither specifically feminine nor, when it is, limited to anything less broad than familial and

---

18   Cf. Thucydides 1.84.1–2: what some call "slowness and delay" (τὸ βραδὺ καὶ μέλλον) ought really to be called σωφροσύνη ἔμφρων ("mental discipline")—it is with εὐπραγίαις ("good action") that one avoids hubris, tolerates misfortune, resists the temptations of risk, and is immune to accusation.

19   *Hipp.* 399, 413, 494, 667, and 731. Cf. Euripides fr. 503: "measured (μετρίων) unions, and measured wives with σωφροσύνη are the best for mortals to find," and, more pungently, *Medea* 634–37 and *Iphigeneia at Aulus* 544–572. In Prodicus's "Heracles" speech, Virtue embodies σωφροσύνη, her eyes being in αἰδοῖ (Xenophon *Memorobilia* 2.1.22); this evidently means that she is not an Aphroditic seductress.

20   358 and 431.

21   1007, 1100, and 1365; reflected back at Hippolytus at 949 and 1402.

22   994–1001. Cf. Euripides fr. 446 (*Hippolytus Veiled*): "Oh blessed hero Hippolytus, what honors you have won thanks to σωφροσύνην: for mortals have no other power greater than ἀρετή: for either sooner or later comes the good grace of εὐσεβία ('pious reverence')."

23   Euripides fr. 505: "the man who bears his fortunes well seems to me to be best and σωφρονεῖν."

domestic excellence.)[24] Euripides seems to be playing up, however, the way sexual restraint *can*—perhaps perniciously—come to *seem* the whole of σωφροσύνη.

In other work I address some cases of σωφροσύνη in Xenophon and in Plato.[25] Their contemporary, Antisthenes, who may have lived until about 365, is worth pausing on. (I will address Isocrates briefly below.) Antisthenes was a prolific and popular author, with literary output spanning the first third of the fourth century, the age of Aristotle's youth. He provides non-Academic evidence for the contemporaneous meaning of σωφροσύνη. His only extant works, the *Odysseus* and *Ajax*, discuss virtue but not σωφροσύνη explicitly, so we will focus on the testimonia and fragments. None even hints at an Aristotelian pleasure-of-touch analysis; together they seem to treat σωφροσύνη as virtually norm-following in general.

Antisthenes' most famous preference is for being mad rather than having pleasure, probably of the erotic sort (fr. 122A–H *SSR*); in one of the reports of this preference, he is said to value σωφροσύνη above all (τὴν σωφροσύνην περὶ πλείστου ποιούμενος καὶ τὴν ἡδόνην μυσαττόμενος, fr. 123B). The throes of pleasure must sap one of rational agency even more than being mad does by definition. Antisthenes must, then, equate σωφροσύνη with the ability to make decisions from stable, presumably long-affirmed reasons. Elsewhere and relatedly, in a context where Xenophon appears to be referring to Antisthenes, Xenophon says that some philosophers oppose σωφροσύνη to *hubris* (*Mem.* 1.2.19 = fr. 103C; cf. Prince 2015, 341), where *hubris* must mean exceeding consensual norms of respect. Similarly, a Cynic letter tasked with clarifying Antisthenic teaching has Simon call Antisthenes a σωφρονιστής ("disciplinarian") and says that he (Antisthenes) might show Aristippus that, though he thinks he imitates Socrates, he is in fact among the ἀφρόνων ("mindless, thoughtless") and lives with much χλιδή (*Soc. Ep.* 12 = fr. 207B). Χλιδή means either "insolence" or "luxury" which it is matters to the goal of the σωφρονιστής. "Luxury" is more likely, I think, since the epistle closes with the injunction to "remember hunger and thirst, for these have great power for those pursuing σωφροσύνη." One practices desire-minimization by minimizing desire-satisfaction. Hunger and thirst are not the sole concerns of σωφροσύνη; they seem only salient or powerful obstacles to the development of σωφροσύνη more generally. Antisthenes interprets a passage of Homer as implying that one would not get to σωφροσύνη

---

24   Women honored for their σωφροσύνη: IG II² 9057, 11162, 13086, SEG 13:181, 222; many more inscriptions honor men for the same.

25   Xenophon: Moore 2018b, 502–7. Plato: Moore and Raymond 2019, xxxi–xxxiv and passim.

QUESTIONING ARISTOTLE'S RADICAL ACCOUNT OF ΣΩΦΡΟΣΥΝΗ   83

through fighting (διὰ μαχῆς), just as one would not get to justice through robbery or to immortality through love of life (fr. 188A-1).[26] Σωφροσύνη here includes peacefulness and keeping to oneself—or, more interpretatively, rational self-control, which is what we have seen already. More idiosyncratically, Antisthenes seems to have said that those who are σώφρων should not learn γράμματα, so as not to be "turned" by others' ideas (fr. 161).[27] This would pertain to the pleasures of touch just if one were to read only decadent culinary or erotic γράμματα. That is surely not Antisthenes' point. He seems to mean either that reading generates new and unwieldy desires or that reading interferes with the toilsome self-work necessary for inner peace. So, reading books either corrupts or distracts from one's project of norm-conformity. Finally, Isocrates seems to have Antisthenes in mind when he notes the oddness in his pedagogical competitors' having ἀρετή and σωφροσύνη as their teaching goals but then not trusting that their students will pay their tuition (*Against the Sophists* 6 = fr. 170).[28] If scholars have rightly identified Isocrates' target, Isocrates associates Antisthenes' education with σωφροσύνη; treats ἀρετή and σωφροσύνη as, when paired, descriptive of a philosophical education; and makes σωφροσύνη a virtue of "doing what one ought," of keeping a contract even if one would prefer to spend money or the time necessary for getting money in some other way. The tight connection between ἀρετή and σωφροσύνη and the purported goals of Isocrates' philosophical competitors shows that σωφροσύνη is the acquisition of a thoughtful attitude toward one's desires and one's obligations.

A few words about Isocrates, who uses σωφροσύνη and cognates frequently. For him, the verb σωφρονεῖν virtually always means "to be reasonable, sensible, prudent"—not acting on impulse or crazily (*Panathenaicus* 14), being thoughtful about what one is doing (*Panath.* 140, 172, 199, 237), and considering long-term consequences (*Busiris* 40, *Plataicus* 22, and *Philippus* 7).[29] Once, in a use

---

26   Prince thinks we cannot document this contrast from Antisthenes' time, so she thinks it may be Stoicizing (2015, 626); but we have already documented this contrast above, in Euripides fr. 282.25–27 K.

27   There are textual problems here: Marcovich 1999 proposes <σοφούς> ἢ σώφρονας, because of the ἢ found in BPF; Dorandi simply replaces the ἢ with τοὺς, following Frobenius (the corrector of Z) and most editors. In favor of Dorandi 2013, Dio Chr. *Or.* 13.17, which probably follows Antisthenes (= fr. 208, see Prince 2015 comm. ad loc), states that learning letters does not conduce to one's leading a city σωφρονέστερον καὶ ἄμεινον ("better and with more σωφροσύνη"); he does not say that it conduces to "wiser" leadership. Further, Dorandi's reading is less paradoxical, and more consistent with Antisthenes' attention to character-development over intellectual learning.

28   Prince 2015, 558; Murphy 2013, 329–37.

29   More cliché uses at *Against Lochites* 22; *Panegyricus* 165; *Antidosis* 242, 304; *Ad Alexandrum* 5. See also the adjective used in the same way at *Nicocles* 51; *Antid.* 290.

84 MOORE

familiar from Thucydides (see n11 above), it has a foreign-policy connotation, opposing πολυπραγμονεῖν, which is imperial meddling; but even here it means acting on longer-term or broader considerations, since in that case, Thebes was said to have overrun its success after defeating Sparta at Leuctra (*Pace* 58). In brief, the verb's use parallels that of the verbal form of προμηθής, προμηθέομαι, "to watch out, take care that" the basic task of rationality.[30]

Isocrates often uses the noun σωφροσύνη in a pair with ἀρετή, as we have seen above, sometimes as the object of philosophers' teachings, treated not really as a subset of "virtue" but as somehow equivalent, or representative, or a salient version of it, and, generally, implying knowing the right thing to do.[31] We might render σωφροσύνη καὶ ἀρετή as "[good] sense and sensibility." Σωφροσύνη is also paired with δικαιοσύνη and treated among the canonical virtues of excellent people,[32] though closer to καρτερία, "hardiness," and ἐργασία, "hard work," than to ἀνδρεία.[33] Sometimes, Isocrates mentions a specific application of σωφροσύνη, though never in a limiting way: as we have seen above, in paying debts,[34] due reverence toward the gods,[35] the bodily comportment of youth,[36] and the erotic restraint of tyrants.[37] It has the geopolitical isolationist implication observed above (*Pace* 63), along with a broader notion of political order and fairness, the opposite of hubris and tyranny.[38] Sparta exemplifies it and its complement, παιθαρχία, "obedience" (*Panath.* 111, 115). Like Xenophon, Isocrates distinguishes it from ἐγκράτεια, "inner force," such that σωφροσύνη is not so much strength with respect to and control over one's desires than the appreciation of the right things to do—at *Nicocles* 44, Isocrates says that it involves foregoing pleasures that provide "no honor" (μηδεμίαν τιμὴν ἔχουσιν; see also *Ad Antipatrum* 4) and aiming, instead, for that

30 See Moore 2015b, 403.
31 Paired with ἀρετή: *C. soph.* 6, 20; *Helen* 31, 38; *Areopagiticus* 37, 38.
32 *Ad Demonicum* 15; *C. soph.* 21; *Nic.* 29, 30; *Pace* 63; *Panath.* 138; *De bigis* 28
33 *Panath.* 197; *Ad Timothium* 3. Thus *Areop.* 4, which claims that ἔνδεια ("lack") and ταπεινότης ("poor condition") bring forth σωφροσύνη rather than power and wealth, which may rather bring about ἄνοια ("thoughtlessness") and ἀκολασία ("indiscipline").
34 *C. soph.* 6, where the matter is connected less to greediness than to doing one's duty.
35 *Bus.* 21; cf. Xen. *Mem.* 4.3.2–18.
36 *Areop.* 45; cf. Plato *Char.* 159b; Xenophon *Constitution of the Lacedaimonians* 3.4, Ar. *Nub.* 962–84.
37 *Nic.* 36, where Isocrates makes clear that at most only a few applications of the respective virtue are being cited; see the gloss on δικαιοσύνη immediately before.
38 *Hel.* 31, 38; *Pace* 119; *Ad Archidamum* 4, and *Ad Timoth.* 3. At *Ad Nic.* 31, speaking of the leader's role in modeling σωφροσύνη for his city, making it more κοσμίως ("coordinated") and less ἀτάκτως ("disordered"), Isocrates avers that having σωφροσύνη is compatible with become wealthier; he appears to have something of the well-run society of the Protestant work ethic in mind here.

QUESTIONING ARISTOTLE'S RADICAL ACCOUNT OF ΣΩΦΡΟΣΥΝΗ   85

reputation that comes from "good character" (ἀνδραγαθία); he thereby makes judgment central. Presumably, as part of maturation and acculturation to a system of values, σωφροσύνη is especially fine in youth (*Evagoras* 22; *Ad Dem.* 15). Isocrates' fundamental view is that σωφροσύνη opposes doing whatever one wants (*Areop.* 37), and, thus, it must mean acting on some principles. His uses of the adjective clarify this: it is contrary to saying whatever one wants (*Panath.* 218), and more generally, contrary to ἀκολασία ("indiscipline"), παρανομία ("law-breaking"), παρρησία ("saying whatever one wants"), and ἐξουσία ("doing whatever one wants") (*Areop.* 20; cf. *Pace* 104). Indeed, Isocrates even has a Socratic moment, saying that σωφροσύνη in students involves their working on themselves rather than acting on conceits of expertise.[39] So, since Isocrates treats σωφροσύνη as a superlative political ideal,[40] it basically means living in accordance with a constitution, a set of norms.

This quick overview of Isocrates' usage of σωφροσύνη cognates, from the 390s until the 330s, shows that the virtue generally refers to norm-following—the disposition for rational choice and deliberation at the personal level; and constitutional stability, fairness, and self-containedness at the political level. Nothing hints, across contexts and decades, of a use primarily or even notably concerned with bodily desires. Against this background, we may now turn to Aristotle.

III   Aristotle's New Idea

A. The Content of the New Idea. Aristotle mentions σωφροσύνη most frequently in his works in lists of three or four virtues that he treats as fundamental examples of the class, generally with bravery, justice, and practical wisdom.[41] When Aristotle focuses on σωφροσύνη and the σώφρων man alone, he gives a remarkably consistent account, in the three *Ethics*, the *Rhetoric*, the *Topics*, and the *Politics*, if at various levels of specification depending on his purposes.[42] A praiseworthy state,[43] σωφροσύνη concerns the appetite or desiderative part of

---

39   *Antid.* 290; cf. *Ad Antipatrum* 2.

40   *In Callimachus* 46; *Pace* 104; *Areop.* 13, 20; *Panath.* 151.

41   *Categories* 8b33 (as stable); *Topics* 107a4; *Problems* 951a6; *Eudemian Ethics* 1218a22 (as good); 1220b19 and 1221a2; *EN* 1103b1–2, 9, 1107a22, 1109a3, and 1109a19; *Magna Moralia* 1185b7, and b14–32; *Pol.* 1323b29–36, 1325a33; and *Rhet.* 1360b24 (secluded in ROT), 1362b12, and 1366b1.

42   He uses the verb only four times: at *EN* 1172b25 and 1173a22 as examples of virtues in quantitative analysis and at *Rhet.* 1364b37 and 1397a10 in exemplary arguments comparing virtues.

43   *EE* 1248b23 and *Rhet.* 1397a10.

the soul,[44] namely, in terms of pleasures,[45] but only certain ones,[46] the bodily ones,[47] specifically, the desires of touch and taste,[48] the beastly ones, though, more properly, the desires related to eating, drinking, and sex.[49] So we see that Aristotle presents σωφροσύνη as much narrower a virtue than anybody else does.[50] Our question is why.

In his fullest and what has come to be the canonical discussion of σωφροσύνη, at *Nicomachean Ethics* III.10–12, Aristotle starts with the assumption that σωφροσύνη concerns pleasures and has as its opposite ἀκολασία ("indiscipline"). He then proceeds by a purported ordinary language analysis, reflecting on the laudatory, wry, or pejorative names we give those whom we deem extraordinary in some desires or other. We do not speak of σωφροσύνη or its opposite, he says, in the context of what we call φιλοτιμία ("ambition"), φιλομάθεια ("curiosity"), or φιλομυθία ("tale-telling") and other modes of talkativeness, all of which involve a taste for non-bodily pleasures. Further, despite its being possible to enjoy visual or auditory pleasures too much or just enough, we do not speak of the intensity of such enjoyment as a failure or success of σωφροσύνη. The same goes for smells. As it turns out, Aristotle asserts, no beasts get special pleasure from sights, sounds, or smells, except incidentally. And so, Aristotle infers, we refer to failures and successes of σωφροσύνη only in relation to the pleasures we share with beasts. Aristotle calls these pleasures "slavish"—probably because an animal's instinctual drive toward them is commanding and not up to negotiation. In humans, those pleasures have a power to provoke our action that seems quite independent of our judgment. Having settled tentatively upon taste and touch as the only relevant perceptual modalities for σωφροσύνη, Aristotle reduces further: it is not the taste of food itself that gives pleasure, at least not to the profligate, and touch seems the only relevant sense for drinking and sex. Besides which, he says, touch is really the most universal sense, and, thus, even more beastly. Thus, σωφροσύνη is a mean with respect to the pleasures of touch. And, once again, Aristotle reduces: σωφροσύνη concerns not all instances of touch—he excludes the "most liberal" sensations, such as rubbings and

---

44 *Top.* 136b13 and 138b3–4; *EN* 1103a6.

45 *EN* 1104a19–25, 34, and b6; *MM* 1186b7–11; and *Rhet.* 1369a21–24.

46 *EN* 1107b5 and *EE* 1232b3.

47 *Rhet.* 1366b13.

48 *MM* 1191a38–b22; cf. 1187b7–11.

49 *EE* 1320a36–b1, *EN* 1117; *Pol.* 1323a28.

50 Curzer (1997) provides a clear and critical analysis of Aristotle's account of σωφροσύνη, but accepts its validity rather more than I do. Young does as well, attending to Aristotle's insight in describing a virtue "acknowledg[ing one's] animality without succumbing to it" (1988, 541).

heating pools in the gymnasium—and, thus, not all surfaces of the body; he implicitly limits it to the pertinent organs of consumption and reproduction.

Transparent and plausible as Aristotle's argumentation may be, fifth- and early fourth-century usage makes Aristotle's claim to follow common or even wise opinion sound wholly tendentious. In the fifth century, there was *no* mention of σωφροσύνη as a virtue of moderation with respect solely to the three desires of touch. Nor do Plato's dialogues confirm Aristotle's assessment of linguistic practice. So, even if there really is no σωφροσύνη with respect to the pleasures of talking too much (as Aristotle says), this does not get Aristotle where he needs to be, that there is no σωφροσύνη with respect to the inclination to talk too loudly, or at the wrong time, or to the wrong people. And yet, there certainly does seem to be such σωφροσύνη, as shown directly by *Charmides* (159b, cf. 154a) and by much else as well.

There are further oddities in Aristotle's account of σωφροσύνη. By contrast to his account of courage in the *Nicomachean Ethics*, where he identifies five types or near-types of courage, sorting out their relative prototypicality, he mentions no subtypes of σωφροσύνη. Are there really none; is he just particularly incurious; or does he believe that the details do not matter here? Further, the argument that touch is the sole relevant sense sounds baldly casuistic. Would the ἀκόλαστος stuff himself with bland food? How much does the desire for wine, and the ensuing buzz or disinhibition, really have to do with the liquid's esophageal descent? Is the person given to excessive sunbathing or reliant on boisterous parties for happiness really failing on a different virtue than the glutton or lush? Who knows.

B. Four Possible Defenses of Aristotle's Idea. Tendentious or odd as it may be, Aristotle's narrow rendering of σωφροσύνη is not inexplicable or indefensible. First, though Aristotle seems driven little by ordinary usage, he does want to find a meaningful coherence among what he takes to be the salient usages. Then he wants to individuate virtues by appeal to the most narrowly tailored sets of feelings concerned with which they would serve as means. And then he wants to make sure those feelings have a narrowly tailored source. Courage, for example, is a mean with respect to pain, the pain of a fear concerned, prototypically, with staying alive, that is, with having any soul at all. Σωφροσύνη is a mean with respect to pleasure, the pleasure of actions at the lowest level of psychic activity, nutrition and reproduction, to both of which touch pertains. Privileging these pleasures excessively is privileging one's animalian self over one's human self. Aristotle is cutting virtues at what could be natural joints and, in this case, deriving the condemnation of the lack of σωφροσύνη from the view that it is bad not to act fully human, where being human is following reason rather than being a slave to specific beastly passions.

Here is a second possible *apologia* for Aristotle. Aristotle does, sometimes, try a little to account for penumbral uses of the term σωφροσύνη and he sometimes belies an awareness of a σωφροσύνη broader than his official version. One instance appears at the conclusion of his main discussion of σωφροσύνη, at *Nicomachean Ethics* III.12. He says that we import the name ἀκολασία (as opposite of σωφροσύνη) to childish faults (ἐπὶ τὰς παιδικὰς ἁμαρτίας), to which it is somewhat alike (τινα ὁμοιότητα) (1119a35–b1). He does not specify which desires children live at the mercy of; he must not think only those of food, drink, and sex. Otherwise, the faults of children and adults would be identical, not "somewhat alike," and he surely does not think that youthful impetuosity concerns only those desires.[51] So, ἀκολασία for children is broader than that for adults. He might, then, think—though he does not say so—that the wider childish use of ἀκολασία (and its opposite, σωφροσύνη) is sometimes applied to adults in, as it were, a derivative or figurative sense. Elsewhere in the *Nicomachean Ethics*, in a gnomic temper, Aristotle says that he who rightly judges himself of little worth is σώφρων, by contrast with the one who rightly judges himself of great worth, who is proud (1123b5). This represents a decidedly Socratic σωφροσύνη of humble self-knowledge. A bit later, Aristotle says we sometimes praise the ἀφιλότιμος ("retiring," "unambitious") person as moderate and σώφρων (1125b13), treating σωφροσύνη here as the disposition not to pursue honor, fame, and so forth—a restraint he otherwise attributes only to ἐγκράτεια (1147b28; see also Isocrates *Ad Antipatrum* 2). Then, Aristotle cites the important moral injunction to be σώφρων, avoiding adultery or hubris (1129b21). This is, at once, a narrower construction on σωφροσύνη than Aristotle elsewhere gives and a more social or political one, as refraining from outrage of domestic or private proprieties. Then, in the *Topics*, he cites as an exemplary dialectical question: how does σωφροσύνη differ from wisdom? (108a2), a Socratic question with *Protagoras* provenance. Σωφροσύνη must be thought enough like prudence, good sense, or knowledge of the good. Aristotle claims, in the same work, that treating σωφροσύνη as harmony *simpliciter* is merely metaphorical (123a34–36 and 139b33). And he opposes a view that justice amounts to σωφροσύνη and courage (150a4–13), a view that makes any sense only with σωφροσύνη referring to more than control of some of the appetites of touch.

---

51   Aristotle acknowledges the conventional view that σωφροσύνη is a virtue for youth: *Top.* 117a31 and *Rhet.* 1361a3–7 and 1390b4. But he says that their being σώφρων is somehow different, given their immaturity: *Pol.* 1259b22–32 and 1277b17–21.

Now, this just about exhausts Aristotle's non-innovative uses of σωφροσύνη.[52] Numerous as they may be, they are many fewer, and much less marked, than the places where he elaborates his theoretical usage. So, there is no reason to believe, I think, that the pleasures-of-touch view does *not* represent Aristotle's settled views or that he means it to describe only a proper subset of σωφροσύνη. What we see, rather, is the novelty and even the counter-intuitiveness of Aristotle's novel idea about σωφροσύνη.

Here is a third possible defense of Aristotle's choice. In ways quite distinct from earlier authors, Aristotle distinguishes sharply between σωφροσύνη, ἐγκράτεια, and φρόνησις, such that what had historically counted as an exercise of σωφροσύνη, for him, often counts as an exercise of one of the other two states, the former not exactly a virtue, the latter not a virtue of character. Getting clear about ἐγκράτεια and φρόνησις, which are at the heart of Aristotle's moral psychology, would take a book. Let me say only the following. For Aristotle, cases of the foolish behavior typically judged as failures of σωφροσύνη have at least three distinct causes: inadequate ethical knowledge, inadequate inner force or compunction against pleasures in general, and inadequately thoughtful moderation with respect to those desires for touch shared with all other animals. The first is a failure of φρόνησις, the second of ἐγκράτεια, and only the third of σωφροσύνη. Perhaps this triple distinction is coherent and helpful. But it does depend on quite controversial general theoretical assumptions: the various levels of soul as described in *De Anima*, the nature of animal perception and desire and the relevance of that nature to our ethical judgments, the distinctiveness of most desires from those of consumption and procreation, and so forth. From this perspective, his analysis of σωφροσύνη is highly factitious.

The fourth avenue in defense of Aristotle may seem the strongest, but it also deploys the trickiest evidence. Some of Plato's dialogues allow for a "conventional" sense of σωφροσύνη as appetite-control. In the *Phaedo*, Socrates says that "what the many call σωφροσύνη" involves being unimpressed by the bodily passions (68c). And σωφροσύνη, for the masses, in the *Republic*, involves (among other things) ruling over the pleasures concerned with drink, sex, and eating (389d; see also 402e3 with 403e–405c8). It would seem, then, that by Aristotle's youth—whenever Plato wrote these two dialogues—the meaning of

---

52   The virtue term arises in some additional cases in the *Nicomachean Ethics* that do not add significantly to the above analysis: 1147b27, 1148a14, 1149a22 (same objects as ἐγκράτεια), 1148a6, 1148b31 (animals only metaphorically called σώφρων), 1150a23, 1151a19 ("ὀρθοδοξεῖν περὶ τὴν ἀρχήν"), 1151b34, 1152a1 (another metaphorical usage), 1152b15, 1153a27, 1153a34, 1168b26, 1171b16, 1177a31, 1178a33 (needing opportunities and other people for the virtue's exercise), 1178b15 (gods are not ever σώφρων).

σωφροσύνη, at least outside esoteric intellectual communities, had changed in Aristotle's direction, or even that the term had long meant what Aristotle says it means but that its history of so meaning has been obscured by the usages found in elite literature. Aristotle is to be seen as theorizing that conventional usage, which is, as it were, the core usage, the meat-and-potatoes referents of σωφροσύνη. The elite, intellectual usages could be seen as derivative, analogical, or, at best, theoretically entailed or suggested by the fundamental-desire account.

I think this is probably the dominant, though implicit, view in the scholarship; but I also do not believe that it can be sustained. The main problem is that it would require a needlessly expansive view of elite literature, whatever it is that presents σωφροσύνη as other than desires-of-touch indexed. It would include almost all literature, including that which is meant for a popular audience—poetry, drama, history, and oratory. Since the "non-conventional" view of σωφροσύνη is so pervasive, elaborated and, so to speak, coherent, we might have to posit two σωφροσύναι, with hardly any interface between them. While not linguistically impossible, it would be argumentatively rash and we, as yet, lack good reason to bifurcate and have much good reason not to.

Here is what I am wondering. Might what "the many" call σωφροσύνη not be any truer to the meaning or purport of σωφροσύνη but just what people have come to talk about when they talk about σωφροσύνη? There is also the Thucydidean angle about the cynicism concerning virtue terms displayed during the agony of the plague. But I mean "what comes to mind first": as, when linking "public leadership" with honesty and deliberation, the latter does not exhaust the former; it just picks out some contemporary talking points. As for speaking of σωφροσύνη in terms of bodily appetites, I hypothesize that this demonstrates an increased popular salience, perhaps in a well-off urban community, of several common, easy-to-diagnose, hard-to-rationalize, and, in the case of sex and drinking, personally and socially damaging failures of self-control. They are problems dispersed enough to be generally familiar and thus easily joined as archetypes, and even stereotypes, of σωφροσύνη. They are also not particularly morally complex by contrast, perhaps, with φιληκοία, φιλοτιμία, or φιλοκερδία, which lend themselves better, as lowest common denominators, to constituting the evident realm of σωφροσύνη. Imagine, in a fictitious parallel, that φιλανθρωπία came to be considered by the masses to be the giving of money to those unable to procure what they need without that help. Money happens to be a good way to help, given its fungibility, transferability, and storability. Financial transactions are easy to understand and see, especially in a coin economy. And, to the extent that any other mode of help could be quantified in money equivalents, gifts of money may even seem logically prior to all other modes of help. So, we can understand the processes by which the masses considered φιλανθρωπία the giving of money. But that does not mean that it is. It may still mean, fundamentally and actually, acknowledging and acting on the vulnerabilities of one's fellow humans. So, too, with σωφροσύνη—the familiar way to talk about it does not crowd out the less-familiar but still quite accessible ways to do so.

Plato's *Charmides* is informative in this context. Its candidate definitions get nowhere close to control of the desires of touch. The issues of alcohol and sex do show up, quite implicitly, as dramatic elements, hinting that Plato knows that σωφροσύνη—whatever else it is—is the virtue that controls one's desire for them. But the proffered definitions are hardly abstruse or theoretical: walking and talking in an orderly and tranquil way is, even if aristocratic, a mundane human way of being; and having a sense of shame is universal and hardly to be restricted to one's self-consciousness of a few bodily desires. Even "doing one's own thing," Critias's riddling definition, meant to show off his cleverness, cannot be so far detached from familiar usage and Critias's defense of it treats it as a virtue of social engagement, not anything so individualistic as consumption. The *Charmides* has had a strange reception in that Aristotle almost wholly ignores it, and ancient discussions of the *Charmides* effectively never deal with any of the candidate definitions. This may suggest that its definitions are absurd—Socratic paradoxes, Platonic juvenilia, propaedeutic jokes. But they are not at all absurd, being, quite to the contrary, very familiar; and the *Charmides'* scarce treatment in later philosophy depends on its aporetic nature (and probably Aristotle's lack of interest in it), not on the views mooted in it.

IV   After Aristotle

I argued in the previous section that Aristotle has reasons for defining σωφροσύνη as he does, but, for all that, he has not said what σωφροσύνη has (really) been or what σωφροσύνη (really) is. My evidence, so far, has been retrospective, comparing his vision of the virtue to the commonplace statements and theoretical views of the virtue. Now, I turn to some prospective evidence. Work by his philosophical associates and successors or epitomizers—the work likeliest to accept Aristotle's word or, should Aristotle be right, to appreciate its truth and defend it—neither accepts nor defends Aristotle's views. Here, I address several prominent anonymous texts and notable authors: the Aristotelian *Problemata*; Theophrastus, the *Divisiones Aristoteleae*, *Virtues and Vices*, and the Platonic *Definitions*; and Aristotle's Academic colleagues, Heraclides, Speusippus, and Xenocrates. This list is obviously not in chronological order, but most of the works are generally unable to be dated, and the argument does not rest on "development." In general, they revert to the mean, so to speak, in not focusing on the pleasures of touch.

Not surprisingly, among the most "Aristotelian" of views is to be found in the Aristotelian *Problemata*.[53] Chapter 28 combines accounts of σωφροσύνη and ἐγκράτεια. Examples of ways to become more σώφρων include drinking and eating less (28.1). Σωφροσύνη—and ἐγκράτεια—pertain only to taste and touch because animals share only these of the perceptions; excess with respect to them is distinctly beastly (28.2). From these remarks, the delimitation of σωφροσύνη looks precisely like that found in Aristotle's canonical works. Indeed, it might even seem more delimited, since σωφροσύνη's apparent synonym here, ἐγκράτεια—a conflation of a virtue and what is not obviously a virtue, which departs from Aristotle's understanding—has, apparently, no wider a scope.[54] Yet, later in the chapter, we see two ways in which *Problemata* 28 widens σωφροσύνη's scope beyond Aristotle's understanding. First, its author says that just as we admire justice in the poor,—their needs making it harder, and, thus, more impressive, for them to give others their due—we admire σωφροσύνη in the young and wealthy, who need enjoyments to fill their leisured days; their self-limitation with respect to them is an impressive self-imposed hardship (28.4). Since we have no reason to think that the young and rich pass their time by enjoying alcohol, food, and sex alone, their self-limitation must cover a potentially expansive range of desires. So, σωφροσύνη involves reining in a broad class of desires, just as justice means giving others their due in a broad range of distributive relations. Second, the author says that we call ἀκρατής those who lack σωφροσύνη in sex, eating, and drinking (28.7; see also 28.2). He mentions these three bodily pleasures, however, not to define the scope of σωφροσύνη but, instead, to explain the connotation of "incontinence," presenting several ways in which one *can* be σώφρων. This provides a sort of evidence that the pleasures of touch are salient but do not provide a natural boundary for the virtue. Thus, the author of the *Problemata*, not so concerned for philosophical niceties, as revealed by the σωφροσύνη–ἐγκράτεια conflation, does not feel committed to maintaining Aristotle's analysis of the virtue.

At somewhat greater distance from Aristotle's theory is that of his leading student, Theophrastus. According to Arius Didymus, Theophrastus maintained an Aristotelian "mean" theory, with σωφροσύνη between the extremes of total

---

53   For a brief introduction to the mix of sources for this Peripatetic assemblage, see Bodnár 2015.

54   For the extent to which Aristotle thinks of ἐγκράτεια as akin to a virtue, see Callard (2017). For a close study of this chapter, attentive to the author's largely "physiological" interests, see Centrone (2017, 327–331 on ἐγκράτεια).

susceptibility to desire and total lack of desire.[55] Arius does not say that Theophrastus specified bodily desires, much less the desires of touch. He says instead that the σώφρων man is the one with appetite for the right things, at the right times, to the right extent, and using reason like a ruler, "making determinations in accordance with propriety" and "in accordance with nature." Now, this is familiar from the final lines of *Nicomachean Ethics* III.12, where, admittedly, they did not get much emphasis. If "appetite" for Theophrastus is restricted to bodily appetites, then not much is new here. But if Theophrastus has a wider conception of appetite, as including any desire, he advances—or maintains—a non-Aristotelian conception of σωφροσύνη. Two considerations support, even if they do not prove, that Theophrastus parts ways with Aristotle. First, Arius shows us that Theophrastus puts σωφροσύνη first in his list of virtues, by contrast with Aristotle's priority of ἀνδρεία (courage). And Diogenes Laertius tells us that Theophrastus wrote a work called Περὶ παιδείας ἢ περὶ ἀρετῶν ἢ περὶ σωφροσύνης, in one book (5.50). Together these testimonies might suggest that Theophrastus saw σωφροσύνη as the first step of maturation into virtue, even the kernel of virtue in general. It might also suggest that he discussed the virtues in the order of training. The *Charmides*, and much else of Greek literature, supports this idea, that training in σωφροσύνη is especially important for the youth and that this training goes beyond moderating the desires for food, alcohol, and sex.[56] Indeed, in the *Charmides*, youthful σωφροσύνη depends on overall bodily and conversational comportment, the right kind of αἰδώς before elders and authorities, and choosing the right pursuits given one's social context. Second, Theophrastus elsewhere addresses, as a linked pair, women's σωφροσύνη and οἰκονομία (fr. 112). While the latter might have tendentious overtones of marital subservience and romantic fidelity, it may also refer mainly to domestic obedience and managerial competence. Σωφροσύνη, then, is probably the dispositional or sentimental side, οἰκονομία the concrete household management skills. Believing that Theophrastus differs from Aristotle about virtue seems vindicated, incidentally, by his differing from Aristotle on other matters as well.

Two works, falsely attributed to Aristotle, clearly diverge from Aristotle's canonical views of σωφροσύνη. The *Divisiones Aristoteleae* defines σωφροσύνη as "ruling over one's desires and being enslaved by no pleasure, but living in an orderly way" (τοῦ κρατεῖν τῶν ἐπιθυμιῶν καὶ ὑπὸ μηδεμιᾶς ἡδονῆς δουλοῦσθαι, ἀλλὰ

---

55   Stob. 2.7.13–25; Theophrastus is mentioned at 2.7.20.

56   Contrast the detailed analysis in Fortenbaugh (2011, 152–155 and 1983, ch. 10), which merely assumes the Aristotelianism of Theophrastus's view.

κοσμίως ζῆν, Diogenes Laertius 3.91).[57] We see no limitation to bodily appetites, much less to the desires of touch. The focus is on autonomy over and from any sort of desire, which amounts to living in something like a principled way.

Virtues and Vices, despite hewing more closely to canonical Aristotle, comes to the same point.[58] On a tripartite view of the soul, it says that σωφροσύνη and ἐγκράτεια both pertain to the appetitive part (1249b27); but still they differ. Σωφροσύνη involves coming to have no drive to enjoy bad pleasures (καθ' ἣν ἀνόρεκτοι γίνονται περὶ τὰς ἀπολαύσεις τῶν φαύλων ἡδονῶν); ἐγκράτεια, by contrast, deploys thinking to check the appetite (1250a7). This is Aristotelian in its distinction between the virtue of character and something else but not in its breadth of subject desires—except that they are "bad." Later, when the author gives more details (§4), we first get a different limitation of those desires: σωφροσύνη is not valuing (τὸ μὴ θαυμάζειν) the enjoyment (τὰς ἀπολαύσεις) of bodily pleasures (or "desires," in Stobaeus's text); and a repetition of what we earlier saw though with stronger moral opprobrium: this non-valuing amounts to having no drive (ἀνόρεκτον) for the enjoyments of any "base" pleasures (πάσης ἀπολαυστικῆς αἰσχρᾶς ἡδονῆς). But here is the change: σωφροσύνη amounts to the fear of being justly dishonored; to being ordered (τετάχθαι) in life both in small and large matters; and is accompanied by good arrangement, orderliness, shame, and caution (εὐταξία, κοσμιότης, αἰδῶς, εὐλάβεια). A question-begger would say that these are all the public and dispositional effects of control over one's pleasures of touch. Yet, the latter may be as primary a set of phenomena as the former's psychological-normative explanation for those public and dispositional effects. Just as centrally, there is simply no reference to pleasures of touch and we have no reason to imagine a tightly circumscribed range of "bodily" pleasures. Whatever the goals of this late-Hellenistic rapprochement between Aristotelian and Platonic views, we see no evidence that Aristotle's fundamental view—that σωφροσύνη concerns the specifically bestial pleasures of touch—dominates.

The Platonic *Definitions*, probably from the fourth century,[59] does not purport to track Peripatetic discoveries. Then again, it hardly aims at idiosyncrasy, either, and it lists seven definitions for σωφροσύνη (411e6–412a2). If Aristotle's

---

57   Though Diogenes attributes this to Aristotle (3.80, 109), and presents it as an analysis of Plato, both claims are hard to accept. Take, for example, the analysis of εὐδαιμονία into five parts—εὐβουλία, εὐαισθησία and bodily health, εὐτυχία ἐν ταῖς πράξεσι, εὐδοξία, and εὐπορία (3.98–99)—which has no obvious parallel in either author.

58   Susemihl and Zeller suggest a Peripatetic first-century BC to first-century AD, aiming to reconcile Plato's and Aristotle's moral philosophy. Rackham accepts this (1935, 486). Doug Hutchinson gives an earlier date: 150 BC +/- 100 years (personal communication).

59   See Hutchinson's comment in Cooper (1997, 1677–1678).

QUESTIONING ARISTOTLE'S RADICAL ACCOUNT OF ΣΩΦΡΟΣΥΝΗ

view got at what everyone understood σωφροσύνη to be, or convincingly articulated what people had not realized it was, we might imagine it to be there, somewhere. And it is not. Σωφροσύνη is defined as:

1. being moderate concerning the desires and pleasures natural to the soul (μετριότης τῆς ψυχῆς περὶ τὰς ἐν αὐτῇ κατὰ φύσιν γιγνομένας ἐπιθυμίας τε καὶ ἡδονάς); or

2. being well-adapted and well-arranged concerning the pleasures and pains natural to the soul (εὐαρμοστία καὶ εὐταξία ψυχῆς πρὸς τὰς κατὰ φύσιν ἡδονὰς καὶ λύπας); or

3. harmony of soul regarding ruling and being ruled (συμφωνία ψυχῆς πρὸς τὸ ἄρχειν καὶ ἄρχεσθαι); or

4. doing one's own thing by nature (αὐτοπραγία κατὰ φύσιν); or

5. having a well-arranged soul (εὐταξία ψυχῆς); or

6. rational discourse of the soul concerning the admirable and disgraceful (λογιστικὴ ὁμιλία ψυχῆς περὶ καλῶν καὶ αἰσχρῶν); or

7. a disposition according to which one can choose and reject as one ought (ἕξις καθ' ἣν ὁ ἔχων αἱρετικός ἐστι καὶ εὐλαβητικὸς ὧν χρή).

Definitions (3)–(7) basically emphasize psychic integrity and rational autonomy. (6) and (7) emphasize being responsive to norms. (3) and (5) resonate with the *Republic*, (4) with the *Republic* and the *Charmides*. The question concerns the first two, what the pleasures or desires "natural to the soul" are. The Aristotle-sympathizer might say that these must be the desires of touch, namely of nutrition and reproduction, since all other, less-basic desires would be culturally mediated and, thus, not natural. But if Academics accept soul-tripartition, spirited and rational desires would seem to be just as natural. Desires for reputation and knowledge would need as much to be moderated, adapted, and arranged.

This seeming hodge-podge of Academic definitions cannot be a sign of unconcern about the real meaning of σωφροσύνη. Three of the first four permanent or acting scholarchs wrote works called Περὶ σωφροσύνης, and all four wrote about the virtue. We have already discussed Plato's *Charmides*, the only such work extant. Let us now look briefly at Heraclides', Speusippus's, and Xenocrates'. What we know about Heraclides', besides its title (Diogenes Laetius 5.86), is that Diogenes Laertius almost uniquely pronounces it written in the "comic" (κωμικῶς, 5.88) mode.[60] The only other work Diogenes calls "comic" is Heraclides' *On Pleasure*. Its fragments are historical anecdotes about people

---

60 Diogenes calls *Of Those in Hades*, *Of Piety*, and *Of Authority* "tragic" it is no clearer what he means about them.

with a wide variety of extravagant tastes.[61] One might wonder whether the Περὶ σωφροσύνης depicted people with a wide range of failures or trials of σωφροσύνη, wide enough that the work could not be called merely *On Drunkenness* or Περὶ ἔρωτος. But here is an alternative way to conjecture at its contents. If Heraclides is really writing in the fashion of comic drama, perhaps his work is in sympathy with Plato's account of comedy in the *Philebus*. There, Socrates presents the comic figure as one who fails to know himself (48c). He misrepresents to himself his possessions, bodily attraction, and overall virtue. Since the implication is that this misrepresentation is voluntary, presumably the self-aggrandizement is the result of pleasure. Thus, if comedies are about failures of self-knowledge, and if Heraclides' comedy is about σωφροσύνη, we might wonder whether Heraclides imagines σωφροσύνη to be self-knowledge (as the *Charmides* suggests).

Of Speusippus's writings about σωφροσύνη, we know only that Michael of Ephesus reports that Speusippus follows a mean theory of virtue, such that σωφροσύνη is neither ἀκολασία ("indiscipline") nor ἠλιθιότης ("silliness," "foolishness," "thoughtlessness").[62] Ἠλιθιότης appears in the *Republic* (560d) as what people scornfully call αἰδός (as "respect"): it must look like diffidence and reserve but depend on stupidity, rather than sensitivity to social norms. Speusippus has thus been influenced by some part of Aristotle—the mean theory—but not by the rest. For him, σωφροσύνη is a preservation of discipline founded in careful thought about, and responsivity to, what matters, not merely inbuilt lassitude or incompetence. There is no hint that Speusippus cares principally or centrally about bodily desires.

Of Xenocrates' Περὶ σωφροσύνης, we know nothing. Only a curious biographical fact remains: he was thought to have been chosen as scholarch over Heraclides and Menedemus for his superior σωφροσύνη (*Index Acad.* 24). Neither was known as particularly intemperate; one's thoughts turn rather toward the anecdotes of Plato's control of anger and political aspiration.[63]

Other fourth- and early third-century authors have interesting views of σωφροσύνη; none has an Aristotelian one.[64]

---

61   On the *On Pleasure*, see Schütrumpf (2009).

62   *In Ethica Nicomachea* 538.35–539.19. Taran doubts that Michael has independent access to Speusippus's works (1981, 442), but the reported view's difference from Aristotle's suggests he knows something about it.

63   Menedemus of Eretria, as it turns out, subscribed to a tight unity of virtue thesis, such that the virtues are one, in particular, temperance, courage, and justice (Plutarch *Moralia* 440e). This suggests a *Charmides*-like view, something quite distinct from Aristotle's.

64   Zeno of Citium and Ariston of Chios, for example (Plutarch *Mor.* 441a).

v Conclusion

In a few sentences, this is how I will leave us. Why does it matter how we evaluate Aristotle's explicit theory of σωφροσύνη? For one, if we accept that it is tendentious—even if we resist the idea that it is false—we can give closer attention to the view in, say, the *Charmides*. We can treat the virtue's connection to self-knowledge seriously, and reflect on its centrality to practical rationality. Indeed, a view of σωφροσύνη loosed from *Nicomachean Ethics* III.10–12 might allow the ancient virtue to play a productive role in contemporary thought about selfhood and agency. There is a broader benefit, too. By assessing the way Aristotle analyzes a specific virtue, we end up having to reflect on our criteria for a good account of a virtue or the meaning of a virtue term. Are we looking for differentiae, or what explains a disposition counting as a virtue, or a sort of evolutionary-biological account, or something about the virtue's socio-linguistic construction? Presumably, our ultimate goal is appreciating a way of thinking about the flourishing human life, namely, through the one-word lens of a virtue term and, so, thinking about any specific virtue will require, at the same time, thinking about that good life. I think the *Charmides* does that, as do other works, and I want to preserve space for them.[65]

---

65   Besides my audience at Saint Anselm College, I would also like to thank an earlier audience at the University of Chicago. I also appreciate the many conversations with Christopher C. Raymond and the thoughtful comments of an anonymous referee.

COLLOQUIUM 3

Commentary on Moore

Jesse Bailey
Sacred Heart University

Abstract

This paper is a response to Christopher Moore's excellent paper, "Questioning Aristotle's Radical Account of Σωφροσύνη." I expand upon some of the themes in the four suggestions Moore makes in his "Four Possible Defenses" of Aristotle that I take to be the most fruitful avenues of research. I then argue that pursuing these avenues will show that Aristotle's thinking in the *Nicomachean Ethics* about σωφροσύνη—and virtues in general—cannot be understood by looking only at the early books. I argue that his deeper analysis of virtue and φρόνησις in book VI demand a revaluation of the apparent finality of his comments in book III. Specifically, I argue that the *Nicomachean Ethics* as a whole is constructed as a dialectical advancement that points to a progressively deepening understanding of the relationship between the discussion of the individual virtues in the early books and the discussion of φρόνησις in book VI must be developed in order to understand Aristotle's conception of any individual virtue.

Keywords

Aristotle – σωφροσύνη – *Nicomachean Ethics* – *Charmides* – φρόνησις

I would like to begin by saying how necessary I find Dr. Moore's paper to be. In his introduction, he describes how he sees the current situation in scholarship regarding σωφροσύνη, and I completely agree with his assessment. I had, myself, begun to take σωφροσύνη as a settled matter. Reading and commenting on this paper has been invaluable for my own work because he has made me wonder about σωφροσύνη again, and for that I am truly grateful.

In my comments, I will try to expand upon some of the themes in the four suggestions Moore makes in his "Four Possible Defenses" of Aristotle that I take to be the most fruitful avenues of research. I will then argue that pursuing these avenues will show that Aristotle's thinking in the *Nicomachean Ethics* about σωφροσύνη—and virtues in general—cannot be understood by looking

---

© KONINKLIJKE BRILL NV, LEIDEN, 2020 | DOI:10.1163/22134417-00351P09

COMMENTARY ON MOORE

only at the early books. I will argue that his deeper analysis of virtue and φρόνησις in book VI demands a reevaluation of the apparent finality of his comments in book III. Specifically, I will argue that the *Nicomachean Ethics* as a whole is constructed as a dialectical advancement that points to a progressively deepening understanding of virtue. As Dr. Moore suggests, an understanding of the relationship between the discussion of the individual virtues in the early books and the discussion of φρόνησις in book VI must be developed in order to understand Aristotle's conception of any individual virtue.

In order to understand how the *Nicomachean Ethics* presents a dialectical advancement in its discussion of ethical life, it is necessary to look at the way the virtues are presented in the text. The order in which the virtues are discussed is no accident, and neither is the fact that courage and σωφροσύνη are discussed in book III, while most of the rest of the virtues are discussed in book IV and the two kinds of justice get all of book V. When Aristotle lists the virtues the text will discuss, the order in the list matches almost exactly the order in which the text deals with them (friendliness changes its place in the order). Aquinas analyzes the order, saying that it begins with a consideration of corporeal life with courage and σωφροσύνη necessary to preserve bare life against the troubles that arise from objects of fear and desire. Then, we consider the external goods, wealth and reputation; then external evils and how to deal with them moderately. Then, we move to external activity and the virtues of the social dimension of human life. Books VIII through X will further expand on this development of the proper locus of concern for someone seeking to live a good human life.[1]

Aristotle begins his discussion of virtue with talk of animals, bodies, and the throat as the location of the pleasures with which σωφροσύνη is concerned. Bodily health serves as the initial *measure* of σώφρων behavior. However, the focus on the body gives way in the dialectic advancement of the text to a discussion of the soul, then of friends, then of the human community, and, finally, even of our relation to the divine as the proper locus of the virtues. To quote Sparshott here:

> The whole discussion proceeds in an order of decreasing materiality and increasing abstractness or spirituality, the controlling logos, as it were, detaching itself more and more from an independent mass of "feeling" that has to be brought under control as the original model of a moral virtue suggested. (1994, 148)

---

1 Cf. Sparshott 1994, 148.

In III.10, Aristotle defines ἀκολασία as applying to the most "common" of the senses. Thus, these pleasures belong to us "not insofar as we are human beings, but insofar as we are animals" (1118b2). As Dr. Moore suggests in his third defense of Aristotle, this does require us to look at the levels of soul outlined in the *De Anima*, but I am not sure I understand why he sees this as a flaw. I want to paint the relation between the *Nicomachean Ethics* and the *De Anima* in a slightly different light from his.

De Anima II.11 and II.12 define touch as the only sense common to all animals and, thus, as definitive of animality. Plants, in the *De Anima*, draw nourishment directly from their environment, but animals lack this ability. As such, they have to hunt. For Aristotle, this requires locomotion and sensation, specifically the sense of touch—this is because he takes the proper objects of nourishment to be wetness, dryness, hotness, and coldness, and it is touch that properly perceives these (*De Anima* II.3). The sense of touch is thus definitive of being an animal that can perceive nourishment and move itself to seize and consume it. This also allows animals, unlike plants, to flee from things that threaten them, predators, and so forth. In the *Nicomachean Ethics* I.7, as Aristotle gives his first definition of the human good as the activity of the soul that has reason, and specifically distinguishes the human good from the good of animals, whose lives operate on sensation (and, we can add, locomotion). So, at the level of children, humans, like other animals, see things we want to experience the pleasure of touching, and we pursue them without measure (as for example, a horse will eat itself to death). We also see things that fill us with fear of pain and we run away without measure. Becoming fully human is using reason to figure out which pleasant things to avoid and which painful things to do despite the discomfort and, by doing that repeatedly, to develop the habits by which we no longer desire the wrong things, and so forth. The point of this short explanation is that Aristotle starts his discussion of the virtues with courage and σωφροσύνη in book III—separated from the discussions of the other virtues in book IV—because these are the virtues dealing with human life *insofar as we are animals*. Thus, he begins from the physical, animal, and *necessary* bodily desires.[2] So, σωφροσύνη initially appears to be about moderating those animal desires with respect to a *measure* that is within the body, health and fitness. I want to suggest that we have to look at the way this measure is transformed in the dialectical advancement of the text to understand Aristotle's full account of σωφροσύνη.

---

2   This is why he so oddly excludes alcohol from σωφροσύνη, since no one requires alcohol to live.

COMMENTARY ON MOORE   101

Famously, in 1.6, Aristotle seems to find fault with Plato's intellectualistic approach to ethics and decries the ethical value of one, universal conception of the Good. However, by book x, it can be argued—as Joe Sachs does in the introduction to his translation—that there is, indeed, one overarching sense of the good revealed through the dialectic advancement the book makes between 1.6 and x, and that standard is the Beautiful.[3] Indeed, Aristotle ends his discussion of σωφροσύνη by saying: "this is why the desiring part of a temperate person needs to be in harmony with reason, for the aim to which both look is the beautiful" (1119b13). Thus, I want to suggest that σωφροσύνη *begins* in the *Nicomachean Ethics* as a virtue for children wrestling with their animalistic needs. In that context, the virtue seems to name the active condition of having desires for pleasures of touch, which are in accord with reason, guided by the *measure* of bodily health and fitness; however, the text does not end there.

The standard for ethical behavior in the *Nicomachean Ethics* transcends the body and even the individual soul. The *Nicomachean Ethics* presents the reader with a process of development from an animalistic child, to an adult person, to contact with the divine, and from concern with body, to soul, to friends, to community, and, finally, to the divine as the measure of ethical living. The closing words of Aristotle's discussion of σωφροσύνη are, in fact, about reason and the Beautiful. Perhaps there is a sense in which the *Nicomachean Ethics*, like Plato's *Charmides*, begins with concerns about sex and overindulgence in bodily pleasures but dialectically advances to a place where the individual virtues and their narrow spheres of relevance can no longer explain ethical living. Perhaps these texts take us on similar journeys from habits of the body and desire to a recognition of the more intellectual aspects of a life well lived in pursuit of the Beautiful.

What does this supposed dialectic advancement in the text, pointed to in the final words of the discussion in book III, indicate? Is σωφροσύνη overcome by something higher in the φρόνιμος, living well with complete friends in a healthy community, contemplating the divine as leisure allows? Could σωφροσύνη be transcended just as justice is no longer needed between friends? Does the fully-developed ethical person look beyond the mere bodily standards of health and fitness, while no longer having any desires with which to wrestle that would violate those limits, and, guided by the Beautiful, attain a level of virtue at which mere σωφροσύνη is left behind or sublated in φρόνησις and in love of the Beautiful?

It is difficult to make a determination with a full discussion of φρόνησις, as Moore says. Perhaps σωφροσύνη is overcome. On the other hand, as Aristotle

---

3   Joe Sachs 2002, xxi-xxv.

suggests in book VI.5, σωφροσύνη might still be necessary to preserve the judgment made by φρόνησις against powerful desires:

> This is why we call temperance (σωφροσύνη) by this name; we imply that it preserves one's practical wisdom (σώζουσαν τὴν φρόνησιν). Now what it preserves is a judgement of the kind we have described. For it is not any and every judgement that pleasant and painful objects destroy and pervert ... [but] judgements about what is to be done. For the originating causes of the things that are done consist in the end at which they are aimed; but the man who has been ruined by pleasure or pain forthwith fails to see any such originating cause—to see that for the sake of this or because of this he ought to choose and do whatever he chooses and does. (1140b10)

This strongly implies that there is an important distinction between σωφροσύνη and φρόνησις that would not allow us to claim that σωφροσύνη is overcome or unnecessary once φρόνησις is developed. However, Aristotle also tells us in book VI, "It is clear from what has been said, then, that it is not possible to be good in the governing sense without φρόνησις, nor to have φρόνησις without virtue of character" (1144b30). Does this mean that individual character virtues lose any specific meaning in the unitary excellent judgment of the φρόνησις, or that they are still there as distinct to preserve the good judgment of the φρόνησις against fear and desire, and so forth? It is not clear. What is clear is that this relationship has to be worked out before we can make any determination about the status of σωφροσύνη in the *Nicomachean Ethics*.

Dr. Moore said it would take a book to figure out φρόνησις, but I am hoping these comments can help push our discussion toward trying to better articulate the relationship between σωφροσύνη and φρόνησις. The closing lines in book III.12 indicate that the beautiful—as opposed to the health of the body—is the proper measure of σωφροσύνη. This strongly implies that the answers to the puzzle of his apparently narrow view of σωφροσύνη lie in this relationship between σωφροσύνη and φρόνησις.

COLLOQUIUM 3

Moore/Bailey Bibliography

Bodnár, I. 2015. The *Problemata Physica*: An Introduction. In *The Aristotelian* Problemata Physica: *Philosophical and Scientific Investigations*, ed. R. Mayhew, 1–9. Leiden: Brill.

Callard, A. 2017. *Enkratēs Phronimos. Archiv für Geschichte der Philosophie* 99.1:31–63.

Centrone, Bruno. 2015. On *Problemata* 28: Temperance and Intemperance, Continence and Incontinence. In *The Aristotelian Problemata Physica*, ed. R. Mayhew, 321–36. Leiden: Brill.

Cooper, J.M., ed. 1997. *Plato: Complete Works*. Indianapolis: Hackett.

Curzer, H.J. 1997. Aristotle's Account of the Virtue of Temperance in *Nicomachean Ethics* III.10–11. *Journal of the History of Philosophy* 35:5–25.

Demos, R. 1957. A Note on Σωφροσύνη in Plato's *Republic*. *Philosophy and Phenomenological Research* 17:399–403.

Donovan, B.R. 2003. The Do-It-Yourselfer in Plato's Republic. *American Journal of Philology* 124:1–18.

Dorandi, T. 2013. *Diogenes Laertius: Lives of Eminent Philosophers*. Cambridge: Cambridge University Press.

Fortenbaugh, W.W. 1983. *Arius Didymus: On Stoic and Peripatetic Ethics*. New Brunswick: Transaction Publishers.

Fortenbaugh, W.W. 2011. *Theophrastus of Eresus. Commentary, Volume 6.1: Sources on Ethics*. New Brunswick: Transaction Publishers.

Howland, J. 2018. *Glaucon's Fate: History, Myth, and Character in Plato's Republic*. Philadelphia: Paul Dry Books.

Laks, A., and G.W. Most. 2016. *Early Greek Philosophy*, (9 Vols.). Loeb Classical Library. Cambridge: Harvard University Press.

Marcovich, M. 1999. *Diogenes Laertius: Vitae Philosophorum*. Stuttgart: Teubner.

Moore, C., and C.C. Raymond, trs. 2019. *Plato: Charmides. A Translation, with Introduction, Notes, and Analysis*. Indianapolis: Hackett.

Moore, C. 2015a. *Socrates and Self-Knowledge*. Cambridge: Cambridge University Press.

Moore, C. 2015b. *Promētheia* (Forethought) Until Plato. *American Journal of Philology* 136:381–420.

Moore, C. 2018a. Heraclitus and 'Knowing Yourself' (116 DK). *Ancient Philosophy* 38:1–20.

Moore, C. 2018b. Xenophon's Socratic Education in *Memorabilia* Book 4. In *Socrates and The Socratic Dialogue*, eds. A. Stavru and C. Moore, 500–520. Leiden: Brill.

Moore, C. 2019. *Promētheia* as Rational Agency in Plato. *Apeiron*.

© KONINKLIJKE BRILL NV, LEIDEN, 2020 | DOI:10.1163/22134417-00351P10

Murphy, D.J. 2013. Isocrates and the Dialogue. *Classical World* 106.3:311–53.

Pendrick, G.J. 2002. *Antiphon: The Fragments*. Cambridge: Cambridge University Press.

Prince, S. 2015. *Antisthenes of Athens: Texts, Translations, and Commentary.* Ann Arbor: University of Michigan Press.

Rackham, H. 1935. *Aristotle: The Athenian Constitution, The Eudemian Ethics, On Virtues and Vices*. London: Heinemann.

Rademaker, A. 2005. *Sophrosyne and the Rhetoric of Self-Restraint: Polysemy & Persuasive Use of an Ancient Greek Value Term*. Leiden: Brill.

Sachs, J., tr. 2002 *Nicomachean Ethics*. Newburyport: Focus Publishing.

Sparshott, F. 1994. *Taking Life Seriously: A Study of the Argument of the* Nicomachean Ethics. Toronto: University of Toronto Press.

Schütrumpf, E., tr. 2008. Heraclides, *On Pleasure*. In *Heraclides of Pontus: Texts and Translations*, eds. W.W. Fortenbaugh and E.E. Pender, 69–92. New Brunswick: Transaction Publishers.

Tarán, L. 1981 *Speusippus of Athens: A Critical Study With a Collection of the Related Texts and Commentary*. Leiden: Brill.

Young, C.M. 1988. Aristotle on Temperance. *Philosophical Review* 97:521–42.

COLLOQUIUM 4

Mythological Sources of Oblivion and Memory

Diego S. Garrocho
Universidad Autónoma de Madrid

Abstract

In this work, I present a selection of mythological and cultural insights from Ancient Greece that make our ambiguous relationship with memory and oblivion explicit. From Plato to Dante, or from Orphism to Nietzsche, and even today, the experiences of memory and forgetting appear as two sides of one essential nucleus in our cultural tradition in general and in the history of philosophy in particular. I intend to present a panoramic view of the main mythological sources that mention these two experiences as well as their unequal consideration. I will thus stress the personifications of both figures, taking up their features and the moral, gnoseological, and even political implications that historically have been associated with them. This is especially apparent in the strong Platonic legacy latent in the history of philosophy, where every time it insists on defining knowledge as a form of memory, the peculiar attributes of forgetting unexpectedly surface, not as a mistake or cognitive error, but as an experience which is truly saving and therapeutic.

Keywords

memory – oblivion – myth – λήθη – μνημοσύνη

I   Introduction: Myth and Memory

Both philosophy and mythology share the common characteristic of dealing with many of the fundamental mysteries faced by human beings. One might even argue that the existence of myth—and, therefore, the existence of the philosophical question—testifies to the quality, depth, or relevance of some disconcerting human concern. For a long time, non-neutral interpreters, such as W. Nestle (1942), attempted to distinguish between mythical wisdom and strictly rational knowledge, establishing a firm border between *muthos* and *logos*. However, with F.M. Cornford's *From Religion to Philosophy* (1912) and,

---

© KONINKLIJKE BRILL NV, LEIDEN, 2020 | DOI:10.1163/22134417-00351P11

especially, with Jean-Pierre Vernant's *Mythe et pensée chez les Grecs* (1965), this interpretation has been challenged. The earlier view turned the birth of philosophy into an abrupt departure from the continuous flow of history. The later scholars, however, showed that it would be neither prudent, nor even cautiously useful, to defend the existence of a strict and discreet break that might allow one to distinguish a transition between the knowledge of the philosopher and that of poets and creators of myths. Not only does any mythical description, obviously, have a rational component, but any experience of meaning or any philosophical strategy purporting to understand the world clearly also has recognizable mythological, fictional, and narrative features.

Accepting this premise as settled, one is forced to assume that a large portion of the veiled or implicit notions that engendered the birth of philosophy owe no small debt to the constellation of persons, values, and characteristics that inspired Greek mythology. Memory and oblivion, essential dispositions of our epistemological tradition, including its various modifications, are not an exception in this regard. Nevertheless, affirming that the border between mythical thought and philosophy is porous, or recognizing its ambiguities and patterns of reversibility, does not necessarily entail the claim that this boundary is non-existent. The works of Plato, for example, are paradigmatic of how one can persistently tend to censure myth for what it does and, at the same time, value the educative function of poets and their risks.

Perhaps for this reason, and with the aim of distancing myself from more typical places that highlight the tension between philosophy and myth, I defer at this point in this paper from expounding the dialectical tension between mythology and philosophical thought within the philosopher. On the contrary, I propose to start, perhaps, from an admittedly unusual and uncommon place: the philosophy of Aristotle. The Stagirite has wrongly been described as less literary, poetic, and, in sum, as tending not to use mythological resources. He himself, however, already indicated in book I of the *Metaphysics* that "it is owing to their wonder that men both begin now and at first began to philosophize" (982b13–14),[1] converting that θαῦμα—something close to surprise or fascination—into the very trigger of philosophical activity and of the love that knowledge inspires in us.[2] In this sense, the identification that Aristotle establishes shortly thereafter, by saying that the "lover of myth" (φιλόμυθος) is in a

---

1   *Metaph.* I, 982b13–14: διὰ γὰρ τὸ θαυμάζειν οἱ ἄνθρωποι καὶ νῦν καὶ τὸ πρῶτον ἤρξαντο φιλοσοφεῖν. All Aristotle's translations in this work are from Barnes (1984). Any changes will be noted in the text.

2   Perhaps, this "love" would be more properly translated as "desire" because with it we want to refer to the term ὄρεξις which, according to Martha C. Nussbaum, would be specifically Aristotelian (1986, 273). Naturally, this mention makes reference to the famous beginning of

certain sense "lover of wisdom" (φιλόσοφος), is singularly significant, since myth consists precisely of the same wonder that excites our philosophical desire to know (*Metaph.* I, 982b18–19). Not far from that intuition, although unsurprisingly much later in his own life, Aristotle came to confess his appreciation for stories and myths. We know that today from a fragment passed on by Demetrius: "For the more I am a selfer (αὐτίτης) and a loner, the more fond of *muthos* have I become" (*De elocutione* 144).[3]

Great problems are those that survive the passage of time. Aristotle himself already pointed out that what is noble (and great problems are, undoubtedly, noble) remains over time (*Nicomachean Ethics* IX, 1168a16).[4] The relation between the concepts of "everlasting" and "quality" in Aristotle is far from being as clear as in Plato. "That which lasts long is no whiter than that which perishes in a day," he states (*EN* I, 1096b4), and this enables us to think that when he establishes the durability of the noble, he refers to the condition of the memorable by the assistance of memory. In this sense, he even notices that remembering of noble things is always pleasant. However, he is also quite explicit asserting that "time wastes things away" and "people forget owing to the lapse of time" (*Physics* 221a33). Somehow, the relations between life and memory, and death and oblivion, are a constant among the Classics in their approach to time.

Time, we may affirm by drawing upon the famous formula, is also said in many ways. It possesses already an essentially mythological meaning. Thus, one of the ways of naming it, Cronos,[5] was prominent as a central deity in Greek mythology to the point of occupying an especially leading role in the Orphic tradition. The emergence of the two faculties or powers, that, in personified form, have the leading role in the following pages, owe their existence to time and the way in which we perceive it. Thus, μνημοσύνη and λήθη, memory and oblivion, are both unthinkable if it were not for the fact that each and every one of us must deal with and possess them only in time and its passing. As we will see, a personified mythological form matches each of these δυνάμεις.

Metaphysics in which it is remembered Πάντες ἄνθρωποι τοῦ εἰδέναι ὀρέγονται φύσει, i.e., "All men by nature desire to know" (*Metaph.* I, 980a21).

3   At this point, I slightly emend the translation by Jonathan Barnes and Gavin Lawrence, preferring to translate φιλόμυθος by "fond of *muthos*" instead of "fond of stories." Cf. *Eloc.* 144 = F 668 R: Καὶ ἐξ ἰδιωτικοῦ δὲ ὀνόματος γίγνεται, ὡς ὁ Ἀριστοτέλης, ὅσῳ γάρ, φησί, μονώτης εἰμί, φιλομυθότερος γέγονα. καὶ ἐκ πεποιημένου, ὡς ὁ αὐτὸς ἐν τῷ αὐτῷ · ὅσῳ γὰρ αὐτίτης καὶ μονώτης εἰμί, φιλομυθότερος γέγονα. τὸ μὲν γὰρ μονώτης ἰδιωτικωτέρου ἔθους ἤδη ἐστί, τὸ δὲ αὐτίτης πεποιημένον ἐκ τοῦ αὐτός.

4   *EN* IX, 1168a16: τὸ καλὸν γὰρ πολυχρόνιον.

5   In classical Greek there are different words that translate what we generically mean with the word "time" in English. Thus, terms like αἰὼν and καιρός will be left out of our analysis.

The soteriological usage of memory seems to open two ways of salvation. In one way, it seems to keep the object of memory away from the destructive action of time. However, in the same way, the action of memory seems to operate a kind of salvation for the one who remembers.

11   The Condition of the Memorable

Before continuing, it is worth highlighting a basic determining feature of myth. Memory, forgetfulness, and their forms do not occupy a secondary or, even less so, an optional role in relation to myth, but the preferred, grounding object of any mythical narration is the nature of the memorable—that is, that which is the object of memory. If, as Cicero already affirmed in the Latin context of his *Philippics*, "vita enim mortuorum in memoria vivorum est posita" (*Philippics* IX, 10), "the life of the dead resides in the memory of the living," then the commitment of myth to memory decides the survival of the individuals and actions that cannot be forgotten. Luc Brisson recognizes precisely that it is the memorable that is distinguished as the constitutive feature of myth. He notes, indeed, that the creation of a message and its transmission are indistinguishable within the context of an oral tradition (1982, 13). In this way, if the memory or retention of a mythical narrative depends strictly on its transmission (that is to say, on its enunciation and its being heard), the memory, creation, and transmission of the myth are, in the end, indistinguishable actions. The memorable is not only the preferred object of mythical narration but, finally, ends up being its true *ratio essendi* or even, to phrase it in Kantian terms, its condition of possibility. Without its role in remembrance, any myth would be inconceivable. This problem, that Brisson hints at in 1982, he revisited decisively in 1995, in the first volume of his *Introduction à la philosophie du Mythe*, where he once again confronts mythological knowledge with philosophy and history. He goes even further to conclude:

> In a civilization in which communication occurred solely by word of mouth, as had been the case in Greece before the eighth century B.C., the transmission of the memorable took a narrative form that, since Plato, we have come to call myths. (Brisson 2004, 162)

Brisson thus underlines the specific and political relevance of myths and highlights its prevalence over history and philosophy.

The proximity between the memorable and the mythical narrative, with little leeway for dispute, also appears to be endorsed by other famous definitions of myth. Carlos García Gual, for example, with his characteristic conciseness and accuracy, defined it as a "traditional story that evokes the memorable and paradigmatic action of some exceptional persons (gods and heroes) in a significant and distant time" (2014, 22). This memorable state of an archetype and the reference to a distant, significant time, perhaps remote, are two other components that justify the close link that I discern among myth, memory and oblivion and that support the thesis I want to defend in this paper.

Let us return, then, to memorable actions, to those actions that the construction of myths is devoted to preserving in memory, if the given definition is complete. Following a saying of Aristotle, it is useful to recall the exhortation that virtually opens his treatise *De memoria*. First of all, he confirms the suitability of specifying what things are the object of memory. This question could be rephrased in a moral and political vein: What is worth remembering? What must we remember? Or, even, what should we remember, though we nevertheless forget? What should we never have forgotten, or what is, by definition, the memorable object? Many centuries later, following the lead of these questions, the most Platonic of Plato's enemies, Friedrich Nietzsche, as usual, formulated a devastatingly total response: "Only what does not stop hurting remains in the memory" (1999, 295). In opposition to Plato, for whom the memory of the forms flows into the joyful exercise of ἀνάμνησις, or even against Aristotle, for whom memory is a cause of pleasure, Nietzsche's traumatic reading connects the unforgettable with pain, memory with damage. It is worth noting, moreover, the following: myths are not told about what is unforgettable in itself but, on the contrary, about what, although it can be forgotten, should not be forgotten. If a memory of pain becomes necessary, the memory of that pain, which the myth turns into its object, will be the memory of something contingent. Something is only worth remembering when, in fact, there is the possibility of forgetting it.

Few things are more eminently Greek than that which concerns oblivion and the object of a command to forget. For example, already in Homer we find several passages in which memory is formulated normatively. Similarly, imposing an oblivion, paradoxical as it seems, is a tradition with ancient roots. For memory, there are several passages in the *Iliad*, where Hector encourages his companions to "remember your impetuous courage," directing the imperative of the verb μιμνήσκω to Trojans, Lycians, and Dardanians insistently. In a contrary sense, oblivion, in this instance referring to pain and evil, also played a notable role in Ancient Greece. Thus, we find evidence of this in Homer's *Iliad*, for example, where Phoebus Apollo is urged to impel Hector's refreshed enthusiasm and make him forget his pain (λελάθῃ δ' ὀδυνάων) (XV, 70). The same topic reappears in several of the tragedies of Euripides, who echoes something that had already become apparent in Hesiod for whom Mnemosyne had cast the Muses as "the oblivion of evils and remedy of worries" (λησμοσύνην τε κακῶν ἄμπαυμά τε μερμηράων).[6]

This unusually positive consideration of oblivion, that is, the almost forced convenience of forgetting the pain, took on an essentially political importance in the restoration of Athenian democracy. We may remember (never better said!), if Nicole Loraux is right, that it was precisely a command to forget that served to restore Athenian democracy after the Government of the Thirty Tyrants (1997, 15). It happened in 403 B.C., after the campaign at Phyle, which definitively tipped the scales in favor of the Democrats.

The phrase attributed to General Thrasybulus was to be enshrined as the founding law of the new Athens. Μὴ μνησικακεῖν: "*Do not remember* the misfortunes," an imperative that forbade remembering the insults and damages committed among fellow citizens during the war. The anecdote is also remembered by Xenophon in his *Hellenica* (II.14, 43) and Aristotle himself, in the *Constitution of the Athenians* (40.2), tells of an execution where the individual was condemned precisely for remembering the proscribed evils.[7] Instead of a foundational agreement or a constitutive law, this old precedent seems to show that forgiveness and oblivion—if their identity is admissible—served as the foundational event for the community of Athenians. However, though memory can be the object of an imperative, it is almost impossible to imagine how oblivion, or at least the rejection of memory, could be formulated in imperative form since the enunciation itself of the law of oblivion makes its fulfillment impossible. Even as a mere formal exercise, if we may try to enforce the oblivion of something, the very mention of it would compel us to remember it. However, despite this impossibility to be "commanded" to forgive, the *Damnatio Memoriae*, for instance, as a classic legal institution, seems to be quite close to it since it is the memory itself that is commanded.

III   Mythical Forms of Memory

So far, I have traced some relationships among myth, memory, and oblivion without specifying the fact that most closely links these three concepts. It is that memory, personified as Mnemosyne (Μνημοσύνη), characterized as a spring or river, the same as Lethe (Λήθη), the river of oblivion, is the protagonist of many Greek myths. In all the Homeric literature, however, there

---

6   Cf. Euripides vid. *Heraclidae* 1043; Cf. *Troades* 606 and *Supplices* 86; Hesiod vid. *Theogonia* 55.

7   Cf. Aristophanes, *Plutus*, 1146.

MYTHOLOGICAL SOURCES OF OBLIVION AND MEMORY

is no reference to Mnemosyne as the personification of memory. In book VIII of the *Iliad,* Mnemosyne is mentioned but merely as a proper name (VIII, 181), though in the "Hymn to Hermes," whose author cannot be Homer, Mnemosyne is already presented as mother of the Muses (*In Mercurium* v, 429). The *locus classicus* for the origin of this mythological character is found in Hesiod's *Theogony,* in a description that will define almost all subsequent reworkings, even to this day. In the Hesiodic poem, Mnemosyne appears as a Titan, daughter of Gaia and Uranus, known for her beautiful hair (*Theogony* v.915).[8] After copulating with Zeus for nine nights, this enfleshed form of memory would give birth to the nine golden Muses who are in charge of those who love festivals and the pleasure of singing. It is significant that the Muses, as I previously intimated, are regarded as the "oblivion of evils," introducing the therapeutic value of oblivion but establishing, especially, a paradoxical relation or common lineage between memory and oblivion. The Hesiodic description, determining the subsequent course of the mythology of Mnemosyne, is regularly referred to in the *Bibliotheca* of the Pseudo-Apollodorus in terms almost identical to those established in *Theogony* (*Bibliotheca,* I, 3).

In a perfectly normal gesture in Greek mythology, the name of the deity is exchanged, almost confused, with the values or faculties it embodies. Thus, just as for Homer Mnemosyne was a common name, Xenophanes also mentions memory as that capacity liable to be nullified by ingesting alcohol. Hence one should praise someone who drinks and still preserves it (memory).[9] Already before this, though with a much more moralizing tone, the poet Pindar made memory the mirror in which to measure noble actions and guarantee the just recompense of our merits. This moralizing is the prelude to the role that memory acquired from the fifth century and takes expression in Aristotle's identification of the noble with what endures.[10] The most common description of Mnemosyne, however, remains reasonably faithful to the Hesiodic foundational portrait, where Mnemosyne, as the mother of the nine muses, harmonizes the task of musicians and poets with memory. In a very close sense, Aristophanes in *Lysistrata* describes memory in terms of poetic inspiration,[11] something Plato will repeat in quite similar terms shortly thereafter. For Plato, the evocation of this Titan always possessed allusions to the memorable, whether appealing to her alliance with the Muses and poets in

---

8   Cf. *Theog.* V, 135,

9   D.K. 21 B1, 19–20: ἀνδρῶν δ' αἰνεῖν τοῦτον ὃς ἐσθλὰ πιὼν ἀναφαίνει, ὡς ἦι μνημοσύνη καὶ τόνος ἀμφ' ἀρετῆς.

10 *Nemea* VII, 14–15: εἰ Μναμοσύνας ἕκατι λιπαράμπυκος / εὕρηται ἄποινα μόχθων κλυταῖς ἐπέων ἀοιδαῖς.

11 *Lys.* 1248: ὁρμαὸν τῷ κυρσανίῳ, / Μναμόνα, τὰν τεὰν/ Μῶάν.

places like *Euthydemus* (275d2) or coining the famous metaphor of the wax tablet as the surface on which memory is registered, as in the *Theaetetus* (191d4ff).[12]

Nevertheless, probably the most concrete and evocative reworking of Mnemosyne is found in the Orphic tradition, a tradition that, indeed, incorporated a strong Platonic influence as well. It suffices to recall Olympiodorus's words that Plato did no more than amend the teachings of Orpheus,[13] which, in one way or another, served to justify the insistence in Platonic philosophy of the link between knowledge and memory.[14]

The presence of both the figure of Mnemosyne and the figure of Orpheus in contemporary culture is also significant. If the old personified name of memory still continues in such momentous texts of contemporary culture as Aby Warburg's *Atlas Mnemosyne* or the proposed title, *Speak, Mnemosyne*, that Vladimir Nabokov gave his memoirs, then the influence of Orpheus and Orphism extends through the whole cultural identity of the West. It travels from Plato to Monteverdi, from Virgil to Titian, reaching an exceptional perfection in Rainer Maria Rilke's sonnets.

Although Orpheus's descent into Hades and his frustrated rescue of Eurydice is the best known scene of the myth, testimonies, such as the ἱεροὶ λόγοι attributed to the Thracian poet, are the most explicit places for poetic and fictional reworking of both memory and oblivion. Among these, probably, the most concrete and extensive evidence is found in the famous archaeological discovery known as the Orphic Gold Tablets.[15] Those small sheets of gold were relegated, for a time, to being mere epigraphic curiosities, although today we know the importance of their discovery and the valuable testimony they give us. These leaves contain short texts, mostly written in verse, in nonprofessional handwriting, riddled with spelling mistakes. They are inscribed on small pieces of gold foil that would be placed in the hand or mouth of the initiates as an obol for Charon and served as instructions or passwords to travel successfully in the most impossible of all trips: the transition to the underworld or the land

---

12 Cf. *Critias* 108d2

13 *In Platonis Phaedonem commentaria* 10.3; Cf. 7.10.

14 Some paradigmatic and emphatic place in the work of Plato related to learning, knowing, recollecting and may be found in the *Phaedo* 72e5–6, *Phaedrus* 249e and 250, or *Meno* 86c. For the link between Mnemosyne and the processus of ἀνάμνησις *vid. Theaetetus.* 191d4.

15 Although, in this work, we will refer essentially to the edition of Fritz Graf and Sarah Iles Johnston (2007), our hypothesis is based on the edition of Alberto Bernabé and Ana Isabel Jiménez San Cristobal (2001) and we also use the information provided in the translation of Bernabé (2003) and in his edition for the Bibliotheca Teubneriana (2004–2005).

MYTHOLOGICAL SOURCES OF OBLIVION AND MEMORY 113

of the dead. These traces vary in antiquity, dating from 400 B.C. to A.D. 260, and show some of the most useful references in the mythological reconstruction of memory and, for some scholars, of the reconstruction of oblivion (Bernabé 2003, 253).

The link or proximity between memory and oblivion is evident, since the inscription on those tablets, as some versions read, would be the work of memory or Mnemosyne. This can be seen, for example, in the Hiponius little sheet, in whose first verse we read, before encountering the instructions for the afterlife: Μναμοσύνας τόδε ἔργον, or, in the translation by Sara Iles Johnston: "This is the work of Memory, when you are about to die."[16] This implies that memory is the custodian of its own advice, contained in the sheets and assisting the initiate. The instruction, in symbolic manner, warns of the existence of a first spring at the entrance of Hades from which one must never drink. This unnamed spring must be avoided in order to reach a second spring later, "the Lake of Memory," in which the initiate prays to quench his thirst. The same advice, with very slight revisions, is also found in the Petelia gold tablet and the Pharsalus tablet, insisting on the fact that, at the entrance to the underworld, the initiate must avoid quenching his thirst at the first of the springs, knowing how to wait patiently for the overflow of memory.[17] The content of these tablets seems to fit perfectly with a series of topics present in other ancient testimonies. The benefit of presenting a series of counsels for the trip to Hades, the presence of an uncontrollable thirst in the transition to the underworld, the image of the cypress and the overflows are usual images in the recreation of Hades. The determining factor, however, is the double value, salvific and positive, given to Mnemosyne. On the one hand, the content of the tablets is guarded and even dictated by memory itself and, on the other, the initiate is told to drink of the fresh water of the Lake of Mnemosyne, in an image consistent with what is told by Plato in the myth of Er in *Republic*. Memory is postulated, then, as a vehicle of salvation in the double sense of the Latin term, as bodily health and as transcendental salvation. If one dealt explicitly with what is expressed in these tablets, there is no reference to oblivion, even though some scholars like Alberto Bernabé use the *Orphic Anthem* 77 to identify the unnamed spring that should be avoided precisely with the River Lethe (2003, 260).

---

16 Bernabé OF 474 (=L1). The text belongs to the Hiponius tablet (ca. 400 BC). It is located in the Archaeological Museum Satale di Vibo. The first edition is that of Pugliese Carratelli and Foti, in 1974.

17 For Petelia Tablet, cf. Bernabé OF 475 = L3; for Pharsalus Tablet, OF=L4.

IV   Oblivion

The prestige of memory, its salvific utility and the value of memory as a resource for the immortality of the finite, has justified that, in some sense, our entire philosophical and epistemological tradition has been designated as an *ars memoriae*.[18] If Platonic philosophy raised the slogan "learning is recollection" to the status of a saving doctrine, confirming evidence, such as that proposed by Orphism or even the detailed speech of the Goddess of Parmenides, reminds us that the insistent affirmation of the dignity of memory has been sustained historically. Despite all this, the fortune was much different for the development of oblivion and its characterizations. Although Nietzsche reminded us in the nineteenth century that "You can live and live happily without remembering, but it is impossible to live without forgetting" (KSA I, 250),[19] the history of oblivion, its mythology and its cultural construction, is far from being its *apologia*. It is true, as mentioned previously, that already in Homer or Euripides the convenience of forgetting damage or pains is recognized and that, in a peculiar political context, the convenience of imposing a form of selective oblivion was mandated in order to give rise to a new community. These almost accidental references in no way thwarted the typically negative regard directed toward oblivion, until it was turned, as in our contemporary context, into a kind of a pathology or cognitive error.

In this sense, the characterization raised by Homer himself in converting oblivion into a form of temptation is emphasized. One can recall, in fact, the passage in which Circe offered the travelers a wine from Pramno, which would make them forget the return to their country (*Odyssey* X, 235–236). Oblivion is a temptation and a risk, a seductive action, but also damning. The theme is constant in Homeric literature because, as we remember, oblivion had already been refashioned in very similar terms in book X when, in the land of the lotus-eaters, the Greeks were warned of the danger of eating that flower. Again, in this passage, the temptation means to succumb to appetite and to eat what will make us forget the way back home (*Od.* IX, 90ff). In both cases, oblivion takes

---

18   What I mean by the expression the "immortality of the finite" is the way in which a mortal entity could endure, or survive over time, following the Ciceronian intuition mentioned before (*Phil.* IX, 10). In that sense, μνήμη could refers to the faculty of memory but it also means the artefacts, practices, and equipment devoted to battle the passing of time and its consequences. Memorials, inscriptions, or tales are, in this sense, not only tools but also forms of μνήμη. Aristotle is paradigmatically clear when, describing honor (τιμή), he notes that commemorations, in verse and in prose, are parts of this honor: μέρη δὲ τιμῆς θυσίαι, μνῆμαι ἐν μέτροις καὶ ἄνευ μέτρων (*Rhetorica* 1361a34–35). Somehow, the noble again is compacted with the condition of the memorable.

19   *Vom Nutzen und Nachteil der Historie für das Leben*, 1874.

MYTHOLOGICAL SOURCES OF OBLIVION AND MEMORY

place as a risky alternative that would prevent the hero from fulfilling his mission and his destiny. In more unqualified and severe words, Hesiod will remind us that oblivion, already personified as Lethe, is the son of the cursed Eris and brother of Fatigue, the hunger and pains that cause a host of evils: wailing, fighting, wars, slaughters, massacres, hatreds, lies, discourses, ambiguities, disorder, and destruction (*Theog.* 227). In such company, naturally, it would be impossible not to conceive oblivion as a superlative evil.

The collection of passages in which the classical tradition attempted to condemn the experience of oblivion becomes virtually uncountable. If Hesiod's version of oblivion presages this recognizable tendency, the passage of time brought even more embellishments. Thus, Pindar himself would link Lethe with Neikos in *Nemean* VIII (verses 24–25) and even Hippocrates, in *De Morbis Popularibus*, would endorse the negative condition of oblivion (VII 1, 3). Finally, Plato ends up emphasizing not only this negative but also the pathological and morally fraudulent character of oblivion. We may remember, as previously noted, that memory in Plato not only fulfills a useful and beneficial function for whoever exercises it, but it is an instrument at the service of knowledge. Its perfection acquires a scope not only epistemic but also soteriological: the salvation and the health of the soul, which are one and the same thing, are given by the reminiscence of ideas, among which, the idea of the Good stands out in power and dignity.[20]

In contrast to this robust defense of memory, oblivion in Plato is not just a mythological theme imagined in the form of a river, nor a transitional experience that guides the passage between life and death. Plato's Lethe is specifically described as a vice or a true moral error: thus, one reads, for example in the *Phaedrus*, in the explanation of another famous myth, the myth of the winged chariot, that the soul is described as unable to see what is true when it loses its wings and falls to the earth. This version of the classic topic of the fall indicates that the soul that abandons the celestial rotation will do so precisely when it is sated with carelessness and oblivion.[21] Finally, Plato's criticism of writing later in the *Phaedrus* rests on the fact that written letters are allies of

---

20   At this point we refer, obviously, to the commented passage from *Republic* VI (509b8–9), which warns that Good is not a mere being but transcends and goes beyond it: ἀλλ' ἔτι ἐπέκεινα τῆς οὐσίας πρεσβείᾳ καὶ δυνάμει ὑπερέχοντος. Proof of the pregnancy of the expression is found in the obsession presented by Derrida, who, throughout his work, did not stop commenting on the expression, ἐπέκεινα τῆς οὐσίας. Already in 1967, Derrida mentions the closeness between Levinas and Plato, linked by this characterization of the good (127, 187, and 150). That same intuition would be retaken, in addition to many other places, in the farewell to the Kaunas-born teacher in *Adieu: À Emmanuel Lévinas* (Derrida 2003).

21   *Phdr.* 248c.

oblivion because they operate from outside the soul and inhibit us from exercising true memory.

The negative evaluation of oblivion attained such a resounding conviction in Platonism that the negativity about the ills of the River Lethe remained entrenched over a long period of time. Thus, for example, the criticism of oblivion clearly persisted in Neoplatonic texts. In the case of Plotinus, we are warned that Lethe is the symbol of the body, a body that is itself cause of oblivion (*Ennead* IV.3[27].26, 55). Iamblichus similarly proclaims that ignorance, insanity, or passions come with the River Ameles, the waters of Lethe, in *De Mysteriis Aegyptiorum* (III, 20). All these features dominated then-contemporary philosophy, where they fit indeed with other mysterious descriptions, recognizable in Proclus's comments on Chaldean Oracles, which reiterated the fluid or liquid condition of oblivion.[22] In a similar context, with even greater force, we read in *Corpus Hermeticum* that oblivion is the origin of evil: ἡ δὲ λήθη κακία γίνεται (X, 15). Such descriptions left little room for hesitation or reassessment, making it impossible, for a long time, to reconsider any therapeutic or vitally useful function of the experience of oblivion.

This mythology of Lethe, despite everything, has provided us with incidents and imaginings where the description of oblivion can be considered, if not positively, at least neutrally. An example of this can be found in Aristophanes' comedy, *The Frogs*, which describes the plane of oblivion in similar terms to its later characterization in *Republic* x (621a–c), but with a much more agreeable connotation, not having the predictably clear moralizing attitude that Plato imposes on it in the myth (*Frogs*, 186).[23] An even more decisive source in the resignification of oblivion and its mythological personification is found, undeniably, in Plutarch. The most important witness concerning the cult of Lethe is found in his *Quaestiones Convivales*, a text in which the construction of an altar in the most prominent site in Athens, the Erechtheion, commemorates both Lethe and Athena (I 612D). This reference confirms the sacral status of oblivion and this occurrence is far from being the only one, since Plutarch also insists, for example, that the ancients assert that Dionysus was Lethe's son. In the same way, and paradoxical as it may seem, Chaeronean also takes up a well-known fragment of Stobaeus in almost literal terms to strengthen the belief that oblivion was deprived of voice and senses, which weakens Lethe's positive appreciation. This privative and incapacitating report is seen again in *De E*

---

22   *Philosophia Chaldaica*, Fr. 2, 25: Πατὴρ ὁδηγεῖ, πυρὸς ὁδοὺς ἀναπτύξας μὴ ταπεινὸν ἐκ λήθης ῥεύσωμεν χεῦμα. We find very similar terms in the *Chaldaic Oracula*: Μηδέ ποτ᾽ ἐκ λήθης ῥεύσωμεν χεῦμα ταπεινόν (Fr. 171). Cf. Fr. 109.

23   Cf. *Rep*. x, 621a–c and Virgil *Aeneid* VI, 705 and 715.

apud Delphos, in which Mnemosyne and the Muses are contrasted with oblivion and silence (394 A 8). This, again, seems to keep Lethe's characterization in an ambiguous status, emphasizing his sacred condition but opposing it unsurprisingly to the benefits of memory.

Another important mention of the cultic condition of the River Lethe appears in Pausanias who, in his *Description of Greece,* Book IX, dedicated to Boeotia, describes access to Trophonius's oracle through a rite. The ceremony, guided by two priests, leads the postulant through the River Hercyna to meet again with the regenerative waters from the Lethe and Mnemosyne.[24] There is one difference: in this instance, it is necessary to drink from the two springs, first from oblivion, to eliminate any previous memory, and then from Mnemosyne, to retain what happens after. Only after this transition can one contemplate the statue of God sculpted by Daedalus (*Desc.* IX, XXXIX, 8).

With the advance of time, many centuries later, the regenerating waters of Lethe and Mnemosyne end up by distinguishing a positive and, once again, salvific role of the function of oblivion. A proof of the strength and importance of the myth and its ability to survive over time is found in Dante, for whom the River Lethe acquires a definitive dignity, rare up until then. Interestingly, the situation taken by Dante towards the end of the Middle Ages is identical to the one we find in Orphism: a *katabasis*, or descent, guided by ritual access, to the spring of oblivion and memory as a condition for the final transition. What is original, however, is that the references to the River Lethe in Dante's *Commedia*, invite us to identify it as an ally for one aiming to forget past misfortunes, perhaps taking up a distant thread that we recognize in Homer, in Euripides, and later in the political register with the use of amnesty. In moral terms, for Dante, forgetting would be equal to eliminating those offenses and sins of which one is guilty. This positive consideration of oblivion in the *Commedia* seems to cross the classical tradition with Christianity to shade in a new common horizon with themes, agents, and tropes that, in principle, started from different points.

The originality of Dante's proposal, as a reader and interpreter of the classical world, is evident in *Inferno*, Canto XIV. There Virgil shows the poet the

---

24   As Pausanias narrates, Hercyna was playing with the daughter of Demeter with a goose. The bird escaped and hid under a Stone. When the Maid picked up the Stone to capture the animal, the water flowed, creating the river which takes her name: the River Hercyna. On the bank of the river, a temple was built, which was devoted to her. Whoever wants to descend to the Oracle of Trophonius should abstain from hot baths, bathing only in the river Hercyna. After other purifications, we could be ready to be taken by the priests to two fountains of water, Lethe and Mnemosyne, rendering it possible for us to remember what we see during the descent to the Oracle Cave.

origin of the mysterious rivers of Hell. He then warns him: "Lete vedrai, ma fuor di questa fossa, là dove vanno l'anime a lavarsi quando la colpa pentuta è rimossa."[25] This may be translated as "You will see the Lethe, but never outside this grave, there where the souls are washed, when their fault is repented (*pentuta*) and removed." This flow is the salvific consequence of regret, ἀμνηστία, or selective *amnesia* that seeks the oblivion of those acts unworthy of remembrance. The Lethe is also mentioned in *Purgatorio*, Canto XXVI, when Guido Guinizzelli issues another warning to the poet. "Tu lasci tal vestigio, per quel ch'i' odo, in me, e tanto chiaro, che Letè nol può tòrre né far bigio."[26] This can be rendered as "leaving such a trace within me, so clear that Lethe could neither erase nor blur it," returning to the theme of memory and writing, oblivion and erasure. In Canto XXVIII, Lethe is mentioned, this time, at the gates of the Terrestrial Paradise, where it is again emphasized that the river of oblivion removes consciousness of Sin. Here, it is joined to the Eunoe, a river of Dante's invention, described as a spring analogous to Mnemosyne that, in this instance, allows us to remember only virtuous actions, insisting on the selective character of oblivion and memory.[27] Dante names the River again when Matilde introduces him into the waters of Lethe in order not to remember, literally, the sad memories.[28] Finally, in a place as prominent as *Purgatorio*, Canto XXXIII, the selective function of both faculties, memory and oblivion, is reviewed, highlighting the necessity of drinking from the water of the River Eunoe which marks the definitive transition from Purgatory to Paradise.

This reconfirmation of oblivion and memory strengthens, once and for all, the appreciation of the therapeutic nature of the experience of oblivion. Its definitive political version, the Edict of Nantes, a few centuries later, repeats the imperative of Thrasybulus in Athens 403 BC, the saying of Euripides, or the old Homeric exhortation. The Edict of Nantes formulates an event that presents another essentially distinct form of harmonizing memory and oblivion, in the context of modernity. The analysis of this new context does not need to be done here, since literal closeness is so firm, decisive, and expressive. It is worthwhile to bring into relief the underlying value of oblivion that took such visible form at the threshold of the modern world. The exhortation in the original French follows: "Premièrement, que la mémoire de toutes choses passées d'une part et d'autre, depuis le commencement du mois de mars 1585 ... demeurera éteinte et assoupie, comme de chose non advenue." Translated into English:

---

25   *Inf.* XIV, 136–138.
26   *Purg.* XXVI, 105–8.
27   *Purg.* XXVIII, 129–132.
28   *Purg.* XXXI, 11–12.

MYTHOLOGICAL SOURCES OF OBLIVION AND MEMORY 119

"First, that the recollection of everything done by one party or the other between March, 1585 ... remains obliterated and forgotten, as if no such things had ever happened." This endorses, finally, that oblivion is both possible and profitable in the face of the catastrophe that memory, or the memory of past crimes, imposes.

v   Conclusion

Throughout this paper, I have tried to rework some features in the classic construction of memory and oblivion, emphasizing Mnemosyne's preferential treatment in opposition to Lethe, but also highlighting the exceptional circumstances in which oblivion stood out for its usefulness, dignity, and profit. It is clear that the philosophical tradition has been considered as mainly an art of memory. From the positive treatment of Platonic memory to the demarcation of the human in Aristotelian thought, philosophy, healing, and memory all presented an intimate connection, still visible today. Memory's natural opposite, oblivion, has been characterized as the fundamental enemy of the salvific experience of knowledge, from Hesiod to Kant. The mnemonic rules, the *Ars Memoriae* of the Renaissance or the call to remember—*memento, homo*—of Christian ritual, insisted on the fittingness of not only the epistemological but also the moral and social power of memory.

Alongside this emphasis on memory, as I have shown, we see beginning already in Homer an opposing or perhaps parallel tradition adumbrating the fittingness of selective oblivion. That oblivion of evils, later affirmed by Euripides as well, took on legal form in the decree of Μὴ μνησικακεῖν when warning that it is not worth remembering absolutely everything. The circumstance of the amnesty, with the stated purpose of resolving the tension between oblivion and forgiveness, shows a normal alternative to the positive consideration of memory. Thus, in contrast to the Orphic, Platonic, and Neoplatonic traditions, with their esteem for memory, there were, over the centuries, notable exceptions, in which not only the convenience but even the sacred condition of oblivion has been justified. From Plutarch to Pausanias, from Dante to Nietzsche, the possibility of exercising a sort of oblivion as a sacred and active experience has emerged with uneven validity over the centuries.

Not long ago, Umberto Eco reminded us of the impossible condition of a science of oblivion, an *Ars Oblivionalis*. This seems to be a subtle provocation but nevertheless, it makes complete sense (Eco and Migiel 1988). Similarly, Harald Weinrich wrote a valuable book devoted to the art and critique of oblivion, exploring some unusual passageways in our culture in which this impossible science was attempted (Weinrich, 1997). Both proposals embody an infrequent possibility, which, however, would open a new way of facing and confronting the classical tradition. If the Greek question par excellence was what we can and what we should remember, we could update the question with a new formulation: What cannot be forgotten, though we should? In what way do we retain the experiences of our life to confront those memories that insist on being remembered, exhibiting an almost unforgettable condition? The mark of the unforgettable cannot be identified with the painful or pleasant condition of a memory since the sign of what is inaccessible for oblivion seems to oscillate between pleasure and pain, making our question about its salvific and positive value urgent and necessary. There is no ideal candidate between a traumatic and happy memory that can perpetuate itself in memory and, by that fact, become inaccessible to oblivion. With Nietzsche, we assume that, in fact, pain is an ally of memory and that the depth of a trauma makes it difficult and even impossible to erase.

However, if the oblivion of a pain seems impossible, the structure of forgetting becomes even stranger because there is also a connection between beauty and memory. We owe a great part of the way in which we still appreciate or condemn memory and oblivion to antiquity: to its myths, persons, and places. Mnemosyne and Lethe, memory and oblivion, are two essentially human dispositions whose prominence has become recognizable in the Western cultural tradition, from art to literature and without a doubt in philosophy. The effort to construct an art of memory ignored for a long time another option, so difficult as to be said to be impossible: learning to forget and not learning to remember may be essential goods that the gods denied us mortals. If philosophy always had a desire to think the unthinkable, perhaps the most necessary, then, building a science, an art, or a virtue of oblivion is something very close to that. Take this test: if you were allowed to remember as much as you want or if, on the contrary, you could forget at will, try to decide which of them you would like to have as your own recourse.

COLLOQUIUM 4

Commentary on Garrocho

Santiago Ramos
Boston College

Abstract

This commentary examines Diego Garrocho's paper, "Mythological Sources of Memory and Oblivion." I argue that Garrocho's thesis hinges on the assumption that two historical continuities exist between myth and philosophy. First, it supposes a continuity of *understanding*: between the mythical conception of memory and oblivion, and the philosophical reformulation of the same, there lies no essential difference; both the mythical and philosophical traditions share a univocal, or at least analogical, concept of memory and oblivion. Second, it supposes a continuity of *appreciation*: memory and oblivion are valued at various stages in the history of thought in univocal or analogical ways. I go on to see whether these continuities have taken place within the work of Plato, who, I argue, is an axial figure between myth and philosophy.

Keywords

Myth – philosophy – Plato – Homer – katabasis – poetry

1 Introduction

Professor Garrocho's paper traces an intellectual genealogy of memory and oblivion, from Homer and Plato to Nietzsche and Nabokov. The purpose for tracing his genealogy is to demonstrate that Western ideas about memory and oblivion have their origin in myth. Garrocho's primary argument is that the imprint of this mythical origin does not disappear when these ideas are recast as philosophical concepts. A second argument makes the case that, while the historical importance of oblivion is subordinate to that of memory (because of the long shadow cast by the Platonic theory of *anamnesis*), nevertheless "there exist exceptional characterizations of forgetting not as an error or cognitive failure, but as a truly redemptive and therapeutic experience."[1] A persistent

---

1 The comment is based on the paper as delivered, so there may be details that no longer apply in the printed version. This quote is from an earlier draft of Garrocho 2020.

© KONINKLIJKE BRILL NV, LEIDEN, 2020 | DOI:10.1163/22134417-00351P12

human need for forgetting and oblivion, Garrocho insists, appears and reappears throughout the history of memory. Garrocho concludes his paper in *aporia*, leaving it to a later investigation to uncover a possible unity between memory and oblivion, perhaps within the experience of nostalgia.

Both of Garrocho's arguments hinge on the persistence of two great historical continuities. First, a continuity of *understanding*: between the mythical conception of memory and oblivion and the philosophical reformulation of the same, there lies no essential difference; both the mythical and philosophical traditions share a univocal or at least analogical concept of memory and oblivion. Second, a continuity of *appreciation*: memory and oblivion are valued at various stages in the history of thought in univocal or analogical ways. However, if it could be shown that a radical rupture has taken place between the mythical and philosophical concepts of memory and oblivion, then both of Garrocho's arguments would be thrown into question.

We might add as documentary support to Garrocho's second argument a few instances where both the mythical and Platonic traditions speak in favor of oblivion. In the *Orphic Hymns*, we find the ode, "To Hypnus," the god of sleep. "You free us from our cares," the poet sings, "and offering sweet respite from toil / you grant holy solace to our every sorrow."[2] In Plato's *Apology*, there is the hint of an appreciation of oblivion when Socrates considers whether death might be "like a sleep in which the sleeper does not even dream," and adds that if it were so, then death would be a "marvelous gain."[3] But can we assume that a concept like "forgetting" is the same when it is deployed by a mythmaking poet as it is when used by a philosopher who is often critical of poetry and myth?

In what follows, I will ask questions that complicate our sense of the continuities mentioned above. I will focus on Plato's attitude toward myth, given that, in many respects, he is an axial figure between mythology and philosophy. My concerns will cluster around three main topics: first, the difference between myth and philosophy in Plato; second, the differences between mythical and Platonic treatments of memory; and finally, the Platonic attitude toward oblivion and forgetting.

II Myth and Philosophy

Does something change when we go from representing memory and oblivion in myth, to contemplating them philosophically?

---

2 "To Sleep," in *The Orphic Hymns*, translated by Apostolos N. Athanassakis, 107.

3 *Apol.* 40d.

COMMENTARY ON GARROCHO

Much scholarship has shown that, within the Platonic corpus, there is not a simple opposition between *muthos* and *logos* or between dialectic, on the one hand, and mythmaking, on the other.[4] Moreover, anyone even superficially acquainted with Plato's writing knows that he has a penchant for making Socrates relate myths to his interlocutors. These myths, it is often argued, serve some sort of philosophical or rhetorical purpose, even if that purpose is merely to provide a dramatic illustration of a difficult subject. Nevertheless, the fact that there is an overlap in purpose between myth and philosophy in Plato does not mean that a difference does not also exist between them. Nor does it mean that this difference might not be especially significant when excavating the genealogy of difficult topics, such as memory and oblivion, which have been treated both philosophically and mythologically in the dialogues.

Plato's dialogues show us a Socrates who maintains a distinction between myth and philosophy, even while creating his own myths. Jean-François Mattéi has spoken of the "distance" that is proper to Platonic myths: "Whatever its inspiration, myth reveals its mysterious character with that voice from beyond that reduces the listener to passivity and arouses in him the sense of being both bewitched and awed by the feeling of immeasurable distance."[5] Myth always summons the tacit assumption that, while it provides an image of the whole of the truth, not every detail or nuance of the truth is in view. Therefore, when beholding a myth, we remain at a certain remove—an "immeasurable distance"—from the whole truth. Myth attempts to give a comprehensive explanation of something while lacking the precision and clarity of discursive reasoning and dialectic.[6]

This structural distance holds whether Socrates happens to be praising or disparaging myth at any given moment. In the *Ion*, Socrates tells the rhapsode: "Surely it is you rhapsodes and actors, and the men whose poems you chant, who are **wise** (σοφοί); **whereas I speak but the plain truth** (ἐγὼ δὲ οὐδὲν ἄλλο ἢ τἀληθῆ λέγω)."[7] In the *Phaedrus*, Socrates says that he would rather believe a myth than go through the laborious process of providing a wise explanation (εἶτα σοφιζόμενος φαίηναὐτὴν) of all phenomena that the myth deals with, a task for which he lacks the leisure time required for execution.[8] In the *Ion*, Socrates appears to be subtly disdainful of myth (though arguably showing some genuine reverence for Homer). In the *Phaedrus*, he seems to be tradition-minded with regard to the value of myth (while also affirming that philosophical discourse could potentially cover the same cognitive ground as myth). In both

---

4 Cf. John Sallis 1996 and D.C. Schindler 2015.
5 Jean-François Mattéi 1988, 69–70.
6 Cf. Schindler 2015, 320.
7 *Ion* 532d.
8 *Phdr.* 229c–230a.

dialogues, however, the "distance" of myth and the distinction between myth and philosophy are preserved: mythical poetry is seen as providing an image of truth, while philosophy provides a dialectical path towards a comprehensive (and possibly never complete) account of the truth. Beyond these examples, there are other instances when a myth may be disparaged for its falsehood. Even then, the distance holds. In the *Symposium*, Diotima rejects Aristophanes' myth of the origin of love for being false, but replaces it with another myth.[9] How could we account for this "distance" in a genealogy of memory?

III   Memory and Recollection

Given this distinction between myth and philosophy, we should explore whether there is a fundamental difference between the mythical approach to memory and the philosophical one.

In Garrocho's paper, myth is defined in the citation from Carlos García Gual: "a traditional story that evokes the memorable and paradigmatic action of exceptional figures (gods and heroes) in an illustrious and distant time."[10] These types of stories are what myth remembers. Garrocho specifies that something is "memorable" if it "might be forgotten but should not be." It should be added that what is being remembered in myth is not strictly speaking *history*, in the modern sense of an accurate account and chronology of past events. Rather, what is being remembered in myth are acts, heroic figures, and cosmological origins that constitute the legendary sources of a culture, and which are described in a poetic mode.[11] Therefore, mythical memory is of an ancient past but one that is not necessarily continuous with the present time. It must be summoned to the present by a poet rather than an historian.[12] Garrocho also claims that the memory of katabasis is a paradigm of mythical memory: "The essential type of memory that provides true knowledge is the remembrance of that which we were able to contemplate in the land of the dead, where past, present, and future converge."[13] This is an experience undergone by both

---

9   *Symp.* 205d–e.

10   As quoted in Garrocho 2020, 109.

11   What I mean by "legendary" is summarized in Jean-Pierre Vernant's account of Hesiod and Homer: "In Homer, it is simply a question of fixing the genealogies of men and gods, of specifying the origins of peoples and royal families, and of establishing the etymologies of certain proper names and the *aition* of the epithets attached to cults. In Hesiod, this inquiry into origins takes on a truly religious aspect and gives on the poet's work the character of a sacred message" (2006, 119).

12   "The poet has an immediate experience of these bygone days. He knows the past because he has the power to be present in the past" (Vernant 2006, 117).

13   Quoted from an earlier draft of Garrocho 2020.

COMMENTARY ON GARROCHO

Odysseus, Orpheus, and later on, Aeneas—a theme developed by many of the great poets in history.

Are these mythical forms of memory the same memory that we discover in Plato? Garrocho argues yes, alluding to the Orphic influence on Platonic philosophy. But if we consider the Myth of Er to be Plato's own version of the katabasis story, we can see meaningful differences between it and the Homeric version.[14] Er tells of the different souls in a heavenly realm, drawing lots and choosing what their next earthly life will be after reincarnation. Er sees the soul once possessed by Odysseus, who chooses a humble and good life, "the life of a private man who minds his own business."[15] Odysseus's former soul is able to make this choice because, thanks to "the memory of its former labors," it had "recovered from love of honor."[16] It is the memory of the experience of the *world* (that is, his "former labors"), and *not* of the underworld, that has taught Odysseus wisdom. This is the reverse of the mythical tradition as articulated by Garrocho above. Moreover, this wisdom consists of, as Socrates later puts it, "the capacity and the knowledge to distinguish the good and the bad life, and so everywhere and always to choose the better among those that are possible."[17] It is wisdom learned from the circumstances of one life (Odysseus's) but that could apply to all lives.

In Homer's account of Odysseus's trip to the underworld, it is difficult to see the same level of explicit ethical reflection that seeks universal applicability. The closest we come is Elpenor begging Odysseus to bury his body and "perform my rites."[18] The performing of rites could be construed as a universal imperative. But to ask someone to fulfill traditional duties is not the same type of philosophically examined moral wisdom that informs the soul of Odysseus in

---

14 The Orphic mystery cult is thought by some scholars to be a later development of Greek religion. This development consists in its being a cult less grounded in public ritual and more in individual participation through reading and thought. As such, it could be interpreted as being closer to philosophy than to previous manifestations of Greek religion. "The characteristic appeal to books is indicative of a revolution: with the *Orphica* literacy takes hold in a field that had previously been dominated by the immediacy of ritual and the spoken word of myth. The new form of transmission introduces a new form of authority to which the individual, provided that he can read, has direct access without collective mediation. The emancipation of the individual and the appearance of books go together in religion as elsewhere" (Burkert 1985, 297). Still, I believe the distinction between Platonic thought and Orphic belief holds, for the reasons outlined below.

15 *Republic* 620c.

16 *Rep.* 620c.

17 *Rep.* 618c. Cf. Marina McCoy, who writes about the Myth of Er as a story meant to teach moral judgment to its listeners: "Plato's myth of Er is intended as a reflection upon moral choice for those who reside in the ordinary and imperfect city, and not the ideal one" (2012, 126).

18 *Odyssey* 10.85.

the *Republic*. Roger Scruton argues that this episode in the *Odyssey* is significant because it shows how ethical norms are expressed in traditional rites. Elpenor is a witness of the social importance of these rites: "The example of Elpenor casts light on this. The rites and customs of a common culture close the gap between emotion and action: they tell people what to do, precisely in those situations where the ethical vision intrudes—where love, grief, anger, or revenge are the proper motives, and where we face each other soul to soul."[19] Yet, Socrates invites us to consider a deeper embodiment of the moral life, one in which our character has been thoroughly transformed by philosophical reflection on our own experience (for example, Odysseus's "former labors") and knowledge of the good, rather than conditioned by traditional rites.

While it is true that certain ethical beliefs concerning virtue and character are embedded in the Homeric myths, it would be a further, and unwarranted, step to claim that they reach the level of self-conscious reflection that is proper to philosophical reflection about ethics. As Alasdair MacIntyre observes with regard to the writers of the Greek epics as well as those of the Nordic and Irish sagas: "The poet is not a theorist; he offers no general formulas."[20] That is not to say, of course, that there is not an implicit or unreflective understanding of the virtues embedded in the epic poetry of Homer and Hesiod. Nor is it to say that Plato's own understanding of virtue is completely universal and theoretical, and that he (unlike the poets) does not see virtue as somehow tied to the particular task of being a good citizen of a Greek city-state. But as MacIntyre's work on the history of ethics makes clear, Plato's thought represents a further step in the development of Greek ethical thought, a step toward a greater critical self-awareness than the epic poets possessed. While in the world of Homer, "morality and social structure are in fact one and the same,"[21] in the time of Plato, a person "is not *only* what society takes him or her to be; he or she both belongs to a place in the social order and transcends it."[22]

The line between mythical and Platonic memory seems even more starkly drawn in the *Meno*. Here, Socrates is explicit about the nature of the knowledge that would be required to answer Meno's question of whether virtue can be taught: "It amounts to the question whether the good men of this or former times have known how to hand on to someone else the goodness that was in themselves."[23] What is required is not knowledge about the past deeds of virtuous men, but stable knowledge about virtue that can be passed from one generation to the next—in other words, the same type of knowledge that

---

19 Scruton 2000, 14.
20 MacIntyre 1981, 128.
21 MacIntyre 1981, 123.
22 MacIntyre 1981, 143.
23 *Meno* 93a–b.

COMMENTARY ON GARROCHO

Odysseus's soul possesses in the Myth of Er. This type of knowledge, Socrates goes on to say, can be recollected in memory.

When we look at the passage in the *Meno* where the theory of recollection is first discussed,[24] we can get a better sense of the nature of the knowledge that Socrates desires. What exactly is it that was "in" the good men of this or former times? The first thing to notice about this section is that Socrates' account of the theory of recollection is embedded in a myth, told through a quotation from Pindar. Yet before he tells the myth, Socrates speaks of the priests and priestesses who know the truth about the myth, and who can give a rational account (*logos*) of it. Thus, the distance of myth is preserved. Next, based on this myth, Socrates speaks of an immortal soul who has learned everything, and could possibly recall the knowledge of virtue. This knowledge must still be sought after—Socrates says that one must not "grow weary" of the search—but the search is somehow within. Moreover, the knowledge of virtue could settle the question of whether virtue can be taught. Socrates has already said that before we can ask that question, we must first know what virtue itself is.[25] This knowledge is distinguishable from "true opinions" (ἀληθεῖς δόξαι); it is unmediated knowledge of the thing itself.[26] Socrates says: "And if the truth about reality is **always** (ἀεί) in our soul, the soul must be **immortal** (ἀθάνατος)."[27] Immortality implies that one is not ultimately vulnerable to the changes that come with time. The soul must be invulnerable in this way because the truths that the soul contains are also invulnerable; they are "always" the same.

This dynamic of mediation is perhaps more clearly manifest in the *Phaedo*. In the account of recollection found in this dialogue, Socrates uses the example of "equality itself" (αὐτὸ τὸ ἴσον).[28] In other words, what is recollected is a fundamental principle. This, too, is an example of "immortal" knowledge, an unchanging archetype that is not tied to any ancient past or legendary ancestral deed—not tied, that is, to events or origins, but rather to a purely ideal realm. The knowledge of equality is not the fruit of contemplating particular examples: "These equal things are not the same as **equality itself** (αὐτὸ τὸ ἴσον)."[29]

---

24   *Men.* 81a–d.

25   *Men.* 71a.

26   *Men.* 85c. Of course, the nature of that "unmediated" knowledge is up for dispute. John Sallis interprets this knowledge in terms of parts and wholes: what is recollected is the whole (Sallis 1996, 79–91). An account of Socratic knowledge as "non-intuitive" and "immediate" is found in Ross 1987.

27   *Men.* 86a–c.

28   *Phd.* 74a.

29   *Phd.* 74c. Commenting on this and adjacent passages, Paul Natorp claims that here Socrates uncovers the priority of thought over sensation: "For originally we only know the copy by means of the archetype (by 'referring' the copy 'back' to it, 75b, 76d), but we cannot know the archetype by means of the copy" (Natorp 2004, 159).

The particular examples appear as equal because of a prior knowledge of equality in the soul. In recollection, the soul has lifted itself beyond the world of becoming toward a timeless realm that both informs and precedes particular objects. Memory is not of the past but of a more fundamental level of reality. In light of this interpretation of the *Phaedo*, we might sharpen our reading of the Myth of Er: the contemplation of Odysseus's "former labors" yields knowledge of the good life not because they are examples of goodness from which we may derive general knowledge of it, but rather because they serve as a spur on the memory of the good, which is already present in one's soul, in the same way that our recognition of the examples of equality reveal our already present knowledge of equality.

Platonic gestures toward the timeless and eternal are, perhaps, echoing the convergence of "past, present, and future" that Garrocho indicates is essential to mythical memory. But the nature of that knowledge that Socrates claims to recollect suggests a deeper rupture with the mythological tradition. Mnemosyne is significant not only for Greek cosmology (and therefore the ancient past), but also eschatology (a timeless future where the soul leaves the body and abides eternally with the cosmic order). This means that for the life of a typical Greek of a certain era, Mnemosyne carried great moral significance for understanding her place in the cosmos, for knowing where she comes from and where she is going.[30] But although Plato wrote his own eschatological myths in various dialogues, in the *Republic*, *Meno*, and *Phaedo* he also seems to be after something altogether different: correct moral judgment and stable knowledge of virtue.[31] What should we make of this difference?

IV   Forgetting and Oblivion

If mythical memory and Platonic memory correspond to different objects, might mythical and philosophical forgetting and oblivion also be of different things? Does the "forgetting" that Nietzsche believes is essential for life correspond with the "memory" of myth or of Plato? Garrocho quotes the following

---

30   Vernant writes that, after a given period in Greek history, Mnemosyne, whose story explains aspects of Greek cosmology, gained eschatological significance as well. In this new worldview, the world, rather than the underworld, was seen as the place of exile (1965, 123–124).

31   "In Plato's theories, mythical thought lives on even as it is being transformed. *Anamnesis* here does not have the function of reconstructing the past and setting it in order, and it is not concerned with a chronology of events; rather, it reveals eternal and unchangeable Being. Memory is not the 'thought of time' but an escape from it. Its aim is not to trace the history of an individual in which the uniqueness of personality would be revealed but to unite the soul with the divine" (Vernant 2006, 135).

COMMENTARY ON GARROCHO

line from Nietzsche's *On the Use and Abuse of History for Life*: "You can live and live happily without remembering, but it is impossible to live without forgetting."[32] It seems clear that Nietzsche means that, in order to live rightly, one must forget previous moments of misfortune or trauma, which can hinder someone from continuing the future-oriented project of creating and re-creating one's self. This type of forgetting is of discrete events in the chronology of one's life. It is not the oblivion of ignorance that Plato seeks to overcome in recollection. It is perhaps closer to mythical memory as defined above. What more could we say about how Nietzsche's idea of forgetting fits within the genealogy of memory and oblivion?

Garrocho speaks about the forgetfulness that lies at the foundations of the Greek political community after the rule of the Thirty Tyrants, and of the paradoxical prohibition against remembering the crimes of the Tyrants. In light of this, what should we make of the curious fact that Socrates seems to have indirectly broken this law, when he mentions his own deeds under the Thirty: "Powerful as it was, the government did not terrify me into doing the wrong action"?[33] In order to remember that Socrates acted justly, one must recall that the Tyrants acted unjustly. Could it be that Plato included this passage in the *Apology* because he wanted future readers to remember these injustices as well? I think this passage might have a bearing on Garrocho's claim that forgetting can be "redemptive." Socrates' redemption, instead, seems to require the keeping of historical memory. How can forgetting be redemptive?

In fact, it seems that Plato wants his readers to remember all sort of historical contingencies, because much of the dramatic irony and moral content of his dialogues would be lost if we did not know these contingencies. How much would we miss if we did not remember the actual personal histories of Charmides, Alcibiades, Hippias, Polemarchus, among others? The *Republic* derives its meaning and significance in part from being a conversation that takes place in the site of a battle between democrats and tyrants. Plato seems to want his readers to connect with the timeless but also to recover what (in our own time) appear as footnotes to history.[34] The timeless investigations of his dialogues are inseparable from the historical moments in which they are embedded, which in turn can only be retrieved in an act of remembering. What should we make of this?

---

32 As quoted in Garrocho 2020, 114.

33 *Apol.* 32d–e.

34 The importance of situation and dramatic context in the Platonic dialogues is discussed in the chapter titled, "The Place of Philosophy," in Hyland 1995.

COLLOQUIUM 4

Garrocho/Ramos Bibliography

Allen, T.W., ed. 1931. *Homeri Ilias*, vols. 2–3. Oxford: Clarendon Press

Athanassakis, A.N., tr. 1977. *The Orphic Hymns*. Missoula: Scholars Press.

Bernabé Pajares, A. 2011. *Platón y el orfismo: Diálogos entre religión y filosofía.* Madrid: Abada Editores.

Bernabé Pajares, A., ed. 2005. *Poetae Epici Graeci. Testimonia Et Fragmenta. II Orphicorum Et Orphicis Similium Testimonia Et Fragmenta.* Fasc. 1/2. Munich and Leipzig: Sauer.

Bloom. A. 1991. *Plato's* Republic. New York: Basic Books.

Brisson, L. 1998. *Plato the Myth Maker.* University of Chicago Press, 1998. Org, 1982. Et Les Mythes. Paris: F. Maspero.

Burkert, W. 1985. *Greek Religion.* Translated by J. Raffan. Cambridge: Harvard University Press.

Burnet, J., ed. 1968 repr. *Platonis opera.* Oxford: Clarendon Press.

Buxton, R., ed. 1999. *From Myth to Reason? Studies in the Development of Greek Thought.* Oxford: Oxford University Press.

Bywater, I., ed. 1894 (repr. 1962). *Aristotelis Ethica Nicomachea.* Oxford: Clarendon Press.

Cooper, J., ed. 1997. *Plato. Complete Works.* Cambridge: Hackett Publishing Company.

Cornford, F. 1912. *From religion to philosophy: A study in the origins of western speculation.* New York: Longmans, Green & Co.

Clark, A. Curtis, ed. 1918. *M. Tulli Ciceronis Orationes: Recognovit breviqve adnotatione critica instrvxit Albertus Curtis Clark Collegii Reginae Socius.* Oxford: E. Typographeo Clarendoniano.

Derrida, J. 1967. *L'Écriture et la différence.* Paris: Éditions du Seuil.

Derrida, J. 1967. Adieu: À Emmanuel Levinas. Paris: Galilée.

Diels, H. and W. Kranz, eds. 1951. *Die Fragmente der Vorsokratiker.* Berlin: Weidmann.

Eco, U., and M. Migiel. 1988. An Ars Oblivionalis? Forget It! *PMLA*, 103.3:254–261.

García Gual, C. 2014. *Historia mínima de la mitología.* Madrid: Turner.

Guthrie, W.K.C., tr. 1956. *Protagoras and Meno.* London: Penguin Books.

Hard, R., tr. 1997. *The Library of Greek Mythology* (Oxford world's classics). Oxford: Oxford University Press.

Hyland, D. 1995. *Finitude and Transcendence.* Albany: State University of New York Press.

Kingsley, P. 1999. *In the Dark Places of Wisdom.* Inverness: Golden Sufi Center.

Lamb, W.R.M., tr. 1925. *Ion.* In *Plato in Twelve Volumes*, vol. 9. Cambridge, MA: Harvard University Press.

Loraux, N. 2002. *The Divided City: on Memory and Forgetting in Ancient Athens*. New York: Zone Book. Org. 1997. La cité divisée : L'oubli dans la mémoire d'Athènes. Paris: Payot.

MacIntyre, A. 1981. *After Virtue: A Study in Moral Theory*. Notre Dame, IN: University of Notre Dame Press.

Maehler, H., ed. 1971. *Pindari carmina cum fragmentis*. Leipzig: Teubner.

Mattéi, Jean-François. 1988. Theater of Myth in Plato. In *Platonic Writings, Platonic Readings*, ed. C.L. Griswold, Jr., 66–83. University Park, PA: University of Pennsylvania Press.

McCoy, M. 2012. Freedom and Responsibility in the Myth of Er. *Ideas y Valores* LXI:125–141.

Natorp, P. 2004. *Plato's Theory of Ideas: An Introduction to Idealism*, tr. v. Politis and J. Connolly, ed. v. Politis. Sankt Augustin: Academia Verlag.

Nehamas, A. and P. Woodruff, trs. 1995. *Plato* Phaedrus. Indianapolis: Hackett.

Nestle, W. 1942. *Vom Mythos zum Logos: Die Selbstentfaltung des griechischen Denkens von Homer bis auf die Sophistik und Sokrates*. Stuttgart: A. Kröner.

Nietzsche, F. 1999. *Sämtliche Werke kritische Studienausgabe (KSA)*, eds. G. Colli and M. Montinari. Berlin: Deutscher Taschenbuch Verlag De Gruyter.

Nussbaum, M.C. 1986. *The Fragility of Goodness. Luck and Ethics in Greek Tragedy and Philosophy*. Cambridge: Cambridge University Press.

des Places, E., ed. 1971. *Oracles chaldaïques*. Paris: Les Belles Lettres.

Radermacher, L., ed. 1901. *Demetrii Phalerei qui dicitur de elocutione libellus*. Leipzig: Teubner.

Ross, W.D., ed. 1961 (reimp. 1967). *Aristotle*. De anima. Oxford: Clarendon Press.

Ross, W.D., ed. 1924 (repr. 1970). *Aristotle's* Metaphysics, 2 vols., Oxford: Clarendon Press.

Sallis, J. 1996. *Being and Logos: Reading the Platonic Dialogues*. Indianapolis: Indiana University Press.

Schindler, D.C. 2015. *Plato's Critique of Impure Reason: On Goodness and Truth in the Republic*. Washington, DC: Catholic University Press.

Scruton, Roger. 2000. *Modern Culture*. London: Continuum.

Solmsen, F., ed. 1970. *Hesiodi opera*. Oxford: Clarendon Press.

Treddenick, H. and H. Tarrant, trs. 2003. *The Last Days of Socrates*. Euthyphro, Apology, Crito, Phaedo. London: Penguin Books.

Vernant, Jean-Pierre. 2006. *Myth and Thought Among the Greeks*, tr. J. Lloyd and J. Fort. New York: Zone Books.

Weinrich, H. *Lethe: Kunst und Kritik des Vergessens*. München: C.H. Beck.

West, M.L., tr. 1966. *Hesiod*. Theogony. Oxford: Clarendon Press.

Westerink, L.G., ed. 1976. *The Greek commentaries on Plato's* Phaedo. Amsterdam: North-Holland Publishing Co.

COLLOQUIUM 5

Final Causality Without Teleology in Aristotle's Ontology of Life

Francisco J. Gonzalez
University of Ottawa

Abstract

The present paper has a negative aim and a positive aim, both limited in the present context to a sketch or outline. The negative aim, today less controversial, is to show that Aristotle's theory of final causality has little or nothing to do with the teleology rejected by modern science and that, therefore, far from having been rendered obsolete, it has yet to be fully understood. This aim will be met through the identification and brief discussion of some key points on which Aristotle's theory differs from teleology as still commonly understood. The positive aim is more controversial as it proposes that we take an ontology of life as the proper context for understanding the significance and nature of final causation in Aristotle. The argument for final causation, in other words, is that, without it, we would lose the phenomenon of life and, indeed, of nature altogether, reducing nature to the inanimate and mechanical.

Keywords

Aristotle – teleology – biology – substance – ἐνέργεια

I   Introduction

Final causality in Aristotle is certainly not a neglected topic and has been the subject of much excellent work in recent years. The question that, arguably, still demands more attention, however, is that of *why* Aristotle finds it neces-sary to appeal to final causes in explaining natural phenomena. *What* exactly do such causes explain that could not be explained without them? And is their explanatory role adequately captured by the modern term with which cri-tiques of Aristotle in modern science have saddled him, that is, *teleology*? The argument of this paper is that, to the extent that we can speak of 'teleology' in

© KONINKLIJKE BRILL NV, LEIDEN, 2020 | DOI:10.1163/22134417-00351P14

Aristotle, it must be not as that thesis about the 'purpose,' 'meaning,' or 'design' of the universe that has received so much modern critique, but as a thesis about the *being* of the natural and living substances that comprise it. In terms of a modern distinction Aristotle himself would not recognize, it is a philosophical, not a scientific thesis.[1] This is why, as I will argue, Aristotle would find the materialistic and mechanistic mode of explanation in modern science not unacceptable or useless, but philosophically impoverished.[2] You *can* explain in that way how things *come to be*, but you cannot explain in that way their *being* or what they are. By invoking nothing but what Aristotle calls 'material necessity,' I can explain how the different parts of an animal come to be, but I cannot explain why the animal, as this particular kind of living thing, has these parts. Life, which is for Aristotle, I will argue, the paradigm of substance, is characterized by a unity and directedness that cannot be reduced to the chance coincidence of different material processes, even if modern biology has found in natural selection a mechanism by which such chance can be argued to yield, over very long periods of time, the consistent and organized results we witness today.[3] There is always an ontological gap, and one that cannot be bridged by

---

1   In the words of Mansion, Aristotle's physics has "un caractère nettement philosophique, au sens moderne de ce dernier mot" (1945, 38).

2   The goal of modern science can be described as that of predicting and mastering natural phenomena, a goal it achieves through the quantification and 'mathematization' of these phenomena. Aristotle's goal is not *incompatible,* but different: that of understanding the being of natural and, especially, living things, in their differentiation from non-natural things. That natural phenomena can be calculated and predicted entirely in terms of material causes without appeal to final causes, as modern science has shown, in no way shows that the being of such phenomena can be explained without appeal to final causes. Mansion make precisely this point when he observes: "Ce n'est pas, sans doute, qu'il estimait inutile ou impossible une application des mathématiques aux objets physiques, mais à son sens cette explication n'était propre qu'à en mettre en lumière le côté quantitative, non à en fournir une explication philosophique atteignant le fond des choses" (1945, 339). He then adds that Aristotle was in principle right because "à moins d'ériger en dogme le mécanisme, la philosophie de la nature ne pourra jamais se limiter à la systematization mathématique et mécanique des phénomènes" (340). Another one to emphasize this point is Patočka: "Il n'y a donc pas chez Aristote de refus de principe de la mathématisation (pour autant qu'elle ne prétende pas saisir l'essence du mouvement) ; simplement, ne tenant pas à prévoir et à maîtriser le mouvement, mais plutôt à l'expliquer et à le comprendre dans son sens, il ne s'y intéresse pas" (2011, 211 ; see also 194, 203, 330, 378, and 410–411). Patočka supports this claim with a crucial point in the context of the present paper: taking the living being as his model, Aristotle does not see movement as having primarily a spatial significance or orientation, but rather a direction towards the plenitude of being (212).

3   C. Johnson (2015) documents, through extensive citation of Darwin's notebooks and other writings, both the extent to which Darwin attributed to chance the variations on which natural selection could do its work and the extent to which he struggled with this notion and its reception, going so far as to eliminate the words 'chance' and 'accident' from later editions of the

FINAL CAUSALITY WITHOUT TELEOLOGY IN ARISTOTLE

any span of time one cares to postulate, between a 'heap' and a 'beautiful arrangement.'[4] But this beautiful arrangement is no evidence of an intelligent designer, a view Aristotle explicitly rejects, though it is defended by Plato before him and is attributed to Aristotle himself afterwards under the name of 'teleology.' On the contrary, the postulate of an intelligent designer assumes the completely anti-Aristotelian thesis that every substance is, in itself, no more than a 'heap,' like the pile of wood lying on the lot before the construction of the house, which, therefore, needs an intelligent designer to give it form and purpose. As Aristotle asserts in *Physics* II.8, "It is absurd (ἄτοπον) not to think it comes to be for the sake of something if they do not see the moving cause deliberating (βουλευσάμενον)" (199b26–28). In short, final causality has no necessary connection to intelligence.

II   Final Causality with Material Necessity

Assuming that this last point requires no defense here, I turn immediately to a second point that does need discussion and defense: that explanation in terms of final causes does not, for Aristotle, take the place of explanation in terms of material necessity. In other words, it is never presented as an *alternative* to material necessity (as is often assumed by critiques of teleology) but, on the contrary, *is seen as inseparable from it*. What I am calling here 'material

---

Origin of Species. By 'chance' is meant here, of course, not the absence of any cause whatsoever, but the 'blindness' towards any future adaptability: variations in an organism are naturally selected because they serve adaptability, but they do not occur in the first place for this purpose, being instead products of purely material (and in cases unknown) causes. Strikingly, this is exactly how Aristotle describes the role that chance plays in the theory of natural selection in his critique of that theory in *Physics* II.8, so that Johnson can even suggest that Darwin took the terminology of 'spontaneous variation,' preferred to 'chance variation' starting with the fourth edition of the *Origin of Species,* from a translation of this Aristotelian text cited for the first time in the 'Historical Sketch' of this edition (130–131). For our purpose here, the most significant lesson to take from Johnson's book is that Darwin and his contemporaries and, indeed, Johnson himself, see intelligent design and chance *as the only options*. In short, for them, the question is, as Johnson at one point phrases it, "But does nature exercise intelligence when it 'gives' 'variations', or does nature simply give them randomly?" (104; see also xix). Johnson is completely unaware, as was Darwin, that for Aristotle the answer is *neither.*

4   The allusion is of course to the famous fragment of Heraclitus, Diels 124, which appears to claim that the most beautiful order (*kosmos*) *is* to be found in a random heap (σάρμα εἰκῇ κεχυμένον ὁ κάλλιστος κόσμος). In any case, Aristotle himself, in the *Parts of Animals*, prefers to cite the story of how Heraclitus told the visitors who found him warming himself in the kitchen that the gods are present there, too: a story Aristotle uses as an illustration of his own claim, to be discussed below, that final causality and thereby beauty are to be found *most of all* in nature and, therefore, in even the most insignificant animals (645a18–25).

necessity' could also be called 'absolute necessity' to distinguish it from what Aristotle calls 'conditional' or 'hypothetical' necessity' (ἐξ ὑποθέσεως, 639b24–25). The latter is completely subservient to final causality and is expressed as follows: in order for this end to come about, such and such is necessary; for example, in order for there to be a house that offers us shelter, wood and bricks are necessary. The other kind of necessity Aristotle recognizes (setting aside as not relevant in the present context the kind of necessity that characterizes eternal beings, 639b24)[5] is described by him in contrast to the first in the following passage from *Parts of Animals*: "For 'necessity' sometimes signifies that if this end is to be, it is necessary for these things to be such and such; and sometimes it signifies that a thing has such and such a state and nature" (ἡ δ᾽ ἀνάγκη ... ὁτὲ δ᾽ [σημαίνει] ὅτι ἔστιν οὕτως ἔχοντα καὶ πεφυκότα, 642a33–35; my translation). The example he gives here is that while respiration occurs for an end, it *also* takes place of necessity in the sense that "the alternate discharge and re-entrance of heat and inflow of air are necessary ... and as the internal heat resists in the process of cooling, the entrance and exit of the external air occur" (642a35–642b2). So, the claim here is not that the alternate discharge and re-entrance of heat and inflow of air are necessary *if* the end of respiration is to be met (conditional necessity), but rather that they are necessary *simpliciter* given the natures of heat and air themselves. Therefore, the necessity that must, according to Aristotle, be demonstrated *in addition to the final cause* is not that conditional necessity that is really only the flipside of the final cause, but, rather, a necessity that lies in the material natures of things and, thus, can be explained with no reference to the final cause. It is this latter necessity that is furthermore described in the *Posterior Analytics* when Aristotle, in summarizing the four causes, uses the following phrase to refer to the material cause:

---

5 Balme assumes that to characterize material necessity as 'absolute' is to attribute to matter the kind of necessity according to which a triangle must have angles equal to two right angles (1972, 76–84). But 'absolute' as applied to material necessity means only *not conditional upon* final causality. To ascribe 'absolute' necessity to eye color, for example, is not to claim that a certain matter *must* produce blue eyes, but, rather, that, if a certain matter produces blues eyes, it does so independently of any final cause. How necessary material necessity is (e.g., must a certain kind of matter *always and invariably* produce the same effect?) is a question left open by its designation as 'absolute.' It might, indeed, be less misleading to speak of 'necessity *simpliciter*' instead. Mansion also identifies the absolute necessity contrasted to hypothetical necessity with the necessity that characterizes what is eternal (1945, 284), oddly because he later recognizes what he calls a 'brute necessity' distinct from, and independent of, hypothetical necessity (286ff.). Mansion, indeed, turns out to be in complete agreement with what will be argued here since he maintains that this 'brute necessity' can act both independently of, and against, final causality (289), concluding that for Aristotle "il y a des phénomènes qui se produisent en dehors de toute finalité, il y en a même beaucoup" (289).

FINAL CAUSALITY WITHOUT TELEOLOGY IN ARISTOTLE 137

"that if certain things hold, it is necessary that this does" (τίνων ὄντων ἀνάγκη τοῦτ᾽εἶναι, 94a21, Barnes, tr. 1993)[6]

There are many examples in the biological works of the co-existence of these two distinct and independent tracks of explanation, the material and the final, in addition to that of respiration just noted. Perhaps the most notorious explanation in terms of final causes is Aristotle's explanation of why man alone among animals stands erect. Yet, the first time Aristotle addresses the question in book II.7 of the *Parts of Animals*, the explanation he gives is exclusively in terms of material necessity: that the region of the heart and of the lung is, in man, hotter than in other animals "again explains why man, alone of animals, stands erect. For the heat, overcoming any opposite inclination, makes growth take its own line of direction, which is from the center of the body upwards" (653a30ff). In short, man stands erect *because* he is hotter, period. It is not until much later, in book II.10, that we get what must be the final cause of man's standing erect, when we are told that only in his case do the natural parts hold the natural position, with the upper part being turned towards that which is upper in the universe. Later in the same work, we are told that man stands erect because the upper part of his body is smaller than the lower part (see 689b: he is given buttocks and fleshier legs to keep his upper part lighter) and because he possesses greater heat. So, we again have an explanation in terms of material necessity, but a final cause is also identified when we are told that this serves man's "godlike nature and substance" (686a27) by not allowing a heavy body to impede the movement of thought and of the common sense (686a31–32) and, thus, allowing him to perform his divine-like function of thinking. Another example concerns man again and, in this case, why he has more hair on his head than do other animals. We are given *two* answers: (1) The greater amount of hair results necessarily (ἐξ ἀνάγκης) from the fluid nature of his brain and the presence of many sutures in his skull; (2) the greater amount of hair is for the sake of protecting the head from excess heat and cold (ἕνεκα βοηθείας), since man's brain is larger and therefore in greater need of protection (*PA* 658b3–7). As for other animals, the ability of serpents to turn their head backwards is a result of necessity *and* for their good (692a4–6); the falling

---

6 Balme recognizes the problem this passage possesses for his thesis that material necessity is always hypothetical and calls it an "apparently anomalous statement" (1972, 83); he eventually retracted his position (1987, 285n33). In contrast, Delcomminette rightly observes: "Il me semble assez clair que la nécessité dont il est question ici doit être une nécessité absolue, puisqu'elle contraste avec la nécessité hypothétique et résulte de la *nature* des chose envisagés" (2018, 301). For an account of why Balme and others have thought that Aristotle accepts only hypothetical necessity and a response, see Cooper (1985).

out of front teeth is for the sake of the good *and* a result of necessity (*Generation of Animals* v.789a8–b8).

The compatibility between final causality and causality by material absolute necessity needs to be emphasized here, as it has been minimized or denied altogether in much of the secondary literature. In her book *Explanation and Teleology in Aristotle's Science of Nature,* for example, M. Leunissen would confine the role of absolute material necessity to what she calls a 'secondary' teleology in distinction from the primary type. Specifically, her distinction is between (1) a primary teleology that "involves the realization of a preexisting, internal potential (or perhaps 'potentials') for form through stages shaped by conditional necessity" and (2) a secondary teleology that "involves the formal nature of a natural being *using* materials that happen to be available (usually residues that have come to be of material necessity and that are not conditionally necessitated) for the production of parts that serve the animal's well-being," as distinct from its mere being (Leunissen 2010, 4–5; see also 18–22). As we can see, according to this distinction, wherever we have primary teleology at work, only conditional necessity is operative; only in the case of secondary teleology do we have nature 'making use of' what is the product of absolute material necessity.

One problem with this view is that the distinction Leunissen defends between a 'primary' and a 'secondary' teleology is simply not sustainable. Aristotle does indeed make a distinction between an animal's *being* and its *well-being*, but he never suggests that final causation works differently in the two cases. Revealing in this regard is a passage from *De Anima* that Leunissen herself cites in support of her thesis: At II.8, 420b13–22, Aristotle draws a parallel between the intake of air serving both the end of breathing and the end of speech, and the tongue serving both the end of taste, which is described as necessary for life, and the end of speech, which is described as being for the sake of well-being. Leunissen expresses the difference as follows:

> The first [capacities] are present because they are conditionally necessary for the animals that have them (i.e., they are the product of primary teleology); the second are present because *nature uses* what is already present—here: what is already present for the sake of performing a necessary function—for the performance of a second function that serves the animal's well-being (i.e., they are the product of secondary teleology. ... (2010, 68)

Yet, here is *what Aristotle says*: "For nature then *uses* the air already breathed in *for two functions*; just as it *uses* the tongue *for both* tasting and articulation" (as

FINAL CAUSALITY WITHOUT TELEOLOGY IN ARISTOTLE 139

cited by Leunissen, 68). Note that Aristotle speaks of nature using what is caused by material necessity in *both* cases rather than only in the case of what serves well-being; he thus makes no distinction between two kinds of teleology (what Leunissen will later refer to as a distinction between nature 'making' and nature 'using' [2010, 91 and 202] is simply not present here). Furthermore, the distinction presupposed by Leunissen between teleological processes "driven by form" (primary teleology) and those "driven by matter" (secondary teleology) (20) is problematic: in *both* of the cases Leunissen wishes to distinguish, that is, the tongue serving the end of tasting and the tongue serving the end of speech, you have material and formal causes.[7]

Furthermore, the two cases cited above where Aristotle presents, independently of each other, an explanation in terms of material necessity and an explanation in terms of final causality, and in which, therefore, the necessity at issue is clearly not simply 'conditional,' do not appear to fit Leunissen's description of *secondary* teleology. While she takes the aim of secondary teleology to be the well-being of the animal, as distinct from its being, in the example of respiration, which Leunissen herself cites (109), the end is clearly not only the well-being of the animal but also its very being. This example, furthermore, clearly shows that material necessity and conditional necessity are *not* mutually exclusive alternatives in the formation of animal parts, as Leunissen's

---

7   Another passage Leunissen uses in support, i.e., *GA* II.744b11–17, while describing a hierarchy of parts with nature as a good housekeeper using the best material for the most essential parts, does not at all indicate, contra Leunissen "that the underlying teleological processes that account for their coming to be and presence must be different" (83). A few pages later, this difference turns into a 'seeming' one that is hardly convincing: speaking of the kidney in particular, Leunissen writes that "since these parts are not themselves a necessary prerequisite for the performance of a necessary function, it seems that their coming to be cannot be conditionally necessitated by an internal potential for form, and is therefore not a case of primary teleology" (91; see also 93). I do not see why a part unnecessary for living but necessary for living well cannot form part of the formal nature of that particular animal and, therefore, be necessitated by an internal potential for form. Leunissen, indeed, grants that even capacities for living well are essential to the animals that have them in the sense that they would be destroyed if these capacities were taken away; in the end, therefore, she can defend the strong distinction she wishes to make between primary and secondary teleology only by claiming that we could imagine *a possible world* in which the animal would not have those capacities that serve only living well (60). Of course, not only would such a possible world not be our world (the only one that exists for Aristotle!) but also the animal deprived of these capacities *would not be the same animal*. It is clear, for example, that Aristotle would not consider a human being lacking the capacity of speech to be *a human being*. As Sorabji observes, "Aristotle speaks of these things as existing partly or wholly for the sake of the *good*, because not all animals need them, but only the higher forms of life. Yet surely they are needed for *existence*, for men could hardly exist as men, if there were no speech and no theoretical or practical knowledge" (1980, 157–158). Gotthelf (2012, 55) makes a similar point.

distinction between two types of teleology assumes ("their [parts] *coming to be* is due to either one of two different kinds of necessity" 110). The circulation of air is the necessary product of the alternate discharge and reentrance of heat *and* is necessary for the end of respiration. As for the case of human erectness, which Leunissen does not discuss, the end is certainly well-being, but in a way indistinguishable from our being; how, after all, could we be human at all without the possibility of thinking? It is also hard to make sense of the idea that nature simply 'makes use of' our materially necessitated erectness after the fact. The reasonable conclusion is that even what Leunissen describes as 'primary teleology' is perfectly compatible in Aristotle's mind with causality by absolute material necessity.[8]

How, then, can Aristotle offer both sorts of explanation? The answer, I suggest, is to be found in a linguistic distinction Aristotle explicitly makes in some cases. In explaining the mesentery, for example, Aristotle tells us that it *comes to be* of necessity (γένεσιν ἐξ ἀνάγκης, PA 678a4), but *is* for the sake of something (οὗ ἔνεκα ἐστιν, 678a16). In the case of the parts of birds, we are again told that the *becoming* of these parts is a matter of necessity (ἐξ ἀνάγκης δὲ τοῦτο περὶ τὴν γένεσιν συμβέβηκεν, 694a23), but they also *are* for the sake of what is best and for the sake of the way of life (τοῦ βίου χάριν, 694b8). What does the language here reveal? That, for Aristotle, it is indeed possible in biology to give a strictly materialist explanation of why something has come into being, but that this is not the same as explaining *why it is what it is*.[9] In other words, the *being* of an organism is not reducible to how its parts come about. I may be able to give a purely materialistic explanation of how the different parts of a bird have come about, but I have not explained the being of the bird until I explain how these parts serve the bird's specific way of life. To use a distinction employed by Sorabji (1980, 151, though he recognizes that Aristotle himself does not consistently make such a distinction, 174), material necessity explains *how* the parts of an organism come about, but not *why* they exist.

Aristotle's teleology is, therefore, not an alternative to the kind of materialistic, mechanistic explanation that has come to characterize modern science nor is it even the claim that such a mode of explanation cannot explain

---

8   For another defense of this view which they call 'irreducible compatibilism,' see Bradie and Miller (1984).

9   Leunissen makes a similar point in claiming, "Whereas the end that constitutes the final cause explains the *presence* of a given natural phenomenon, the *coming to be* of that end must itself be explained further in terms of either the operation of formal-efficient causation or of material-efficient causation" (2010, 7–8; the latter disjunct is made in support of her distinction between primary and secondary teleology critiqued above).

FINAL CAUSALITY WITHOUT TELEOLOGY IN ARISTOTLE 141

outcomes;[10] instead, it is the claim that such explanation, however sufficient and valuable within its own domain, cannot claim to explain the being of an organism, indeed, cannot help but *eliminate this being altogether*.[11] The parts of

---

10   M.R. Johnson argues that there are not two independent types of explanation here since the materialist, mechanistic explanation is always subservient to the teleological explanation. But, as shown in the main text, Aristotle clearly distinguishes between a kind of necessity that is hypothetical (and, therefore, dependent on a final cause) and a kind of necessity that is not. Furthermore, contrary to what Johnson maintains (2017, 142), the example of respiration (along with the other examples I cite here) is clearly meant to illustrate the latter necessity as independent of the final cause (see also Bradie and Miller 1984, 140). Johnson is perfectly right to maintain that there is nothing in Aristotle's teleology "that precludes him from offering mechanistic explanations" (2017, 149); he is also right to maintain that such explanations are perfectly compatible with teleological explanations. Where I disagree is with the claim that Aristotle's mechanistic explanations have no independence from, and are always completely subservient to, teleological explanations. Certain material causes *will by themselves* produce anger or respiration and are therefore sufficient to explain these as effects; but Aristotle's view is that anger and respiration cannot be reduced to material causes nor therefore fully understood solely in terms of them. In terms of the other example considered here, material causes can fully explain the secretion on the head of that substance we call hair without any appeal to final causes; but hair, as the functional part of an organism, is *more* than such a secretion and this 'more' requires teleological explanation. While I agree that "teleological explanation can be neither potentially reducible to, nor merely a heuristic for, mechanistic or materialist explanation" (Johnson 2005, 184), I would add: nor can teleological explanation *take the place of* materialist, mechanistic explanation. Cooper, while arguing that Aristotle recognizes an absolute necessity distinct from hypothetical necessity, still like Johnson insists that the former is always subsumed under the latter (1985, 160). Indeed, he seems to treat all teleology in Aristotle as being like what Leunissen calls "secondary teleology": nature *makes use of material necessity for its own ends* (see 163–164).

11   R.J. Hankinson expresses well the problem raised by Aristotle's acceptance of explanation in terms of material necessity: "If antecedent material factors necessitate (i.e., are sufficient for) a particular result, how can a final cause also play a role in the outcome …?" (1995, 130). The same problem is used by Balme to argue against the view that material necessity is ever 'absolute' for Aristotle (1972, 79; though, as noted above, he later abandoned the view that all necessity within living bodies is 'hypothetical' [285n33]). The only solution Hankinson appears to arrive at parallels the one suggested here: the need for final causes arises from the *gap* between the form of the living organism and "what can and should be explained in a reductionist manner on the basis of the elemental properties" (134). Significantly, Balme makes a similar point, though he does not exploit it, to reconcile 'absolute' necessity with final causality: "The essential x-properties are not deducible from the matter-of-X, because the matter-of-X is by definition lacking in x-properties. True, the proximate matter must include all the properties needed to compose the product, but they still do not add up to the product's own character. The tissues out of which an eye grows must be translucent, tough, watery, etc., but the eye's ability to see is not necessitated by them" (1972, 77). See also Leunissen: "In short, for Aristotle an animal is the primary example of a natural substance, whereas for the materialist an animal is merely a coincidental conglomeration of elements (2010, 24)."

an animal have material causes and are thus products of material necessity. But as Aristotle shows in *Physics* II.8, to explain them *only* through an appeal to material necessity is to treat their functions in the organism as *accidental,*[12] which is, in turn, to treat the organism itself as only an *accidental unity*.[13] Empedocles' ox-faced ox progeny *are no more natural* than his human-faced ox progeny since *both* are accidents; but this means that neither can be, in Aristotle's view, a natural substance. What Aristotle's teleology opposes is not explanation through material necessity, but the elimination of living organisms as substances that results from recognizing no form of explanation but material necessity.[14]

She, therefore, describes what Aristotle is opposing as not only 'reductionism' but 'eliminativism,' i.e., the denial that plants and animals are substances at all. See also S. Meyer (1992, 820–825). But, as Gotthelf notes, Aristotle's objection against his opponents appears to be that they eliminate the nature of living things, whether they recognize this or not (and most likely they do not!), *as a consequence of* their reductive explanation in terms of material causes (2012, 77–85).

12   This, in my view, explains something dwelt on by Mansion: the coexistence of determinism and contingency in Aristotle. As Mansion claims, "dans l'ordre naturel, dans la mesure où en sont exclues les interventions dues à l'action humaine, le déterminisme causal régne en maître, sans aucune limitation" (1945, 325; contrast Kullmann [1979, 41], who later appears to defend a similar view [58–59]). As Mansion also notes, Aristotle's account of chance in nature and fortune in human action in *Physics* II.4–6 limits them to the realm of final causes. As Mansion, apparently, does not note (see 307–310), however, the latter is explained by the former: if everything that occurs in nature is fully determined causally, then the only thing that can be called 'accidental' is the achievement of an end other than the one normally expected.

13   T.L. Short captures the crucial point here when he writes, though not in connection to Aristotle in particular: "My point is that a pattern discernible in events is an aspect distinct from the sum of the individual events that compose the pattern. Thus, the pattern requires an explanation—unless, indeed, it *is* coincidental—distinct from the logical union of the explanations of the individual events. The logical union of the explanations of the individual events composing a pattern explains the factual existence of that pattern, but it does not show that the pattern is not just a mammoth coincidence" (2002, 331). Mansion makes a similar point more succinctly when he writes that "la conception téléologique exige une comprehension des faits beaucoup plus large, car il ne suffit pas de poursuivre leur enchainement, il faut encore découvrir leur convergence" (1945, 209). I can, therefore, agree with Cooper that "so far as the *whole* living thing is concerned, the flat rejection of absolute necessitation does fully accord with Aristotle's position" (1985, 162); but Cooper is wrong in thinking that, therefore, "on Aristotle's view, *nothing* [my emphasis] that happens in the formation of a living thing *does* happen by absolute necessity" (162).

14   The case that Aristotle's defense of teleology in *Physics* II.8 is not a rejection of material necessity has been strongly made by Meyer (1992) and C. Byrne (2018, 119). See also Sorabji (1980, 151–152).

FINAL CAUSALITY WITHOUT TELEOLOGY IN ARISTOTLE 143

To clarify further the roles of necessity and explanation here, let us consider an objection that has been formulated by Allan Gotthelf,[15] who also defends Leunissen's distinction between primary and secondary teleology, though weakened to the point of disappearance.[16] According to Gotthelf, the part of an organism can be said to *be* for something only if it *has come to be* for

---

15   His specific target here is Sorabji, who has argued that final causality in Aristotle is compatible with necessitating causes (1980, 153). Before explaining how they are compatible, Sorabji makes the obvious point that texts like those I cite above show that *Aristotle* considers them compatible (see also 173). Indeed, as Sorabji notes, Aristotle states the compatibility as a general principle in the APo. 94b27–29: "It is possible for the same thing to be the case both with some aim and from necessity" (Barnes, tr. 1993). But I do not find Sorabji's explanation of how the two explanations are compatible very clear: he seems to say little more than that one or the other is appropriate in different contexts.

16   In a paper Gotthelf co-authored with Leunissen, we find the same distinction between nature 'producing' and nature 'using' materials and the demonstrably false claim that the causation of parts in the case of primary teleology "is *wholly* due to form (for even the material used in that process is produced of conditional necessity by the organism's—or its mother's—form)" (Gotthelf and Leunissen 2012, 131): demonstrably false because, as we have seen, even in the case of parts Gotthelf and Leunissen attribute to primary teleology, Aristotle speaks of causation by absolute material necessity and not only by necessity as conditioned by the final cause. It is also revealing that while Gotthelf and Leunissen in this paper offer to provide something lacking in Leunissen's book (see Leunissen 2010, 61), i.e., "a *non-metaphorical* characterization of secondary teleology" (Gotthelf and Leunissen 2012, 131), what they actually provide is an analogy with the art of woodworking and its capacity to make good use of excess wood shavings (132). If we recognize that the metaphor or analogy is, in fact, nothing more than that, nature *not* being a deliberative agent making choices about materials already at hand (see n30), then it is hard to see what remains of the supposed difference between secondary and primary teleology. The co-authored paper, in any case, contains two important and significant revisions to the account of secondary teleology found in Leunissen's book. First, the parts attributed to secondary teleology are described as "necessary *for an animal of that form to live or* to serve the animal's well-being" (131). Assuming we have two options here, the first italicized option, presumably conceding the point made by both Sorabji and Gotthelf himself as cited above, is an important addition that makes secondary teleology much harder to distinguish from primary. We find later on the same page, the qualification that nature's use of materials in secondary teleology "in all *or most cases* adds just to the well-being of the animal" (131, my italics). But even more significant is the concession that the potential for form realized in primary teleology *includes* the potential realized in secondary teleology. As they write, "we think it is the case for Aristotle that the one nature, the one potential for form, *includes* the potential to act for the best on (excess) material of a certain sort (should such material happen to be around), at some point in the process *later* than the initial activation of that potential" (132). But if in the case of both primary and secondary teleology we have *one* potential for form, *one* being-towards-the-end, however we may distinguish its different aspects, and, in both cases, this one potential works with what is produced through material necessity, then why and how distinguish here between them?

something. Therefore, if it has *come to be* out of material necessity, it cannot *be* for something. Final causality thus rules out material necessity as a sufficient cause (2012, 35–44). His position is expressed most clearly and succinctly in the following passage:

> If parts came to be of material necessity (and thus animals were as they were because of the way they came to be—the force of the rejected alternative, 'being for the sake of coming to be'), teleological explanation of the presence of these parts by reference to their contribution to the being of the animals of which they are a part would not be warranted. Given that they *come to be* for the sake of such a contribution, their *being* can be *explained* by reference to that contribution. (2012, 42)

As is made clear by the last sentence, and as Gotthelf explicitly acknowledges, his view makes 'coming to be' logically prior to 'being': it is how something comes to be that explains what it is and not *vice versa*. The problem is that, as Gotthelf recognizes, Aristotle repeatedly asserts the opposite, that is, that being is prior to coming to be. Gotthelf, of course, attempts to deal with this problem. But I would rather take as my *starting point* what Aristotle repeatedly says: that it is because a part universally or for the most part *is* for something in the context of the developed organism that it *comes to be* for something. What I take this to mean, and will further explain in what follows, is that we cannot deny final causality without denying the integrity of the organism. The function of the part in the organism is not accidental but is why this part exists *and, therefore,* why it came to be. But let us imagine that we now look at the process of the part coming to be not from the end, but from the other direction, from the temporal beginning. Then what would we see? Not a part popping out of nothing, but a part coming to be as a result of a series of material processes, that is, out of material necessity. Aristotle does not need to deny that the part, thus, comes to be out of material necessity in order to claim that *being for something* it must *also* have *come to be for something*. Gotthelf would, of course, reply that coming to be out of necessity and coming to be for an end are mutually exclusive. But would this not be the claim, against Aristotle's explicit doctrine, that material and final causes are mutually exclusive?[17] The point is that

---

17   C. Byrne rightly argues that "there is no inconsistency between Aristotle's use of final causes in his biology and elsewhere, and his account of the non-teleological physical necessity operating in all perceptible objects" (2018, 107), emphasizing the different roles played by final and material causes. He seems to do so, however, at the cost of depriving final causes of any real causality. Thus, he revealingly claims: "Stated in more contemporary language, final causes are effects, not causes" (108). Byrne indeed appears to see Aristotle's teleology as nothing but *a description of beneficial consequences.* This is why he has no

FINAL CAUSALITY WITHOUT TELEOLOGY IN ARISTOTLE   145

we can explain, and even experience, an embryo developing a vital part
through material necessity, but what is missed if this is our full explanation is
the 'directedness,' for want of a better word, of the material processes towards
a living integral organism.[18] Could nature produce animals with ox-heads and
human bodies through a random mixture of elements, as Empedocles be-
lieved? Aristotle does not need to deny this: his argument is that it could not do
so consistently or 'for the most part' and, most importantly, that the result
would not be a natural organism but a 'monster.'

III   Material Necessity without Final Causality

If final causality never replaces material necessity, Aristotle in addition recognizes cases in which there is no final cause at work and that, therefore, can be

---

problem with attributing a 'global teleology' to Aristotle on no more evidence than the
passage from the *Politics* to be discussed below and the surprising assumption that
Aristotle is, in *Physics* II.8, presenting as his own view the absurd claim that it rains in
order for crops to grow (115): "In both individuals and groups of individuals, however, the
final cause explains only the additional or incremental effect, that is, the beneficial
consequences that the activity of one thing produces for something else" (116). Can
'explains' mean anything other than 'describes' here? How does final causality *explain*
that animals are good for humans to eat? In line with the statement quoted above, Byrne
sees the efficient cause as, by itself, producing the beneficial result when the latter is not
the outcome of chance (111). Thus, while Byrne claims that "final causes and material
causes *explain* different features of the physical world" (114, my emphasis), the better
word would be 'describe' because it is not at all clear what causal, or even explanatory,
work final causes are left to do on his account.

18   Gotthelf writes that in a continuous change resulting in *B* "this change is (in part) the
actualization of a potential for B which is not reducible to a sum of actualizations of
element-potentials whose identification does not mention the form of *B*" (2012, 12).
Gotthelf must insert the qualification 'in part' because the change resulting in *B* consists
at least in large part in the sum of actualizations of the element-potentials. The problem
is how to understand the 'part' contributed by what Gotthelf calls the potential for *B*.
Would it not be better to understand this according to the idea that the whole is greater
than the sum of its parts? *B* as the resulting organism is a whole greater than the sum total
of its parts even though it does not have 'parts' other than these. *Therefore*, the potential
for *B* is irreducible to the potentials of its element parts *even though it is through the
actualizations of the potentials of all these element parts* that the potential for *B* is itself
actualized. Bradie and Miller object against Gotthelf that the potential for form is not in
Aristotle's texts irreducible *in principle* since its being irreducible to the potentials of the
four elements does not show it to be irreducible to other material principles (1984, 142).
Apart from the fact that Aristotle could not be expected to rule out reducibility to material
principles whose existence he did not recognize, a whole is irreducible to its parts *in
principle*, whatever those parts are.

explained *only* by appeal to material necessity.[19] If nature does nothing in vain, much within nature occurs in vain. An example often cited is that of 'bile' (*PA* 677a13). In the context of discussing the gall bladder, Aristotle asserts that bile is a necessary residue that does *not* exist for the sake of anything (οὐχ ἕνεκά τινος, 677a15; also 29–30). Nature, Aristotle asserts, *sometimes* makes use of residues for something beneficial (for example, the ejection of ink in cephalopods is the result of necessity, but 'nature uses' this residue for the protection and safety of the animal, 679a28–30), but we should not, therefore, look for a purpose in every case; some things exist *only of necessity* (677a16–18). Furthermore, there are parts of animals that Aristotle explicitly claims serve no purpose, such as a lobster having one claw randomly larger than another,[20] or an octopus having only one row of suckers, which Aristotle explains as *necessary* but *not for the best* (οὐκ οὖν ὡς βέλτιστον ἔχουσιν, ἀλλ᾽ ὡς ἀναγκαῖον διὰ τὸν ἴδιον λόγον τῆς οὐσίας, 685b15–16). There is, indeed, at least one notorious case of a part of an animal being *harmful* to it. Aristotle believes that horns are, in the case of many animals that have them, not only useless, but even detrimental (663a9–12): deer have been given speed as another form of defense because the size and branching of their horns do them more harm than good (μᾶλλον βλάπτει ἢ ὠφελεῖ). So why, then, do these animals have horns? Presumably, because of natural necessity: an excess of earthy matter in larger animals is secreted as horns (663b30ff.).[21] Finally, book v of the *Generation of Animals* is

---

19 As Pellegrin rightly maintains, "Il faut d'autant plus conserver une place à la nécessité absolue dans l'approche aristotélicienne, que certains processus vitaux sont régis par ce seul genre de nécessité" (2011, 42). Cooper, in contrast, by not discussing these cases of absolute necessity working in living things *without* final causality, maintains that Aristotle, while not *reducing* absolute necessity (what he calls 'Democritean necessity') to hypothetical necessity, nevertheless *subsumes* the former to the latter (1985, 160).

20 In lobsters, and only in them, which claw is larger is a matter of chance (τύχωσιν) since, though having claws belongs to their genus, they have them in an indeterminate way (ἀτάκτως) because they are deformed (πεπήρονται) and do not use them for their natural purpose but rather for locomotion (*PA* 684a30–684b2).

21 Yet, Aristotle, at the end of the chapter, suggests that this earthy matter can be secreted either as horns or as teeth and that nature employs one or the other necessity according to a final cause. This is why Aristotle introduces this part of the chapter as follows: "Let us consider the character of the material nature whose necessary results have been employed by nature according to a principle for a final cause" (Πῶς δὲ τῆς ἀναγκαίας φύσεως ἐχούσης τοῖς ὑπάρχουσιν ἐξ ἀνάγκης ἡ κατὰ τὸν λόγον φύσις ἕνεκά του κατακέχρηται, *PA* 663b23–24). Yet, since this talk of *nature making use of materials for the sake of some end*, as if nature were a deliberative agent like the carpenter making choices about materials already present at hand, cannot be taken literally (see n30 below), the meaning must be only that the results of material necessity, ideally, are integrated into the specific ends of the organism. Furthermore, the problem of the useless, even detrimental horns remains as an exception to this ideal case. After explaining that nature has stripped does of horns

FINAL CAUSALITY WITHOUT TELEOLOGY IN ARISTOTLE

dedicated to characteristics animals have of necessity and not for a purpose. For example, Aristotle asserts that while an animal has an eye out of necessity, it has an eye of a certain color out of a different kind of necessity, which he describes as the necessity of naturally acting or being acted upon in such and such a fashion (ἐξ ἀνάγκης μέν, οὐ τοιαύτης δ᾽ἀνάγκης, ἀλλ᾽ἄλλον τρόπον, ὅτι τοιονδὶ ἢ τοιονδὶ ποιεῖν πέφυκε καὶ πάσχειν, 778b16–19). We have here a very clear distinction between hypothetical or conditional necessity, that is, eyes being necessary in order to see, and 'absolute' necessity, that is, eyes being of a certain color because their matter is naturally disposed in a certain way. It is of the latter he is speaking when he asserts that certain characteristics animals have come to be only out of necessity and through the moving cause and not at all for a final end (ὅσα γίνεσθαι συμβαίνει μὴ ἕνεκά του ἀλλ᾽ἐξ ἀνάγκης καὶ διὰ τὴν αἰτίαν τὴν κινητικήν, 789b19–20).[22]

Therefore, what Aristotle objects to in a view like that of Empedocles is the claim that *all* of an animal's parts and characteristics are like this, that is, that *all* of them come about *only* out of necessity and do not exist for an end. Pointless claws and detrimental horns do not threaten the unity and integrity of the organism as long as many or most of the organism's parts exist for an end. Aristotle is not intent on finding a final cause for everything in nature and knows that, in some cases, it is simply not to be found. For him, it suffices to maintain that final causes are often operative in nature since this is all that is needed to preserve nature against the random and unnatural assemblages of Empedocles.

---

because they are useless, Aristotle must grant that they are useless in the males too, though not as detrimental on account of the males' strength. Theophrastus in his *Metaphysics* also pointed to these cases as limits to final causality, in agreement with, rather than in criticism of Aristotle: see Gourinat (2015) and also Patočka (2011, 322); the latter, however, sees Aristotle's teleology as undergoing some revision in Theophrastus.

22 For the general principle that many things come to be out of necessity *rather than* for an end, see also *PA* I.642a2 and *GA* II.743b16–18. Another interesting but ambiguous example is Aristotle's claim in the *Generation of Animals* that animals that lack testes do so *not* because this is better, but *only* because of necessity (διὰ τὸ ἀναγκαῖον μόνον, 717b34), where this clearly refers to absolute material necessity. What makes the example ambiguous, however, is that despite the 'only,' Aristotle immediately adds that these animals lack testes also because it is necessary that their copulation be speedy! This may be another example of how material and final causality can work independently without excluding each other.

IV   No Global Teleology

The next point to be made is that if Aristotle's major work on animals is on the *parts* of animals, this is because only the parts can be explained in terms of final causes. In other words, a whole animal species cannot be explained in terms of final causality (by saying, for example, that one type of animal exists in order to serve as food for another type). The *telos* is always *internal* to the organism and explains the functioning of its parts. There can be a purpose for which a particular kind of animal has a particular part (or there may not be), but there is no purpose for which that particular kind of animal itself exists.[23] Aristotle does claim in *Generation of Animals* II.1 that the final cause "has its principle higher up" (ἄνωθεν ἔχει τὴν ἀρχήν, 731b23). This higher principle turns out to be the divine. As Aristotle goes on to explain, and as he also asserts elsewhere, reproduction in animals, and even in plants, has the end of partaking of the eternal and the divine (*An.* 415a26–415b7; *GA* II.731b31–732a1). But it is wrong to characterize this as an *external* end in the way that the purpose of sheltering humans is external to the house: the end described here is each living thing preserving itself by reproducing itself in form (εἴδει), though not in number (ἀριθμῷ). Similarly, if the unmoved mover is said to cause motion as a final cause at *Metaphysics* XII.7, this reinforces, rather than violates, the autonomy of natural substances. It is through being most itself, through being 'active' in such a way as to be its own end, that a natural substance approximates or moves towards the one substance that is absolutely active and

---

23   This is something that has been noted by Pellegrin: "Un animal n'est pas, en lui-même, à proprement parler, *explicable*", by which he means "téologiquement' (Introduction to Le Blond 1995, 32); see also Pellegrin 2011, 48–49. Therefore, he describes Aristotle's zoology as a 'moriologie,' suggesting that this is why Aristotle shows little interest in animal *taxonomy* (2011, 16). His approach is much closer to what today would be called 'comparative anatomy.' P.-M. Morel has distinguished between "une téléologie cosmique ou globale" and "une téléologie locale [ou interne] et relative"; he focuses on showing the latter at work in *De Motu Animalium* and, if he claims not to wish to "réduire l'explication finale en zoologie à un pur localisme organique, à l'idée selon laquelle il n'y aurait d'explication finale correct qu'au niveau de l'organisation interne du vivant" (2016, 28), it is not because he defends a strong version of cosmic teleology, but only because he sees Aristotle's biology as also submitting the different organisms and species to common rules.

FINAL CAUSALITY WITHOUT TELEOLOGY IN ARISTOTLE

absolutely its own end.[24] The good towards which it is directed in approximating the divine is, in other words, its own good.[25]

There are, indeed, two notorious passages that have received much discussion in the literature as appearing to suggest that animals have an end or purpose outside of their own self-preservation. But note, first, that we are talking about only two passages out of the entire corpus. If these passages truly show that Aristotle was a global teleologist, then he was a remarkably reticent one. But they need not, in fact, show any such thing. The one passage is the only one in all the biological writings in which Aristotle appears to suggest that a feature of one animal serves another animal. When explaining why the shark has its mouth placed underneath rather than in front (Aristotle offers δελφῖνες as an example, but that is clearly incorrect), Aristotle gives as one reason that nature thereby provides a means of salvation for other animals (PA 696b27–32). But

---

24 This point is well expressed and defended by F. Baghdassarian who asserts that "la actualité divine est une finalité des êtres naturels, dans la mesure où chacun, visant son acte propre, vise aussi l'Acte pur" and concludes that "la finalité divine ne se surajoute pas à celle qui oriente chaque être vers sa perfection propre. Elle la prolonge au contraire, en en proposant une illustration parfaite. Ce sur quoi repose l'aspiration des êtres naturels au divin est exactement ce sur quoi repose leur tendence vers leur fin propre" (2016, 180–181). See also Gotthelf: "So, in aiming at divinity, animals are not aiming at something other than self-preservation; divinity here *just is* eternal self-preservation, eternal self-continuation" (2012, 58); and Leunissen (2010, 45). Kahn, though defending the existence in Aristotle of what he calls a 'cosmic teleology,' appears to see it as coinciding with the teleology immanent to each living thing (see 1985; 193, 195, and 203). It is, therefore, not correct to claim with Kullmann that here "we have a finality which does not contribute anything to the essence of the thing aimed at" (1985, 172; see also 1979, 35–37). Sedley also assumes that the only kind of global teleology possible is the one he defends as completely distinct from the internal teleology that receives the emphasis in Aristotle. Thus, he claims that in addition to its own end of self-perpetuation, the pig also exists for the end of providing food for humans, where these two ends are obviously completely distinct (though Sedley oddly insists that there is no conflict between them [2010, 28]). Sedley's overall argument in the article also assumes, without evidence, that it was Aristotle's decision to identify god's activity with pure contemplation that put him in the 'dilemma' of having to explain the purposiveness of nature without appeal to divine craftsmanship (11). Could it not, on the contrary, have been his realization that the purposiveness of nature not only does not need, but is incompatible with being the product of divine craftsmanship (since only what has its source of motion within itself can count as 'natural') that led him to his own unique conception of the divine?

25 Miller and Miller make this relevant and important observation: "Aristotle, by contrast [to his predecessors], conceives of 'the good' as entirely integral to the existing and coming to be of self-sufficient entities as *ousia*, not as an efficient cause (whence the motion) and not as existing separately from *ousia*. Conceiving *ousia* as entity that exists through the good (functional) fit of its parts, which in turn is (hypothetically) necessitated by the unity of the whole, was a revolutionary and difficult idea then—and remains so today" (2005, 89n104).

two things are to be noted here: first, the whole sentence in which Aristotle offers this reason is qualified by the word φαίνεται, 'it appears'; it is, therefore, by no means certain that Aristotle is himself committed to what thus 'appears.' Secondly, he immediately provides two other reasons that, in appealing both to final causality and necessity, would of themselves fully explain the characteristic in question: the shark has its mouth underneath for the purpose of preventing it from giving way to its gluttonous appetite and thus perishing from over-repletion *and* because its snout is too round and small to allow for a sufficiently large opening in front. Note how the final cause here, as in every other case in the biological writings, has to do with the shark's self-preservation. Since, indeed, two final causes are adduced here, Balme sees Aristotle as substituting the correct teleological explanation (preventing gluttony) for a faulty one (saving other animals; 1987, 279).[26]

The other passage is the rather infamous one from the *Politics* in which Aristotle, after describing how animals, both tame and wild, provide us with food and clothing, asserts the following: "So if nature makes nothing either incomplete or in vain, it is necessary for all of these [animals] to have been made by nature for the sake of human beings" (1256b21–23). One reaction to this passage has been to assert that Aristotle simply cannot mean what he says here since it is so inconsistent with the rest of his teleology.[27] The limitations of such a response are obvious. Another is to note that this claim is made within the context of political, and not natural, philosophy. According to W. Wieland, for example, the passage "should not be interpreted as implying a universal teleology. For Aristotle is not concerned there with the philosophy of nature, but with the practical question of how man establishes himself in the world and makes things in the world ... the passage cannot be taken without qualification as a proposition of theoretical philosophy" (1975, 158). The problem with this response is Aristotle's appeal in the *Politics* passage to the principle that nature does nothing in vain. The most sensible interpretation is that of M.R. Johnson who, while not simply dismissing the passage as do other interpreters, makes the case that it does not commit Aristotle to an anthropocentric

---

26   On this case, see D. Charles who rightly argues that "Although the location of the shark's mouth benefits the other fish, their being benefitted is not, it seems, teleologically caused by that benefit" (2012, 244); also M.R. Johnson who, along with other reasons for not taking Aristotle as offering the saving of the other fish as a genuine teleological explanation, also cites the uniqueness of the passage (2005, 209). Leunissen, in contrast, takes it as a genuine case of teleology, though what she calls 'secondary teleology' (2010, 25, 43–44).

27   See Leroi: "He really can't mean this since the rest of his teleology is, as I've said, overwhelmingly directed at the survival of individual animals" (2014, 324). Balme likewise asserts that "it is impossible he could have meant this literally" (1987, 279). See also Charles (2012, 244).

FINAL CAUSALITY WITHOUT TELEOLOGY IN ARISTOTLE 151

teleology but, rather, is consistent with his usual view that "teleological explanations always refer to the benefit of specific natural kinds" (2005, 229–237).[28]
There would be an inconsistency only if the *Politics* passage were claiming that
animals primarily function for the benefit of man, but it need not and cannot
be claiming that: there is nothing about an animal's functioning, as discussed
throughout the biological writings, that has anything to do with its serving as
food for another animal. That the function of an animal is to be eaten would be
considered by Aristotle an absurd claim. What, then, is the *Politics* passage saying? Aristotle goes on to claim that hunting is natural and is so because it is
natural for human beings to eat other animals. And why is *that* natural? Since
the work of nature would have been *incomplete* (ἀτελές; and significantly, the
principle as stated here is that nature does nothing in vain *or* incomplete) if it
had not provided humans with a food source, it must be considered natural for
animals to provide such a food source. We can find here the assertion of some
kind of crude global ecology, but that falls well short of an anthropocentric
teleology. Such a teleology was not unknown to Aristotle: Socrates, for example, is shown defending a very strong version of it in Xenophon's *Memorabilia*
IV 3.3–12. It is, therefore, significant that it appears nowhere in Aristotle's biological writings and is suggested at all only in this one passage from the *Politics,*
a work that is, by its very nature, of course, anthropocentric.[29] The emphasis
here on what human beings need and on animals serving this need, with the
explanation that nature would not leave man or any other animal unprovided
for (the same passage asserts that plants exist for the sake of animals!), does
not imply a doctrine that would be incompatible with Aristotle's biology: that
a living thing's functioning serves any other end than its own self-preservation.[30]

---

28   Leunissen, in contrast, takes the passage as expressing a genuine case of teleology that is
      anthropocentric, but she tries to avoid the problems this causes by classifying it as a case
      of what she calls 'secondary,' rather than 'primary,' teleology (2010, 41–42). A similar
      solution is proposed by Kullmann who, appealing to Aristotle's distinction between two
      senses of 'final cause,' i.e., that 'for the sake of which' (οὗ ἕνεκά τινος) and that 'to the
      benefit of which' (οὗ ἕνεκά τινι), claims that animals are, in the *Politics,* said to exist for
      man only in the latter sense (1979, 25–28; 1985, 173).

29   Sedley, in contrast, takes the passage as expressing a robust global teleology and even
      describes Aristotle as following Xenophon's Socrates here (2010, 27). He attempts to
      explain the almost complete absence of any expression of a global teleology outside of
      this passage, and in the biological writings in particular, but his claim of a corresponding
      silence in Plato is hardly persuasive (24–25).

30   Apart from its particular application to the case of the relation between humans and
      other animals, the personification of nature in the considered passage from the *Politics,* as
      well as elsewhere, can itself be seen as posing a problem. Is not the very description of
      nature as doing nothing in vain, disposing everything for the best, making good use of
      materials, *etc.*, evidence of a global teleology in which, beyond the natures of individual

V Teleology and Evolution

The above points make possible another possible misunderstanding of Aristotle's teleology. This teleology is often characterized as essentialist and ahistorical.[31] It is true that Aristotle appears to regard species as fixed and eternal. However, there are two aspects of Aristotle's position that suggest he could accommodate an evolutionary perspective.[32] First, while Aristotle's *scala naturae* is most often cited for its suggestion of a hierarchy among natural beings, what Aristotle himself stresses is the *continuity*. Thus, in the context of explaining why it is in some cases unclear whether something is a plant or an animal, Aristotle writes:

> For nature passes from lifeless objects to animals in such unbroken sequence (συνεχῶς), interposing between them beings which live and yet are not animals, that scarcely any difference seems to exist between two neighboring groups owing to their close proximity. (*PA* 681a12–15; Ogle tr. 1882)[33]

Aristotle, thus, does not recognize sharp, clear boundaries between plant and animal or even been living and non-living; why, then, should he be committed to sharp boundaries between species? Central to his explanatory method in the *Parts of Animals* is, indeed, to note *analogies* between the parts of

---

 things, there is a Nature acting with deliberation to ensure that each thing serves a good beyond itself? This problem has been raised most forcefully by A. Mansion who is intent on defending Aristotle against any charge of anthropomorphism: see 1945, 261, for the presentation of the problem and the citation of all the Aristotelian texts in which this anthropomorphized nature is found, and 262–269 for the discussion. Mansion's solution, in the end, is a simple one and one I share: given that taking such anthropomorphic expressions literally is inconsistent with the final causality Aristotle *argues for* at the end of *Physics* II, we should not take them literally (263; see also 337); the same position is taken by Kullmann who also cites the relevant texts (1979, 24). More positively, Mansion argues that the order of nature described figuratively in such expressions can be explained without them (270–281).

31 Though see in contrast Balme (1980).

32 See O'Rourke: "I propose that in the light of his basic metaphysical principles, with minimal modification to this philosophy of nature, Aristotle might readily accommodate an evolution of species" (2004, 38). See 38–42 that parallel my argument.

33 See the parallel passage in *HA* 588b4–18. Aristotle's emphasis in both passages on the 'continuity' between living and nonliving, plant and animal, has the strong implication that there are no gaps between them: "I mean that two things are continuous [συνεχές] when the limits of each by which they make contact become one and the same thing and are, as the name indicates, contained in each other. But continuity is impossible if these extremities are two" (*Physics* 227a11–13, Reeve, tr. 2018)

FINAL CAUSALITY WITHOUT TELEOLOGY IN ARISTOTLE

otherwise radically different species of animals: "For most animals have parts that are the same by analogy" (τὰ γὰρ πολλὰ ζῷα ἀνάλογον ταὐτὸ πέπονθεν, *PA* 644a23). A wonderful example is Aristotle's explanation of a bird's beak:

> For supposing that one were to cut off a man's lips, unite his upper teeth together, and similarly his under ones, and then were to lengthen out the two separate pieces thus formed, narrowing them on either side—then we should at once have a bird-like beak. (659b20–25; Ogle, tr. 1882)

As already noted, the primary object of explanation in Aristotle's biology is not one individual animal species as distinct from others, but the individual animal part as found analogously with regard to function across a wide range of species.

Secondly, given the role we have seen Aristotle grant to material necessity, nothing rules out, in principle, the parts of animals undergoing transformations that run counter to the actual function of that animal and its survival.[34] Aristotle himself notes at the end of book IV of the *Generation of Animals* that nature is prevented from numbering generation and destruction according to the numbers that rule the stars by the indeterminateness of matter and the multiplicity of principles that often cause accidents against nature (πολλὰς ἀρχάς, αἳ τὰς γενέσεις τὰς κατὰ φύσιν καὶ τὰς φθορὰς ἐμποδίζουσαι πολλάκις αἴτιαι τῶν παρὰ φύσιν συμπιπτόντων εἰσίν, 778a4–9). If a sufficient number of such accidents took place over time, the very way in which the animal functions could be altered, thus making it a different animal. Indeed, in another extraordinary thought-experiment from the *Parts of Animals*, Aristotle describes a kind of 'devolution' resulting from material necessity that he would need only to

---

34   We can, thus, dispel one possible objection against Aristotle: if nature works for a purpose, should not all the transformations and changes organisms undergo benefit them? As we have seen, Aristotle has no problem acknowledging that animals have parts or characteristics that come about solely through material causes and serve no purpose. C. Johnson recounts what is, in this context, an interesting criticism of Darwin made by Asa Gray, namely, that Darwin "did not see the logical possibility of an intelligent designer preordaining variations that he (or it) nevertheless knew were preordained to obliteration by the action of natural selection. That may be a difficult intelligent designer to understand—why would an intelligent designer *do* that—but the conception is not internally riven by contradiction. Gray was correct on that score" (2012, 153–154). But what is difficult here to understand as the action of an intelligent designer is less difficult to understand as the action of a nature acting for an end *without intelligence or design*. See also Kullmann's suggestion that if Aristotle had thought through to its logical end his own recognition of the absence of "a comprehensive finality in animal bodies," "he would have reached the theory of evolution by natural selection" (1985, 174).

reverse to imagine a process of evolution (686a25–687a2). As noted earlier, Aristotle gives as the necessary cause of man standing erect the fact that the upper part of his body is smaller than the lower part, something, in turn, explained—and the details do not concern us here—by the possession of greater heat. Noting, however, that, in children, the upper part of the body is larger than the lower part and that this is why they crawl on the ground rather than walk, Aristotle claims that quadruped animals are like children in this respect (and both are described as 'dwarf-like,' ναν⟨δες). Specifically, children illustrate how human arms could become a third and fourth leg if the top of their bodies were heavier than the bottom. The greater material on top and the resulting closeness to the ground make quadrupeds less intelligent since "their psychical principle is corporeal and impeded in its motions" (ἡ τῆς ψυχῆς ἀρχὴ πολλοῖς δὴ δυσκίνητός ἐστι καὶ σωματώδης, 686b27–28; Ogle tr. 1882). Aristotle then imagines a further decrease in heat as resulting in more earthy matter that brings the animal even closer to the ground, thus, causing it to develop more feet than four. As this process proceeds further, the animal would lose its feet altogether and slither along the ground with its whole body. Finally, through yet further decrease in heat and the development of more earthy matter, Aristotle imagines the animal sticking its head in the ground, losing all capability of motion and sensation, and becoming a plant! Reverse this, and we can imagine, again as a result of purely necessary causes, the plant evolving into a snake, the snake into a centipede, the centipede into a lizard, the lizard into a four-footed mammal, and the four-footed mammal into a two-footed mammal capable of standing erect.

The point here is not that Aristotle was even close to developing a theory of evolution: the point rather is that his teleology need not be incompatible with such a theory.[35] Nor is the intention here to deny the substantial differences

---

35   Paradoxically, perhaps, one idea in Aristotle that might make him more open to the idea of evolving, or at least new, species is an idea discredited today: spontaneous generation (see GA11.762a10–33). As Johnson notes, while things that are spontaneously generated have forms, in their case "the form is largely determined by the matter" (2012, 137) ('largely' because, as Bradie and Miller note [1984, 139–140], there is a role to be played here by what Aristotle describes as 'vital heat'). If, according to one estimate, as much as one fifth of the animals Aristotle considers are seen by him to be exclusively spontaneously generated (see Johnson 2012, 134–135, and Johnson 2013, 118n27 for references), much opportunity is created for the kind of spontaneous variation the theory of evolution requires. We have here also a rather large exception to the final causality of species reproducing themselves in imitation of the divine: as Johnson again notes, "If inanimate materials do happen to combine to produce insects and oysters, they do not do so 'for the sake of' producing these kinds of living things. Rather they do so by an incidental cause and spontaneously" (2012, 139).

FINAL CAUSALITY WITHOUT TELEOLOGY IN ARISTOTLE 155

that still exist between Aristotle and Darwin, differences that are not all necessarily to Darwin's advantage. Even if it has been argued that Darwin was a teleologist and identified himself as such,[36] even if he was overcome with boundless admiration when, at the very end of his life, he finally began to read the *Parts of Animals* in the English translation of his friend W. Ogle, it is nevertheless doubtless true that whatever teleology can be found in Darwin is quite different from the Aristotelian version. Darwin can be said to be a teleologist to the extent that, on his theory, a certain characteristic is naturally selected *because* it serves the organism's survival. To the extent that this is true and if I am right in suggesting that Aristotle's theory does not, in principle, rule out evolution, the scientific approaches of Aristotle and Darwin are reconcilable. But Aristotle's teleology is stronger than Darwin's in the claim that it makes about the *being* of the living organism as characterized by an *inner directedness* that could not be reduced to mere adaptation.[37] This is, indeed, the key point of Aristotle's final causality that I wish to pursue further in what follows.

VI   Final Causes in Nature as Ontological Thesis

Given the points that have been made, our reasons for exercising caution in using the term 'teleology' in connection with Aristotle are not limited to its association with the notion of 'intelligent design.'[38] We could follow the lead of certain contemporary biologists who, finding themselves in agreement with Aristotle, while seeking to avoid being mocked by their peers, have begun to speak of 'teleonomy.'[39] But we, in any case, now arrive at the more positive aim

---

36 See Lennox (1993), but also the rebuttal of Ghiselin (1994). As Gotthelf suggests, we probably need to distinguish here between a stronger and a weaker teleology: in the weaker form, which one can ascribe to Darwin, a certain characteristic is naturally selected "*because* it contributes to the life of the organisms possessing it"; in the stronger form, which is Aristotle's, the process *aims* at an end (though unconsciously and unintentionally), where this "*directiveness on an end*" is irreducible, i.e., cannot be explained in terms of anything simpler (Gotthelf 2012, 368–369). The question, then, is whether the weaker teleology of Darwin renders obsolete the stronger teleology of Aristotle.

37 Von Uexhüll, whose biology shows important affinities to Aristotle's, rejects 'adaptation' as an explanatory concept in biology (Weiss 1948, 52).

38 The term 'teleology,' as M.R. Johnson notes (2005, 30), is not attested before its use by Christian Wolff in 1728. Furthermore, the motivation of this coinage could not be more anti-Aristotelian: as again noted by Johnson (30–31), Wolff coins the word to designate a special science *distinct from physics.*

39 Philosopher and historian of science, David Hull, thus, joked: "Haldane [in the 1930s] can be found remarking, 'Teleology is like a mistress to a biologist: he cannot live without her

of this paper: once we understand what an Aristotelian final cause *is not*, what can we say it *is* and what function does it serve?[40] If final causes do not, in Aristotle, supplant explanation in terms of material necessity, if they clearly are not at work at all in the case of certain phenomena, and if they provide no global explanation of why the things that exist, exist at all, then why appeal to them?

As Aristotle himself notes in rejecting any hypothesis of intelligent design in nature, the challenge here is to understand a kind of 'purposiveness' distinct from any purpose aimed at by some deliberative agent. To attribute final causality to the parts of an organism is to attribute to them a certain *directedness* that cannot be reduced to the material necessity of 'if A, then B.' It is to claim that explanation must proceed not only from A to B (if this happens, then something else follows of necessity), but also from B to A (in view of this, something else must occur). This is, therefore, a point Aristotle explicitly defends near the beginning of the *Parts of Animals*. There, he surprisingly claims, contrary to his usual habit, that natural science is *not* a theoretical science,[41] the reason being that theoretical science has as its object *what is,* while natural science has as its object *what will be* (τὸ ἐσόμενον, 640a1–9; see also *Phys.* 200a15–30). We fail to make this distinction, Aristotle argues, when we treat

---

but he's unwilling to be seen with her in public.' Today the mistress has become a lawfully wedded wife. Biologists no longer feel obligated to apologize for their use of teleological language; they flaunt it. The only concession which they make to its disreputable past is to rename it 'teleonomy'" (1982, 298). An example is Jacques Monod, who in writing of 'teleonomy' contrasts it to final causality, identifying the latter with the notion of a 'project' or 'plan' (1970; see, for example, 37–38); in fact, as Kullmann notes (1979, 61), Monod's 'teleonomy' is nothing other than what Aristotle understands by final causality. Chase reviews the work of three recent theorists of science, Robert Rosen, René Thom, and Ilya Prigogine, who "devoted a good part of their careers to arguing that it may be time to rehabilitate some aspects of the Aristotelian four-cause system, and especially final causation, abandoned as a result of the dominance of the Newtonian paradigm" (2011, 522).

40 As Gotthelf notes, this is not a question that Aristotle ever explicitly answers: "Readers of the corpus will search in vain for a detailed analysis of what it is to be (or come to be) for the sake of something" (2012, 3).

41 There have been attempts to read the text as not making this distinction (by turning it into a distinction between theoretical sciences and arts, or, as in Pellegrin (2011, 485–486), between theoretical physics and a physics for physicians), but they have not been convincing: see M.R. Johnson (2005, 163–165). Johnson himself takes the distinction to be one between theoretical sciences of things that are natural, which, therefore, change, and theoretical sciences of things that do not change (e.g., mathematics). This is not incorrect, but the difference that interests Aristotle here is not between what changes and what does not change but between what *is* and *what is to be,* where the latter is a reference to the final cause, as Le Blond notes: "La fin n'est pas encore réalisée et l'être qui devient y tend" (1995, 72).

FINAL CAUSALITY WITHOUT TELEOLOGY IN ARISTOTLE   157

health or a man as only a necessary *consequent* of what already is. Rather, health or man is *that for the sake of which* this and that necessarily comes to be and is, therefore, an *antecedent*. In other words, 'if A is, then B is' is the proper form that explanation takes in the theoretical study of what is. However, in the study of what *will be*, the proper form of explanation is: 'if B is to be, then A must necessarily be.' In *starting* with the consequent, we treat it not as a *result*, but as an *end*.[42] Aristotle proceeds to give an example of the kind of explanation he considers appropriate here:

> It is because it [the end that 'will be,' such as a human being or health] is such, that its coming to be must be such and take place in such a way; it is for this reason that this one of its parts comes to be first and then this one. And similarly in this way for all the things that are constituted by nature (640b1–4; my translation).[43]

We can see in this passage why Aristotle is denying here that natural science is a theoretical science, since the methodology he describes seems to be that of a *productive* science: in building a house, too, we begin with 'what will be' (the house) and then think back to what must occur, and in what order, if this end is to come to be. Yet, Aristotle cannot be claiming, in contradiction to what he says everywhere else, that the science of nature is actually a productive science like carpentry.[44] Instead, he wants to highlight an affinity with productive sci-

---

42 Le Blonde is right to suggest that this point commands all the reflections to follow (1995, 72). Aristotle makes the same basic point at *Phys.* 11.200a15–20, though there the contrast is specifically with mathematics. Significantly, Short, without citing the passage under discussion here, gives the following as the reason why Darwin's idea of traits being selected due to their consequences is not, as such, teleological: "the consequences that explain the existence of adaptive traits are the consequences those traits *have had*; they are not the consequences that they *will have* or *can have*. As the consequences precede the effect they explain, a consequence etiology is consistent with a mechanistic account of that effect" (2002, 324).

43 I take this to be a general formulation that includes all the types of explanation that Aristotle outlines in what immediately precedes (*PA* 640a33–640b1): it is because this is the essence of man that he develops these parts; it is because man could not exist without these parts that he develops these parts; it is because man could not live well without them that man develops these parts. But the passage is obscure and has been interpreted differently. Leunissen takes the passage cited to refer only to what she calls 'secondary teleology' (2010, 97–98).

44 Contra W. Ogle who interprets the difference here as one between theoretical science *and art* (constructive science), thus, turning nature into art! "The artist, on the other hand, or nature, the chief of artists, starts from an ideal conception, not yet existent in matter, but to be realized in the future (τὸ ἐσόμενον). Starting from this, he reasons backwards through the antecedent steps that are necessary, if the conception is to be realised" (1882, 142).

ence, which distinguishes natural science from other theoretical sciences: the fact that it starts and works back from 'what will be,' rather than starting and working forwards from what was or is.

The significance of this passage becomes clearer if we consider Leunissen's neglect of its central point throughout most of her study[45] and the fact that, when she finally gives it some serious consideration (198–199), she takes Aristotle's identification of the starting point with 'what will be' as meaning that the final cause will figure as the major term of a syllogism and, therefore, *not* as the middle term (199). Consider one syllogism she offers as an example: (1) Birds are essential flyers; (2) flyers necessarily have wings; (3) birds necessarily have wings. This appears to be precisely the kind of explanation Aristotle is *ruling out* when he writes (on Leunissen's translation): "not 'since this is or has come about, that from necessity is or will be'" (2010, 198). The syllogism that would better fit Aristotle's purpose is the following: (1) Birds essentially have the end of flying; (2) wings are necessary for the end of flying; (3) therefore, birds have wings. (Leunissen's objection that some birds do not fly is equally a problem for her premise that birds are essential flyers!) Significantly, Leunissen provides no formulation for her example of what she considers 'secondary' teleology, claiming it is 'not easy' (203). But the formulation in line with what Aristotle says would be something as follows: (1) All animals have the end of defending themselves; (2) in some animals, only horns serve the end of self-defense; (3) some animals have horns. One could also, as we have seen, provide another explanation that makes no reference to final causality but explains horns simply as the result of material necessity.

---

45   Leunissen appears simply to ignore the passage in maintaining that demonstrations of teleological natural processes, like scientific demonstrations in general, "ought to reflect the chronological order of causation in the world, moving from the start or origin of the natural development to its end. ... This means that final causes can never take the position of a middle term, which picks out the causally *primary* factor in a chain of development" (2010, 7). When she first cites, without quoting, 640a1–9 (80; see also 100), she completely misses its central point, insisting that biology is a theoretical science and that it differs from another theoretical science like mathematics only in that its conclusions "do not hold always and without exception" (80). Later, Leunissen quotes the passage again and explicitly treats the distinction between theoretical science and natural science as one between science of eternal substances and science of perishable substances, claiming that the reason why natural science cannot proceed from prior to posterior is that, in the case of perishable substances, the prior does not necessitate without exception the posterior (108). But this is not Aristotle's own explanation and is also false given that, as Mansion has shown (1945, ch. 9), contingency, as Aristotle understands it, is perfectly compatible with thoroughgoing causal determinism. In her discussion of the *Posterior Analytics*, Leunissen, again, asserts that the chronological order of causation rules out final causes being middle terms (197; see also 211).

FINAL CAUSALITY WITHOUT TELEOLOGY IN ARISTOTLE 159

An example Leunissen takes from the *Posterior Analytics* as an example of teleological explanation most clearly shows the untenability of her reading. She reconstructs the explanation of walking being for the sake of health as follows: (1) walking prevents food from floating in the stomach; (2) food not floating in the stomach is healthy; (3) walking produces health. This fits exactly the form of explanation Aristotle *rejects* at the beginning of the *Parts of Animals* and it is easy to see why: the end of health is deprived of any real causal role. Health is here simply a result, rather than the 'what-is-to-be' that must come *first* in the order of explaining walking.[46] The price of mistaking Aristotle's point in the crucial passage from the *Parts of Animals* is that the final cause, in being denied, in principle, the position of the middle term in a demonstration, is denied any causality, whatever Leunissen might want to say to the contrary.[47] The final cause becomes always the *effect* of another cause and never itself the cause. Thus, Leunissen writes:

> It is my contention that whereas the importance of final causes lies in their explanatory priority (they are easily identified through observation and often form the starting points of explanations), material or formal features constitute the causally primary factor in explanations. That is, the coming to be and presence of ends that constitute the final causes are themselves—depending on whether the teleology is primary or secondary—primarily driven by either material factors ... or formal factors ... which have causal priority. (2010, 135–136)

I have already questioned the distinction between primary and secondary teleology, but Leunissen's discussion of examples from the *Parts of Animals* also shows her making too strong of a distinction between the final and the formal cause. What she wishes to claim, for example, is that the cause of fish having fins is not the end of swimming but their formal nature as swimmers; but is this a meaningful either/or in the case of living substances? For reasons that will become clearer in what follows, I believe the answer to be plainly negative. As Aristotle openly asserts in the context of his critique of the natural selection

---

46   Delcomminette, thus, makes the helpful suggestion that "contrairement à la representation que l'on a tendance à s'en faire, la téléologie est donc un mode d'explication tourné non pas vers l'avenir, mais vers le passé, précisément parce qu'elle consiste à *partir* de la fin" (2018, 304).

47   She denies saying final causes have no causal force, only that they have 'no causal primacy' (211); she denies that they have only a heuristic value (220).

160   GONZALEZ

theory in *Physics* II.8, the cause in the sense of the end must be the form (199a30–32).[48]

If there has been some resistance to understanding the method of biological science in the way suggested by Aristotle in the passage from the *Parts of Animals*, of which Leunissen's study is only one example, it is due to fear of what has been called 'backward causation.'[49] We can understand talk of the end of a house causing the materials to be assembled into a house because, in this case, the end takes the form of an *intention* that, as such, temporally precedes the making of the house. But to say that an end has causal efficacy *in nature*, where nature is not taken to be an intentional agent, is to suggest that 'what will be' can exert causal force on the present. This is absurd, however, only if we confuse final causality with efficient causality[50] and, thus, take the claim to be that the end existing in the future sets something in motion in the present. A good example of this confusion[51] is the following statement by a prominent biologist, C.S. Pittendrigh: "the recognition and description of end-directedness does not carry a commitment to Aristotelian teleology as an efficient causal principle" (1958, 394). The irony is that a pseudo-Aristotelian teleology is here rejected in defense of the position that could be described as genuinely Aristotelian: the existence of end-directedness in living organisms. As Aristotle emphatically asserts in *De Generatione et Corruptione*, "The productive power is a cause as that from which the motion originates, but the for-the-sake-of-which is not a productive power (therefore health is not a productive power, unless metaphorically" (ἔστι δὲ τὸ ποιητικὸν αἴτιον ὡς ὅθεν ἡ ἀρχὴ τῆς κινήσεως. τὸ δ᾽ οὗ ἕνεκα οὐ ποιητικόν [διὸ ἡ ὑγιεία οὐ ποιητικόν, εἰ μὴ κατὰ μεταφοράν], 324b13–15; my translation). But we do not avoid the same mistake if we claim that final causes have only *explanatory*, as opposed to *causal*,

---

48   As Delcomminette observes, "la fin, c'est simplement la manière dont l'essence se manifeste dans le devenir, à savoir comme le *but* auquel tend le processus de generation lui-même" (2018, 304).

49   This motivation is very clear in Leunissen.

50   As M.R. Johnson shows, what prepares the rejection of final causes in the modern period is their identification with efficient causes in the medieval period (2005, 16–23). Speaking of the characterization of the soul as *telos* in *De Anima*, Miller and Miller observe: "Unfortunately, this mechanism by which functional parts dynamically fit together and hold themselves in an optimal configuration as *telos* has generally been misunderstood as 'teleology' in the pejorative sense—as a kind of backward efficient causation from something existing separately from the functional parts" (2005, 82–83). Then, with the support of *Physics* 198a35–b9, they rightly insist in a note (83n98) that what they call "*hou heneka* causation" is not understood by Aristotle as acting like an efficient cause. See also Bradie and Miller (1984, 137), though they suggest a qualified sense in which the final cause can operate as an efficient cause.

51   Cited by M.R. Johnson (2005, 167n12).

FINAL CAUSALITY WITHOUT TELEOLOGY IN ARISTOTLE

priority, since we thereby assume that final causes cannot really *cause* anything because only efficient causes do that. As Aristotle makes clear in a passage from the *Generation of Animals* (II.6, 742a19–22), the priority of the end, in relation to that which is for the sake of the end, is not a priority merely in explanation, but a priority *with respect to substance* (Τὸ τε γὰρ οὗ ἕνεκα καὶ τὸ τούτου ἕνεκα διαφέρει, καὶ τὸ μὲν τῇ γενέσει πρότερον αὐτῶν ἐστι, τὸ δὲ τῇ οὐσίᾳ). What does this mean? If the being of the substance in question is to be inherently directed towards some end, then the end has priority in substance and, therefore, *causal* priority in the strongest sense of causal priority. Because a living thing has *to be* this or that (where this will specify both its form and, inseparably, its end), it has this or that part, and not: because it has this or that part, it is this or that kind of living thing. The end of flying does not 'backwards cause' the wings of a bird to start growing nor is it only a heuristic principle that 'explaining' what the wings are for motivates us to look for their real causes (Kullmann [1979, 41] comes close to this latter position). Having wings is necessitated by what the bird *has to be*.[52]

It is also the final cause that gives functional *unity* to the parts of the organism and, therefore, unity to the organism itself. Indeed, once we stop giving the term ἐντελέχεια the terrible translation of 'actuality' (terrible because missing entirely the notion of possessing an end key to the term's construction), we can see the final cause or *telos* as a necessary ontological feature of a substance[53]

---

52 In the context of the description of the *telos* as an unmoved mover, Miller and Miller rightly observe the following: "An important consequence of this characterization of the causal role of the *telos* is that it cannot occur by *dunamis-dunamis* interactions between whole (qua *telos*) and its parts, i.e., *not* by backward or 'downward' efficient causation. Instead, the species-configuration (*telos* as *ousia* according to the *logos*) as unmoved mover is the optimal pattern of mutual enablement among the functional roles of the parts for the best overall functioning of the organism" (2005, 87).

53 Mirus also makes the case that "Aristotle's teleology is firmly grounded in his understanding of being. More specifically, as we have seen, it is rooted in the claim that actuality is prior to potentiality, both in λόγος and in οὐσία" (2004, 724). He shows that the *telos* is not to be understood only as an end of motion, but as the limit that defines the *being* of a thing and he recognizes the importance in this regard of *Metaphysics* IX 1048b18–30, where Aristotle distinguishes activity (ἐνέργεια), which possesses its end within itself, from motion (κίνησις, 709–711). On this text, see Gonzalez (2019). But, in claiming that Aristotle's teleology is rooted in his metaphysics and *not* in his biology (699–700), Mirus is making a false opposition: could not Aristotle have arrived at his understanding of the ontological role of the final cause through his understanding of how final causality works in living substances? Gotthelf, in contrast, appeals to the biological work to make the case that the concept of *telos* in Aristotle is to be understood by reference to his conception of 'actuality' rather than by reference to some conception of what is good (2012, 47–57). The thesis that he defends is largely assumed in my account here, i.e., that "Aristotle's notion of goodness is rather itself defined in terms of the notions of actuality and end (and that Aristotle's

and also see why the *living* substance is the paradigm for what counts as a substance. That the artifact needs to be given its *telos* from the outside makes it lacking in true substantial unity and, therefore, not a substance in the strictest sense. It is in this context that we are to understand an extremely important claim that Aristotle makes in the *Parts of Animals* and a surprising one since it runs completely counter to the kind of argumentation that usually supports teleology: the that-for-the-sake-of-which and the beautiful, he claims, are to be found *more* in the works of nature than in the works of craft (μᾶλλον δ'ἐστι τὸ οὗ ἕνεκα καὶ τὸ καλὸν ἐν τοῖς τῆς φύσεως ἔργοις ἢ ἐν τοῖς τῆς τέχνης, 639b19–21). How can Aristotle claim this?[54] Is it not obvious that final causes are to be found most of all in the products of human craft and in nature, if at all, only to the extent it approximates human craft? But it is not hard to see what Aristotle means. A product of craft, like a bed, does not contain its final cause within itself; its final cause is external to it. Its final purpose must be given to it from the outside because, in itself, it lacks purpose and is not more than a random collection of wood or metal. A natural object, in contrast, contains its purpose within itself, making it 'beautiful' in a sense in which no product of craft can be beautiful.

The very externality of the *telos* in the case of artifacts makes it easier to identify, and Aristotle therefore himself uses artifacts to help us understand final causes in the case of nature. This is a case of explaining the prior and less familiar through the posterior and more familiar. There is, however, a real danger in such a procedure: we may, thereby, make the mistake of interpreting final causes in nature as if they were simply an instance of the final causes we find in craft, whereas, for Aristotle, it is craft that imitates and falls short of nature in this regard, not *vice versa*.[55] Furthermore, even in using the *techne*

---

theory here is not circular)" (49). See also Mansion (1945, 276), who, however, regrets that Aristotle did not provide in his *Metaphysics* a theory of the good in its relation to being.

54　Balme suggests two possible meanings: that nature achieves its ends more successfully than art or that "finality penetrates nature more completely" in the sense, for example, that the body of a man is more inseparable from his end (his soul) than marble is inseparable from the end of the statue of a man (1972, 76). The latter seems the more likely meaning. Le Blond suggests that it is precisely the absence of deliberation that allows the final cause a greater role in nature: "L'hirondelle qui construit son nid par une impulsion naturelle, par instinct, est davantage dominée par la fin, plus proche d'elle, que l'architecte qui délibère sur la façon de construire une maison" (1995, 68).

55　Though Charles begins his analysis of teleological causation by acknowledging that Aristotle "is not seeking to analyse natural teleology as an instance of craft teleology" (2012, 238), he nevertheless himself proceeds to do precisely that. Never even asking *how natural teleology differs from craft teleology,* he simply assumes that because the latter requires that the good be the object of "needs and desires," or that there be present a "sensitivity to the good," the same must be the case with natural teleology. Thus, we are

FINAL CAUSALITY WITHOUT TELEOLOGY IN ARISTOTLE 163

model heuristically, what Aristotle sees as paralleling final causes in nature is the end-directedness of the *techne* itself and *not* the intentionality, desires, or needs of the agent using the *techne*. This is made perfectly clear in the continuation of the important passage from *Physics* II.8 cited above:

> It is absurd [for them] to think that [it] is not coming to be for the sake of something if they do not see the moving cause deliberating. On the contrary, *craft too does not deliberate* (καίτοι καὶ ἡ τέχνη οὐ βουλεύεται). And if the art of shipbuilding were inside the wood, it would produce in the same way nature does. So that if the for-the-sake-of is *inherent in* craft (ἐν τῇ τέχνῃ ἔνεστι), so is it in nature. (199b26–30; my translation)

Thus, the parallel with nature depends on the claim that *even in craft* the relation to an end is inherent in the craft itself and does not exist simply in the deliberation or intentionality of the agent.[56] In other words, what parallels final causality in nature is *not* the doctor's desire to produce health, as a state she judges to be good, but the directedness towards health inherent in the very craft of medicine, whatever the doctor may or may not want.[57] It is indeed this *internal* directedness existing in both craft and nature that explains why both exhibit a certain order in attaining their ends: a parallel that Aristotle appeals to in one of his arguments for final causality in nature (199a8–20). The differ-

---

confronted with the problem of how we can sensibly speak of a plant needing, desiring, or being sensitive to its good (254–5). See, in contrast, Patočka, who denies that Aristotle took his fundamental principles from the experience of the artisan, asserting that he was, instead, in his conception of nature, the adversary of all 'artificialism' (2011, 428–431), and Furth, who devotes an entire section of his book to the topic of "Why artifacts are bad examples" (1988, 181–184), though acknowledging that, once their weakness is understood, "there is no harm, in itself, in using them as illustrative examples where such strengths as they enjoy may prove helpful" (183). Given his general neglect of teleology, however, the weakness Furth diagnoses in the artifact examples has nothing to do with their relation to their ends.

56   Sedley appears to believe that the claim that craft does not deliberate, in narrowing the gap between craft and nature, brings Aristotle closer to Plato (2010, 14–18). The very opposite is the case. For Plato craft *does* deliberate and the purposiveness of nature is a product of craft in the sense of being a product of deliberation on the part of a divine agent. Aristotle's position is diametrically opposed in arguing that nature is purposive without deliberation *and that even craft is like nature in this respect.*

57   It is revealing that W. Ogle, who recognizes no alternative to material necessity other than intelligent design (1882, i) and must therefore place Aristotle on the side of the latter, must, in paraphrasing this passage, so qualify it as utterly to misrepresent it: "If you ask me whether this hidden force acts, as the builder or the shipwright, with conscious deliberation, and conscious adaptation of means to ends, *I do not know*. Even art does not *always* deliberate" (vi, my emphases).

ence between craft and nature lies in whether this being-towards-an-end is in the thing itself that comes to possess this end or not. In the case of shipbuilding, the end towards which this craft is inherently directed comes to be in wood that is distinct from it. But if the art of shipbuilding were in the wood itself, the wood would make itself into a ship *and without the intervention of any deliberative agency*. In this case ships would be natural. We therefore gravely misinterpret the other example Aristotle proceeds to give, that of nature being like a doctor who cures herself, if we interpret this as attributing some kind of deliberative agency to nature. On the contrary, what we are asked to imagine is a case in which the art of medicine would exist in the body in such a way that the body would cure itself *without the intervention of a doctor*.[58] This is why the present passage does not contradict Aristotle's claim at the beginning of book II that a doctor curing herself is, in fact, *not* an example of nature (292b24–30). Because a craft, in fact, does not exist in the materials out of which its product is made (the body in the case of the production of health, the wood and bricks in the case of the production of a house), it requires the intervention of a deliberative agent in order to reach its end. No such intervention is required in the case of a natural substance since such a substance contains its principle of motion and, thus, its end within itself.[59]

---

58   So, one could claim that Charles has misunderstood even craft teleology. In contrast, Leunissen writes: "It is important to note that conscious intentionality plays no significant role in the analogy between art and nature in the second book of the *Physics*" (2010, 17). See also Broadie (1990, 398). Broadie, however, is led astray by assuming, despite Aristotle's explicit assertions to the contrary (e.g., *Phys.* 199a16–17), that "it is craft that provides the model for nature, not the reverse" (390) and, further, that "if we take one thing as a model for another, we expect the latter's structure to exhibit all that is essential in the former" (401). She then objects that craft is not an appropriate model because "from craft alone nothing comes about"; that a craft is exercised at all depends on ulterior values possessed by the craftsman (400). But this is precisely why, for Aristotle, craft imitates nature and not the other way around: though a craft is like nature internally and, of itself, directed towards an end (health in the case of medicine, e.g.), it, unlike nature, depends on an agent and an end external to itself to be exercised. To use Aristotle's example, if the art of ship-building were in the wood, then ships would come into being without an external agent or an external end, i.e., they would come to be *naturally*. But a craft, in fact, is not in the thing it makes and, thereby, *falls short of, while approximating* natural final causality. Surprisingly, Broadie herself recognizes that her considerations "may set us wondering whether the analogy's true direction is not the reverse of what it seems" (403), since it is the natural activity of organisms that can help us understand the "end-directed automation" of craft and not the other way around (403).

59   M.R. Johnson suggests that what is comparable to the building art being present in the wood is 'spontaneous generation' (2012, 118), i.e., Aristotle's view that certain living things are generated directly out of matter and not by a parent possessing the same form. But what Aristotle explicitly compares to the building art being present in the wood is *nature*

That the living thing as thus containing within itself its own principle and end is the paradigm of substance for Aristotle and that artifacts, in contrast, are not, strictly speaking, substances, is a point that has been forcefully argued by A. Kosman. As he expresses the point, this is because in genuine substance there can be "no separation between what is a substance and what a substance is" (2013, 88). I suggest expressing the point differently: in genuine substance there can be no separation between what a substance is and *what it is for*. The *telos is* the form, as Aristotle explicitly maintains in the case of living things: the soul of a living thing is equally its *eidos* and its *telos* (*An.* 415b15), something that clearly cannot be said of an artifact like the bed. It is significant in this context that Aristotle, in criticizing Democritus for explaining all the operations of nature as results of material necessity (*GA* v.789b2–4), does not deny that Democritus speaks of 'form' as well, but, rather, charges him with misinterpreting form in equating it with mere 'configuration' (σχῆμα) or 'color' (χρῶμα). Material necessity can, of itself, produce various configurations of atoms or parts, but the form of a living thing is not a certain configuration or shape, but rather *its function* (τὸ ἑαυτῆς ἔργον, *PA* 641a2). A dead hand has the same configuration or shape as a living hand and, yet, is a hand only equivocally.

Here, we can return to the notion of ἐντελέχεια. Blair (1992) has suggested understanding this term to mean 'having the end within' (see also von Fritz 1938, 66), an understanding Aristotle himself implies at *Metaphysics* 1050a21–23 in making the connection there between *telos* and ἐντελέχεια. M.R. Johnson has also rightly noted the importance of the ἐν- prefix of both this term and the term ἐνέργεια, along with its loss in the usual translations of 'activity' and 'actuality': in both terms, the prefix stresses the *internality* of the function or end (2005, 90; see entire discussion on 85–90). In a passage from the *Physics* in which Aristotle is explaining the different senses of ἐν, he indeed gives the 'for-the-sake-of-which' as one sense (ἔτι ὡς ἐν τῷ ἀγαθῷ καὶ ὅλως ἐν τῷ τέλει. τοῦτο δ'ἐστὶ τὸ οὗ ἕνεκα, 210a22–23). Very much worth noting in this context is the attempt of W.E. Ritter, in an article from 1932 published in *The Quarterly Review*

---

and, thus, natural generation, e.g., a human being producing a human being. It might seem that natural reproduction is, instead, comparable to the builder building the house, since, in both cases, we appear to have the transfer of the form from one thing to another thing, i.e., from the building art in the builder to the wood and from one human being to another. But it is clear that, for Aristotle, a human being producing another human being is an example of a thing having its source of motion *in itself*: a human *reproduces itself* and this is what makes it *natural* (see Mansion 1945, 238 and 260–261). The point of the example is that houses would be natural if the art of building were in the wood, *not* because, in this case, they would generate spontaneously, but because, in this case, they would be capable of *reproducing themselves*.

166   GONZALEZ

of Biology, to interpret the notion of ἐντελέχεια within a biological context. In-sisting that the word *telos*, as implied in ἐντελέχεια, should be understood as more akin to wholeness and completeness than to purpose and favoring, for this reason, Ross's translation of ἐντελέχεια as 'complete reality,' Ritter inter-prets ἐντελέχεια as expressing the complete wholeness of an organism and, therefore, equates the rejection of Aristotelian teleology with the failure to see this phenomenon:[60]

> The teleology for which Aristotle is roundly condemned by many pres-ent-day biologists he was not at all or very slightly guilty of. On the other hand those who condemn the teleology which he did hold, that of com-pleted wholeness as essential to the adequate interpretation of any phe-nomena of nature whatever, are in so far not only failing, themselves, in reaching such interpretation, but are tacitly denying the possibility of it. (1932, 382; for how this 'completed wholeness' is understood, see espe-cially 390)

While Ritter neglects the aspect of internal directedness I wish to highlight here, he does emphasize the role of *genesis towards the telos* as essential to the wholeness in question. What is, in any case, now easy to see is why the term ἐντελέχεια would naturally suggest itself to Aristotle as the one appropriate for describing the being of the soul of the living thing, the being-at-work or activ-ity (ἐνέργεια) of the living thing, which alone has its end within itself (ἐντελέχεια) and, thereby, grants the living thing its completeness and wholeness. This is true of natural substance in general, for which the form and the end are the same,[61] but not of artifacts.[62] If one imagines a hierarchical continuum with, at

---

60   Though they do not cite Ritter, Miller and Miller (2005) clearly share his understanding of ἐντελέχεια.

61   "And since nature is twofold, the matter and the form, of which the latter is the end, and since all the rest is for the sake of the end, the form must be the cause in the sense of that for the sake of which" (*Phys.* 199a30–32, Hardie and Gaye, trs. 2014). As Mansion succinctly expresses the essence of Aristotle's teleology: "La nature agit en vue d'une fin et cette fin, c'est la nature elle-même: ces termes peuvent résumer la doctrine d'Aristote relative à la finalité naturelle" (1945, 251–2).

62   Miller and Miller (2005), in contrast, do not appear to make a fundamental ontological distinction between livings things and artifacts, and nowhere suggest that the latter are not truly *ousiai*. While they, at one point, acknowledge some ontological distinctions between organisms and artifacts (53), they insist that despite these differences "the same dynamic, holistic causal ontology that accounts for the existing and stability of artifacts (and resolves their basic *aporiai*) also accounts for the existing and persisting identity of organisms (and resolves the same *aporiai*)" (53). In explaining Aristotle's use of artifacts

FINAL CAUSALITY WITHOUT TELEOLOGY IN ARISTOTLE

the top, substances that are their own ends and, at the bottom, substances whose ends lie outside themselves, then one must locate the unmoved mover at the top and artifacts at the bottom.

To believe that all final causes are external and the products of an intelligent agent is to collapse this distinction between an organism and an artifact or machine since what distinguishes the former from the latter is an *internal* purposiveness or directedness. What is lost when the claim, "The bird builds a nest in order to lay its eggs," is reduced to the claim, "The bird builds a nest and then lays eggs," or when the claim "The carnivore has sharp teeth in order to tear its meat well," is reduced to the claim "The carnivore has sharp teeth and then can tear its meat well," what is lost, in short, when we eliminate the "in order to" of final causality, is what distinguishes a natural organism from a mechanism. This is why, for Aristotle, to reject final causality is simply *to destroy nature*. As he writes in critique of Empedocles: "But the person who asserts this does entirely away with nature and what exists by nature. For those things are natural which, *by a continuous* [συνεχῶς] *movement originated from an internal principle, arrive at some end*" (*Phys.* 199b14–17, Hardies and Gaye, trs. 2014). Essential to what is natural is precisely this movement from an internal principle towards an internal end. Aristotle repeats this criticism in *De Generatione et Corruptione* when he asserts, with a malicious allusion to the supposed title of Empedocles' poem, that Empedocles "says nothing about nature" (οὐδὲν ἄρα περὶ φύσεως λέγει, 333b18). Here, Aristotle explicitly identifies the nature of a thing with its good, in contrast to chance (ἀλλὰ μὴν καὶ τὸ εὖ τοῦτο καὶ τὸ ἀγαθόν, 333b19). If Empedocles, in not recognizing final causes, implicitly eliminates nature, modern philosophy, in rejecting final causes, does so explicitly. This is nowhere clearer than in the following claim of Descartes in his *Principia Philosophiae:*

> For clearly there are no principles of mechanics that do not also apply to physics of which it is a part or species; and the clock, composed of these or those gears so that it should indicate the hour, *is not any less natural* than the tree, arising from this or that seed so that it should bear such fruit. (1644, 4.203.307–308; my translation and emphasis)[63]

---

as examples, they suggest that they are simply less complex ontologically than organisms (39).

63 As Weiss observes, "The physicist's world order is one thing, the 'orderliness' which the teleological theory envisages is another. ... It must be maintained that the orderliness of nature which Aristotle had in view has not found and cannot find a satisfactory interpretation by means of the most perfect mechanism" (1948, 46).

The French edition even adds, after the first clause cited, that "all the things that are artificial are thereby natural" (1647, 480; my translation). If later modern philosophers are less radical in wanting to preserve a distinction here, they are, arguably, also less consistent, as we see especially in the case of Kant.[64]

The continuity of movement towards an end from within that Aristotle considers essential to a natural substance is, furthermore, what gives it the unity that allows it to be called a substance at all. Thus, in *Metaphysics* VII.16, Aristotle writes that the parts of animals exist in potency "when they are one [organism] and continuous by nature, but not brought together through force or fused together, since such a thing would be a deformation" (ἀλλ'ὅμως δυνάμει πάντ' ἔσται, ὅταν ᾖ ἓν καὶ συνεχὲς φύσει, ἀλλὰ μὴ βίᾳ ἢ συμφύσει. τὸ γὰρ τοιοῦτον πήρωσις, 1040b14–16, my translation). This claim, furthermore, can be seen as preparing the suggestion in the crucial following chapter, VII.17, that only natural substances count as substances: "Since some things are not substances, but those that are substances are composed according to nature and by nature, it would seem that nature itself is substance, being not an element but a principle" (ἐπεὶ δ'ἔνια οὐκ οὐσίαι τῶν πραγμάτων, ἀλλ'ὅσαι οὐσίαι, κατὰ φύσιν καὶ φύσει συνεστήκασι, φανείη ἂν [καὶ] αὕτη ἡ φύσις οὐσία, ἥ ἐστιν οὐ στοιχεῖον ἀλλ'ἀρχή, 1041b28–31, my translation). The implied reasoning is not hard to make out: something that is merely 'put together,' like a bed, lacks the continuity and unity required to count as a substance, while such continuity or unity is precisely what characterizes what exists by nature and the living organism, in particular, in its inner directness towards an end. Note the extraordinary implication: teleology is here ontology, that is, it is the continuous internal movement towards an end that gives a natural substance the unity that not only makes it a substance but makes it the only true substance. As Gotthelf, considering the same passages from the *Metaphysics,* puts the point: "the very

---

64   A pivotal figure here is indeed Kant. For an excellent volume on Kant's relation to biology, see Marques (2012). While Kant rejects Descartes's identification of the organism with a mechanism (see the *Kritik der Urtheilskraft*, AK V, 374–375) and recognizes that understanding the former requires talk of nature acting for an end, he considers this final causality in nature to be, in principle, *unknowable* and this because he shares two of Descartes's assumptions: first, that science can only recognize material and mechanistic causes and, two, that final causality, as implying an intelligent designer, is, in principle, *supernatural.* The result is summed up well by one contributor to the cited volume, Zöller: "In Kant's view, on the contrary, the following would need to be said about the life sciences: to the extent that they have to do with life, they are not sciences and, to the extent that they are sciences, they have nothing to do with life. In the Kantian perspective, the life sciences would thus be an absurdity [*ein Unding*]" (2012, 107; my translation). One can, therefore, say that if Kant saves life as a phenomenon against Descartes, he does so only to render it, in principle, unknowable.

FINAL CAUSALITY WITHOUT TELEOLOGY IN ARISTOTLE 169

same irreducibility that underwrites Aristotle's natural teleology underwrites his theory of substance" (250). But, then, Empedocles can be accused of destroying not only nature, but substance itself.[65]

We must again remind ourselves that what is lost here has nothing to do with intentionality or intelligent design. The organism does not need to be directed by some intelligent agent because it has its own inherent directedness. For Aristotle, what generates man is not God nor a conjunction of material processes; instead, as he repeatedly asserts, it is man that generates man.[66] This seeming triviality is in fact the by-no-means-uncontroversial ontological claim that an animal like man is its own source of motion and its own end and

---

65 It is a peculiar and unfortunate feature of the book by Furth that, while insisting that Aristotle's metaphysics was informed by his biology and that "the actual Aristotelean substances are pre-eminently the biological objects, living things" (see 1988, 67–68; also 171) and while also recognizing as an important feature of living things that "they are constantly and at all levels engaged in natural processes and routines that are *future-oriented*, i.e., ones that are aimed at natural *telê*, 'completions'" (73), it nevertheless says practically nothing of final causality. While what Furth calls the 'teleological aspect' is acknowledged in his discussion of *De Anima* (147), it is simply ignored when, in the chapter "Bio-Metaphysics," he proceeds to draw lessons for metaphysics from the biology (163–173), and this even though he will later note that the subject matter of *Metaphysics* VIII.2, so essential to the understanding of substance, is *the same as* that of *De Anima* 2.1–5 (251). He does acknowledge at the start of the next chapter that the lessons he has drawn "are by no means exhaustive of the metaphysical morals derivable from the biology" (175), but why would he leave out the teleological aspect in particular, given that he, at least once, recognizes the importance of the 'for-the-sake-of' in understanding substance (230)? As he notes at one point, the type of form that Aristotle takes to be operative in nature must be "a powerful *integrative agency* that is the *cause* of unity" (243), but, as he does not note, the form can exert this power only *as end*. When, towards the end of the book, Furth remarks that the metaphysical question that has concerned him, i.e., "Why are there material individuals?" can be understood as asking "To what end?", he says that "we have touched upon this aspect of the matter" but that "the main burden of the account thus far" has understood the question as asking instead "*what causal agencies must be at work in the world to bring it about?*" (276). The opposition here between "To what end?" and "By what causal agency?" with its implication that final causes are not causes, is itself revealing.

66 Γεννᾷ ὁ ἄνθρωπος ἄνθρωπον (*PA* 640a25–26; *Phys.* 193b8–9; 194b13). These three passages, together, reveal the different dimensions of this claim. In the first passage, the claim is made against Empedocles' attempt to attribute certain characteristics of the animal to what happens to it in the process of formation (the vertebrae of the backbone are explained through the fetus being twisted and, thereby, having its backbone broken into pieces). In the second passage, the claim is made in contrast to the fact that a bed does not beget a bed and, thus, in support of the distinction between nature and craft. In the last passage, the *sun* is added as a cause producing man in addition to man. Here, we see clearly that Aristotle's teleology is not incompatible with explanations in terms of material necessity.

therefore *not a product, whether of an intelligent designer or of mere material necessity.* As W.E. Ritter rightly notes, Aristotle "never proposed an explanatory theory of organisms that would make artificial products of them—as is really the case with the modern mechanistic theory of life" (1932, 388).

The conclusion, therefore, is that final causality in Aristotle should be understood primarily within the context of an ontology of life, where life is to be seen as paradigmatic for ontology period. This means that it is not to be understood within the context of what we have come to call 'teleology.' It is not a thesis about the aim or purpose of natural substances, but, rather, a thesis about the *being* of those living things that, for Aristotle, were the paradigm of substance: substances that, on the one hand, are neither simply products of material processes nor products of intelligent design—indeed, are not products at all—substances which, on the other hand, are characterized by a certain directedness that is neither intentional nor intelligent.[67] Such a "sober conception of finality," as Mansion has called it (1945, 255), is neither anachronistic nor outdated; on the contrary, it can be judged a contemporary philosophical challenge.

In an important but easily overlooked article published in 1948 in the *Classical Quarterly*, Helene Weiss, who was a student of Martin Heidegger and the author of a book on causality and luck in Aristotle, compares Aristotle's teleology to the theory of the great theoretician of biology Jakob von Uexküll, whose work merits more attention today. Von Uexküll rejected the mechanistic science of living nature because, while he did not ignore but, rather, made use of its important contributions, he saw it as missing what he considered the central phenomenon of life: what he called *plannedness, Planmässigkeit* (Weiss, 48).[68] This notion does not imply, for von Uexküll, any planning intelligence and therefore cannot be identified with an aim, but, on the contrary, is an attempt to express the self-ordering and agency (without thought) that appear to characterize life, especially as shown by the experiments of another great biologist Hans Driesch: in one of his experiments, for example, Driesch removed

---

67   I agree with Gotthelf that "Aristotelian teleology, in fact, is neither vitalist and mystical, nor 'as if' and mechanical. The notion of an irreducible potential for form supplies the proper content to the awareness that, for Aristotle, organic development is actually direc*tive,* without implying ... that it is direc*ted*" (2012, 28). However, I disagree that this teleology, for Aristotle, is an *empirical* thesis. If what I argue here is at all correct, then it is simply false that "There is nothing in the fundamentals of Aristotle's philosophy, and nothing in his philosophical or scientific method, which would prohibit the adoption of the reducibility thesis, should the scientific evidence warrant it" (28). When Aristotle claims that the rival Empedoclean view *destroys nature*, he obviously is saying more than that it is empirically false.

68   For more on this, see Brentari (2015, 57–63).

FINAL CAUSALITY WITHOUT TELEOLOGY IN ARISTOTLE   171

from an animal embryo the material that would normally be used to develop a determinate organ or limb, only to see the embryo subsequently produce the same organ or limb by transforming some other material (Weiss, 49). Von Uexküll also saw this phenomenon of a plan as implying the wholeness or completeness of the organism; indeed, he speaks of 'perfection' (Weiss, 53). After suggesting that, with these notions of the plan and perfection, von Uexküll is expressing what Aristotle expressed with the word *telos* and, in particular, with that possessing-the-*telos*-in-itself that he called ἐνέργεια, in the important passage from *Metaphysics* IX, 1048b18–36, and ἐντελέχεια elsewhere (54), Weiss makes what I judge to be the crucial point: "Teleology does not so much mean the striving after some aim as it means the phenomenon that natural processes are directed from a whole (*Ganzheit*)" (55). It is this 'directedness from a whole" that defines the being of the living substance and that can be identified neither with the blind chance of material causation nor with intelligent agency. Weiss thus sees both Aristotle and von Uexküll as acknowledging "a third and intermediary ontological region:"

> The causation found in nature is *sui generis*. A *plan* is at work, as Uexküll puts it, or, in Aristotle's words, a causing for the sake of the τέλος, but without νοῦς. The understanding of this third region causes difficulties to the modern mind. (57)

This comment captures precisely what is at stake. While the modern mind thinks in terms of the opposition between blind material determination and intelligent design, Aristotle's defense of final causes is a defense of nature as a third region and such a defense, once distinguished from a rightly rejected and outdated 'teleology,' has lost none of its philosophical relevance.[69] It is not only philosophers who recognize this. No less a figure than the Nobel Prize winning biophysicist Max Delbrück, after suggesting that Aristotle himself deserves a posthumously awarded Nobel Prize for his discovery of the principle behind DNA,[70] attributes the lack of appreciation for Aristotle among most scientists to "our having been blinded for 300 years by the Newtonian view of the world" (55).[71] Words in a similar vein written by the great microbiologist Carl Woese

---

69   The important article of Miller and Miller (2005) illustrates this contemporary relevance in detail, even if not emphasizing the distinction between artifacts and living organisms. See also Bradie and Miller (1984, 143–144).

70   For assessments of this claim, see Furth (1988, 119–120n26), and Johnson (2012, 141).

71   Or the Galilean view: "The triumph of Galilean thought meant that the primary model for understanding the world was no longer, as it had been for Aristotle, that of the organism, but rather that of the machine" (Chase 2011, 516).

are perhaps even more significant because, as far as I have been able to determine, Woese knew nothing of Aristotle. In 2004, Woese published in *Microbiology and Molecular Biology Reviews* a manifesto with the modest title, "A New Biology for a New Century." Here, he rails against "a biology that operates from an engineering perspective, a biology that has no genuine guiding vision!," a biology that has become no more than "an engineering discipline," that seeks to change the living world without understanding it and that is, therefore, a danger to society (2004, 173). Aristotle's defense of final causes will be of no interest to the biological engineers, though it is also, I have argued, not incompatible with their work. But I suggest, in conclusion, and in full modesty and in full recognition of my ignorance of such a complex topic, that, for the reasons given here, Aristotle's defense of final causes should be of much interest to those who seek to understand life and, thus, to the new biology envisioned by Carl Woese.[72]

---

72   I wish to acknowledge the very helpful written comments of M.R. Johnson, from all of which the present paper has profited; even where I have stubbornly resisted some suggestions, they have helped me make my position clearer. I also owe a debt to the thoughtful remarks of my commentator for the Boston Area Colloquium in Ancient Philosophy, Brian Julian, as well as to the many challenging questions of the audience at Assumption College. I presented an earlier version of this paper at the Federal University of Rio de Janeiro in 2017 and am grateful for the discussion there in helping me develop the paper further.

COLLOQUIUM 5

Commentary on Gonzalez

Brian Julian
Boston College

Abstract

This commentary argues that, in contrast to the view of Professor Gonzalez, Aristotle's account of final causation is not very helpful for addressing contemporary concerns. Aristotle presents it as a type of cause, but, when one considers Aristotle's distinction between facts and explanations, a final cause is better viewed as simply a fact. It is true *that* organisms show an internal directedness towards an end, but one can still ask *why* this is the case. Because of its limitations, Aristotle's account of final causes is not a third ontological region between materialism and intelligent design, but its lack of explanation leaves it open to attack from either side.

Keywords

Aristotle – final cause – fact – explanation – intelligent design

This paper by Professor Gonzalez is quite helpful in illuminating Aristotle's account of final causation. He argues that, when Aristotle makes use of final causes, he is discussing the being of living organisms. To be living is to have an internal directedness towards an end and this directedness is what makes the living thing a unified substance. If we ignore this directedness, then we end up losing the phenomenon of life and are left simply with machines. Professor Gonzalez reminds us that final causes are different from efficient causes, so we should not think in terms of "backward causation," where the end is spurring on the development of the organism by reaching back in time, as an intention allows a housebuilder to start work by envisioning the future. Nor are final causes to be overruled by the material cause, since material necessity is compatible with an explanation in terms of ends.

All of this is a fruitful way to think about Aristotle. My own thinking was especially stirred by the distancing of final causation from efficient causes and the identification of it with the phenomenon of being internally directed. In

© KONINKLIJKE BRILL NV, LEIDEN, 2020 | DOI:10.1163/22134417-00351P15

174   JULIAN

particular, this led me in the opposite direction from Professor Gonzalez. He sees in Aristotle's account its potential uses, whereas I have been struck by its limits. I am wondering whether a final cause that is stripped of any efficient causality has any explanatory power left. In order to explore this issue, I am going to assume in what follows that Professor Gonzalez is correct in the description of Aristotle that I just outlined. What I will draw attention to is the potential limits of Aristotle's account of final causes and, in turn, the limited help that Aristotle could supply in addressing contemporary questions.

To understand the potential limits of Aristotle's account of final causation, it is necessary, first, to recall the point of the four causes. As he states at the beginning of the account of causes in *Physics* II.3 (194b17–20, Irwin and Fine, trs. 1996), "our inquiry aims at knowledge; and we think we know something only when we find the reason why (τὸ διὰ τί) it is so, i.e., when we find its primary cause (αἰτίαν)." And, as he reminds us elsewhere, such as in *De Anima* II.2 (413a13–16), the account that shows the cause (τὴν αἰτίαν) is preferable to one that only states the that or the fact (τὸ ὅτι). Given this distinction between a fact that something is the case and the cause that shows the reason why, I would argue that Aristotle's final cause is really not a cause at all. It is simply a fact about natural organisms and artifacts, because it is not really explaining anything.

Let me illustrate this by telling a story about a hypothetical exchange between Empedocles and Aristotle. Suppose that Empedocles wrote a book explaining the formation of clouds, a treatise he titled *The Silent Heavens*. In this book, he explains how seedling clouds are delicate things and are easily destroyed by sound waves. Many seedling clouds do not survive their infancy due to the sounds in the sky, but those that do survive grow larger and fluffier, eventually absorbing all the sounds and allowing more clouds to grow. Thus, once the heavens are silenced, a gray, cloudy sky may appear. Now, this is a very interesting theory, but Aristotle comes along and points out that Empedocles' theory is inadequate. It has ignored a common phenomenon: thunder. Thunder, as everyone knows, is a noise in the clouds, so, clearly, clouds do not absorb all the sounds and make the heavens silent.

But as Aristotle also argues in *Posterior Analytics* (II.10, 94a7–9, Barnes, tr. 1993), it is not adequate simply to say that "thunder is noise in the clouds," since it is only to state the "conclusion of the demonstration of what it is." It is only to state the fact *that* thunder is, not to explain it. In order to explain why thunder happens, one needs to state that it is "a noise of fire being extinguished in the clouds" (*APo.* II.10, 94a5, Barnes, tr. 1993). Thunder is a noise in the clouds due to the extinguishing of fire there. In this imaginary exchange, then,

COMMENTARY ON GONZALEZ   175

Empedocles is actually two steps removed from a good account of clouds, because not only has he failed to explain thunder, but he failed to even mention
it.

The same thing is also happening in the real exchange between Empedocles
and Aristotle over final causes in nature, except this time neither thinker is going as far as he should. In explaining the coming to be of living organisms,
Empedocles and the other advocates of necessity ignored a crucial feature: organisms develop towards ends. In doing so, these thinkers were eliminating the
phenomenon of life and of nature. Their mistake, however, was not that this is
something they tried to explain and failed, but that it is a phenomenon they
did not notice at all. They were trying to explain how an animal can obtain a
good result, such as having sharp teeth in the front or being a calf-headed calf
(*Phys.* II.8, 198b23–32), not why there is a *directedness* towards something
good. Aristotle is right to identify the whole phenomenon that organisms have
an internal motion towards an end that is good, but it can very reasonably be
asked why it is that organisms display this striking feature. Since Aristotle does
not offer an explanation for this fact, a more sophisticated materialist than
Empedocles could potentially offer an explanation that no longer requires
mentioning it.

Aristotle fares no better when addressing the proponent of design. As Professor Gonzalez notes, Aristotle argues against a certain kind of intelligence in
nature at the end of *Physics* II.8. In this passage, Aristotle states that neither
craft nor nature deliberates, but "the for-the-sake-of is inherent in" both
(199b30; Gonzalez 163). If one could implant the craft into its material—put
the art of shipbuilding into the wood—then the crafted product would eventually materialize. The end, the ship, would come about on its own just as with
the development of a living being. Thus, someone should not be looking for an
intelligent agent to be directing the development of a natural organism towards the end, but "it is absurd [for them] to think that [it] is not coming to be
for the sake of something if they do not see the moving cause deliberating"
(199b26–28; Gonzalez 163). Professor Gonzalez takes this passage as an Aristotelian argument against an intelligent designer:

> the postulate of an intelligent designer assumes the completely anti-Aris-
> totelian thesis that every substance is in itself no more than a 'heap,' like
> the pile of wood lying on the lot before the construction of the house,
> that therefore needs an intelligent designer to give it form and purpose.
> (Gonzalez 135)

I would contend that this is actually not an argument against an intelligent designer, but against an intelligent builder. This matters, because it means that Aristotle is leaving unexplained the design-like elements that most need explanation.

Suppose I were standing next to a shipbuilder and each of us had a pile of wood nearby. Someone with magical powers then takes the shipbuilding craft that is in each of us and implants it into our piles of wood. Our ships then start to grow from an internal principle in the wood, and eventually there would be one ship—and one piece of sculpture that vaguely resembles a ship. That is, there is a difference between a craftsperson and an ignoramus. And, importantly, there is a very interesting account to be given as to why the craft of the shipbuilder is different from the "craft" in me—an account that Aristotle does not mention. David Bostock notes this piece of the craft analogy that Aristotle omits, when he comments on the claim that craft does not deliberate:

> Aristotle is apparently thinking that, once you have learnt how to make something, you no longer have to plan how to do it. But one will of course object that in nature there is neither planning *nor* a learning process. (Waterfield tr., and Bostock, ed. 1996, 245)

Aristotle is saying that, while a craft needs a deliberative agent to move the material towards the end product, nature does not need such an agent to assist in moving the natural thing towards its goal. But he leaves out the fact that we can and should give an account of why the craftsperson has a principle that is able to move material towards a good, organized product. Even if there is no need for a deliberative agent to move the organism along from seed to maturity—no need for an intelligent builder—it still makes sense to ask why natural things move towards something good rather than towards chaos, to ask whether they need an intelligent architect or programmer. Aristotle simply does not raise this question. As in the discussion with Empedocles, Aristotle's argument here is against the need for a very limited kind of intelligence in nature, but he leaves the discussion wide open for other kinds of intelligent design to be the explanation for the phenomenon observed.

Aristotle's account of final causation, then, is limited. It is only stating a fact rather than offering an explanation and this, in turn, limits its helpfulness in addressing contemporary concerns. Professor Gonzalez cites Helene Weiss approvingly when she suggests that Aristotle's account could be a third ontological region between intelligent design and strict materialism, one that preserves the "phenomenon that natural processes are directed from a whole" (Gonzalez 171) or, as Professor Gonzalez puts it, "the phenomenon of life" (Gonzalez 170).

My worry is that this account is not really a third, distinct region. It only looks like one because it is unexplained. It seems perfectly appropriate for a materialist to explain why life is a phenomenon we do not have to mention, why only machines exist. It also seems appropriate for a proponent of design to explain how the fact of directedness in organisms is evidence for their position, since they can explain why it happens. Nor is the middle position helped by stating that the fact in question concerns the *being* of an organism. One could easily make the case that free-willishness is a part of the being of humans, that it is intrinsic to the idea of a human that we behave as though we have free will. But of course, this answer will satisfy no one who wants an *explanation* of free will or to know whether or not humans *actually* have it.

In conclusion, I would like to thank Professor Gonzalez for writing a stimulating paper that has forced me to think about Aristotle's account of final causation in a way I had not before. Even if a final cause turns out not to be a full explanation, it is, nevertheless, an important phenomenon to consider.

COLLOQUIUM 5

Gonzalez/Julian Bibliography

Baghdassarian, F. 2016. *La question du divin chez Aristote: Discours sur les dieux et science du principe.* Louvain-la-Neuve: Peeters.

Balme, D.M. 1972. *Aristotle's* De Partibus Animalium I *and* De Generatione Animalium I [*with passages from II.1–3.* Oxford: Clarendon Press.

Balme, D.M. 1980. Aristotle's Biology was not Essentialist. *Archiv für Geschichte der Philosophie* 62:1–12.

Balme, D.M. 1987. Teleology and necessity. In *Philosophical Issues in Aristotle's Biology,* eds. A. Gotthelf and J.G. Lennox, 275–285. Cambridge, UK: Cambridge University Press.

Barnes, J., tr. 1993. *Aristotle, Posterior Analytics.* 2nd ed. Oxford: Clarendon Press.

Blair, G.A. 1992. Energeia *and* Entelecheia: 'Act' in Aristotle. Ottawa: University of Ottawa Press.

Bradie, M., and F.D. Miller, Jr. 1984. Teleology and Natural Necessity in Aristotle. *History of Philosophy Quarterly* 1.2:133–146.

Brentari, C. 2015. *Jacob von Uexküll: The Discovery of the Umwelt between Biosemiotics and Theoretical Biology.* Dordrecht: Springer.

Broadie, S. 1990. Nature and Craft in Aristotelian Teleology. In *Biologie, logique et métaphysique chez Aristote: acts du Séminaire CNRS-NSF,* eds. D. Devereux and P. Pelligrin, 389–403. Paris: Editions du centre national de la recherche scientifique.

Byrne, C. 2018. *Aristotle's Science of Matter and Motion.* Toronto: University of Toronto Press.

Charles, D. 2012. Teleological Causation. In *The Oxford Handbook of Aristotle,* ed. C. Shields, 227–266. Oxford: Oxford University Press.

Chase, M. 2011. Teleology and Final Causation in Aristotle and in Contemporary Science. *Dialogue* 50:511–536.

Cooper, J.M. 1985. Hypothetical Necessity. In *Aristotle on Nature and Living Things: Philosophical and Historical Studies*, ed. A. Gotthelf, 151–167. Pittsburgh: Mathesis.

Delbrück, M. 1971. "Aristotle—totle-totle." In *Of Microbes and Life*, eds. J. Monod and E. Borek, 50–55. New York: Columbia University Press.

Delcomminette, S. 2018. *Aristote et la nécessité.* Paris: j. Vrin.

Descartes, R. 1644. *Principia Philosophiae.* Amsterdam: apud Ludovicum Elzevitum.

Descartes, R. 1647. *Les Principes de la Philosophie, escrits en latin par René Descartes, et traduits en François par un de ses amis* [*l'abbé Picot*]. Paris: H. Le Gras.

Furth, M. 1988. *Substance, Form and Psyche: An Aristotelian Metaphysics.* Cambridge, UK: Cambridge University Press.

Ghiselin, M. 1994. Darwin's Language may Seem Teleological, but his Thinking is Another Matter. *Biology and Philosophy* 9:489–92.

Gonzalez, F.J. 2019. Being as Activity: A Defense of the Importance of *Metaphysics* 1048b18–30 for Aristotle's Ontology. *Oxford Studies in Ancient Philosophy* 56:123–191.

Gotthelf, A. 2012. *Teleology, First Principles, and Scientific Method in Aristotle's Biology.* Oxford: Oxford University Press.

Gotthelf, A. and M. Leunissen. 2012. What's Teleology Got to Do with It? A Reinterpretation of Aristotle's *Generation of Animals* v. In Gotthelf 2012, 117–142.

Gourinat, J.-B. 2015. Les limites du finalisme chez Aristote et Théophraste. In *La Métaphysique de Théophraste: Principes et Apories,* eds. A. Jaulin and D. Lefebure, 147–177. Louvain-la-Neuve: Peeters.

Hankinson, R.J. 1995. Philosophy of Science. In *The Cambridge Companion to Aristotle,* ed. J. Barnes, 140–167. Cambridge, UK: Cambridge University Press.

Hull, D. 1982. Philosophy and Biology. In *Philosophy of Science,* Contemporary Philosophy: A New Survey 2, ed. G. Fløistad, 280–316. Hague: Nijhoff.

Irwin, T., and G. Fine, trs. 1996. *Aristotle: Introductory Readings.* Indianapolis: Hackett Publishing Company.

Johnson, C. 2015. *Darwin's Dice: the Idea of Chance in the Thought of Charles Darwin.* Oxford: Oxford University Press.

Johnson, M.R. 2005. *Aristotle on Teleology.* Oxford: Oxford University Press.

Johnson, M.R. 2012. The Medical Background of Aristotle's Theory of Nature and Spontaneity. *Proceedings of the Boston Area Colloquium in Ancient Philosophy* 27:105–152.

Johnson, M.R. 2013. Nature, Spontaneity and Voluntary Action in Lucretius. In *Lucretius: Poetry, Philosophy, Science,* Daryn Lehoux, A.D. Morrison, and Alison Sharrock, eds. 99–130. Oxford: Oxford University Press.

Johnson, M.R. 2017. Aristotelian Mechanistic Explanation. In *Teleology in the Ancient World,* ed. J. Rocca, 125–150. Cambridge, UK: Cambridge University Press.

Kahn, C. 1985. The Place of the Prime Mover in Aristotle's Teleology. In *Aristotle on Nature and Living Things: Philosophical and Historical Studies,* ed. A. Gotthelf, 183–205. Pittsburgh: Mathesis.

Kosman, A. 2013. *The Activity of Being: An Essay on Aristotle's Ontology.* Cambridge, MA: Harvard University Press.

Kullmann, W. 1979. *Die Teleologie in der aristotelischen Biologie: Aristoteles als Zoologe, Embryologe und Genetiker.* Heidelberg: Carl Winter.

Kullmann, W. 1985. Different Concepts of the Final Cause in Aristotle. In *Aristotle on Nature and Living Things: Philosophical and Historical Studies,* ed. A. Gotthelf, 169–175. Pittsburgh: Mathesis.

Le Blond, J.-M, tr. 1995. *Parties des animaux, Livre I.* Paris: Flammarion.

Lennox, J.G. 1993, Darwin *was* a Teleologist. *Biology and Philosophy* 8:409–421.

Leroi, A.M. 2014. *The Lagoon: How Aristotle Invented Science.* New York: Viking.

Leunissen, M. 2010. *Explanation and Teleology in Aristotle's Science of Nature.* Cambridge, UK: Cambridge University Press.

Mansion, A. 1945. *Introduction à la Physique Aristotélicienne.* Deuxième edition, revue et augmentée. Paris: J. Vrin.

Marques, Ubirajara Rancan de Azevedo. 2012. *Kant e a Biologia.* São Paulo: Barcarolla.

Meyer, S. 1992. Aristotle, Teleology, and Reduction. *Philosophical Review* 101:791–825.

Miller, A.E., and M.G. Miller. 2005. Aristotle's *Metaphysics* as the Ontology of Being-Alive and its Relevance Today. *Proceedings of the Boston Area Colloquium in Ancient Philosophy* 20:1–107.

Mirus, C.V. 2004. The Metaphysical Roots of Aristotle's Teleology. *The Review of Metaphysics* 57.4:699–724.

Monod, J. 1970. *Le Hasard et la Nécessité. Essai sur la philosophie naturelle de la biologie moderne.* Paris: Éditions du Seuil.

Morel, P.-M. 2016. 'La Nature ne fait rien en vain': Sur la causalité finale dans la *Locomotion des animaux* d'Aristote. *Philosophie antique* 16:9–30.

Ogle, W., tr. 1882. *Aristotle on the Parts of Animals.* London: Kegan Paul, Trench and CO.

O'Rourke, F. 2004. Aristotle and the Metaphysics of Evolution. *Review of Metaphysics* 58.1:3–59.

Patočka, J. 2011. *Aristotle, ses Devanciers, ses Successeurs,* tr. E. Abrams. Paris: J. Vrin.

Pellegrin, A., tr. 2011. *Aristote: Les Parties des animaux.* Paris: Flammarion.

Ritter, E. 1932. Why Aristotle Invented the Word *Entelecheia. The Quarterly Review of Biology* 7.4:377–404.

Sedley, D. 2010. Teleology, Aristotelian and Platonic. In *Being, Nature and Life in Aristotle,* eds. J.G. Lennox and R. Bolton, 5–29. Cambridge, UK: Cambridge University Press.

Short, T.L. 2002. Darwin's Concept of Final Cause: neither new nor trivial. *Biology and Philosophy* 17.3:323–340.

Sorabji, R. 1980. *Necessity, Cause and Blame: Perspectives on Aristotle's Theory.* Ithaca: Cornell University Press.

Von Fritz, K. 1938. *Philosophie und sprachlicher Ausdruck bei Demokrit, Platon und Aristoteles.* New York: Stechert.

Waterfield, R., tr. 1996. *Aristotle, Physics,* ed. with intro. and notes by D. Bostock. Oxford: Oxford University Press.

Weiss, H. 1948. Aristotle's Teleology and Uexküll's Theory of Living Nature. *The Classical Quarterly* 42.1/2:44–58.

Wieland, W. 1975. The Problem of Teleology. In *Articles on Aristotle,* vol. 1: *Science,* eds. J. Barnes, M. Schofield, and R. Sorabji, 1–141. London: Duckworth.

Woese, C.R. 2004. A New Biology for a New Century. *Microbiology and Molecular Biology Reviews* 68.2:173–186.

Zöller, G. 2012. Uma 'ciência para deuses' –as ciências da vida na perspectiva de Kant. In *Kant e a Biologia,* ed. Ubirajara Rancan de Azevedo Marques, 83–108. São Paulo: Barcarolla

Index of Names

Alexander Aphrodisias 6–8, 16, 25–26
Altham, Jimmy 35n8, 40
Ammonius Hermiae 2, 17, 18n19, 19n20, 20–21
Antiphon 79–80
Antisthenes 82–83
Aristippus 82
Aristophanes 80, 110n7, 111, 116, 124
Aristotle 1–27, 31–67, 73–102, 106–107, 109–111, 114n18, 133–177
Arius Didymus 92–93

Balme, D.M. 136n5, 137n6, 141n11, 150, 152n31, 162n54
Bernabé, Alberto 112n15, 113
Blair, George A. 165
Blumenthal, Henry 2, 5, 25n4, 26, 26n6
Bossier, Fernand 1–2, 24–26
Bostock, David 176
Brisson, Luc 108
Buchak, Lara 27
Burnyeat, Myles 26, 26n7

Chaeronean 116
Charles, David 40–41, 42n21, 54–56, 58, 58n40, 150n26, 150n27, 162n55, 164n58
Cicero, Marcus Tullius 108
Cornford, F.M. 105

Damascius 2, 15, 18, 26
Dante Alighieri 105, 117–119
Darwin, Charles 134–135n3, 153n34, 155, 155n36, 157n42
De Haas, Frans 3, 3n2, 5n5, 7n7
Democritus 79–80, 165
Descartes, René 167, 168n64
Dillon, John 3, 3n2, 14
Diogenes Laertius 23, 93–95
Driesch, Hans 170

Eco, Umberto 119
Empedocles 77n7, 142, 145, 147, 167, 169–170, 174–176
Epicharmus 77, 80
Epictetus 5, 7, 16

Euripides 78n10, 81–82, 83n26, 109, 110n6, 114, 117–119

Finamore, John 3, 3n2, 14, 22n23

Gotthelf, Allan 141–142n11, 143–144, 145n18, 149n24, 155n36, 156n40, 161n53, 168, 170n67
Griffin, Michael 7n8, 19–20, 22n23
Gual, Carlos García 109, 124

Hadot, Ilsetraut 1n1, 3, 3n2, 6–7, 15, 20
Heidegger, Martin 170
Heraclides 91, 95–96
Heraclitus 74, 78, 135n4
Hesiod 76n5, 110, 110n6, 115, 119, 124n11, 126
Hippocrates 7n7, 115
Hipponax 77
Homer 19, 76, 76n4, 82, 109, 111, 114, 117, 119, 121, 123, 124n11, 126
Huby, Patricia 1–2
Hume, David 33n5, 35, 62

Iamblichus 1n1, 3, 3n2, 5–7, 7n7, 9, 14–16, 116
Isocrates 82–85, 88

Johnson, M.R. 141n10, 150, 150n26, 154n35, 155n38, 156n41, 160n50, 164n59, 165, 171n70, 172n72

Kant 119, 168, 168n64
Kosman, A. 165

Lautner, Peter 1–2
Leunissen, M. 138–141, 143, 143n16, 149n24, 150n26, 151n28, 157n43, 158–160, 164n58
Loraux, Nicole 110
Luna, Christina 1–2

MacIntyre, Alasdair 126, 126n20, 126n21, 126n22
Mansion, Auguste 134n1, 134n2, 136n5, 142n12, 142n13, 151–152n30, 158n45, 161–162n53, 164–165n59, 166n61, 170
Mattéi, Jean-François 123, 123n5
McDowell, John 40, 43n22, 50n33

INDEX OF NAMES

Menedemus   96, 96n63
Michael of Ephesus   96, 96n62
Moss, Jessica   32–33, 33n4, 33n5, 34n6, 35,
  44, 46, 47n30, 48n31, 53n36, 54, 60n1, 60n2

Nabokov, Vladimir   112, 121
Nagel, Thomas   37, 43n22, 45, 45n24, 50
Nestle, Wilhelm   105
Nietzsche, Friedrich   105, 109, 114, 119, 129,
  132, 133, 140, 141

Olympiodorus   18–21, 112

Pausanias   117, 117n24, 119
Philoponus, John   4, 8, 16, 18, 21, 54n37
Phocylides   77, 80
Piccolomini, Francesco   1–2
Pindar   77, 81, 111, 115, 127
Pittendrigh, C.S.   160
Plato   4, 6, 7–13, 15–21, 23–24, 26, 73–75,
  78–79, 80n14, 82, 82n25, 84n36, 87, 89, 91,
  94n57, 94n58, 95–96, 101, 105–109, 110–116,
  119, 121–123, 125–126, 128–129, 135, 151n29,
  163n56
Plotinus   7n7, 13, 16, 116
Plutarch   96n63, 96n64, 116, 119
Porphyry   5, 7–9, 13, 19n20
Priscian of Lydia   1–2, 3n2, 6–8, 14–15, 19,
  25n4
Proclus   7n7, 13, 21, 116
Protagoras   78–80

Ritter, W.E.   165–166, 166n60, 170

Sachs, Joe   101, 101n3

Semonides   77
Simon   82
Simplicius   1–27
Sinhababu, Neil   36n10, 37–38, 49, 62, 62n4
Smith, Michael   36, 37n12, 41n20, 43n22
Sparshott, Francis   99, 99n1
Speusippus   91, 96
Steel, Carlos   1–6, 13–16, 24–25, 25n4, 26
Stobaeus   78n9, 94, 116

Themistius   7n7, 17–18, 19n20
Theognis   76n4, 76n5, 77, 81
Theophrastus   6, 7n7, 19, 91–93
Thrasymachus   78–80
Thucydides   79, 79n11, 80n17, 81n18, 84, 94

Urmson, J.O.   1–2, 4–5, 10, 13, 16, 24n3

Vallat, Phillipe   1, 3
Vernant, Jean-Pierre   106, 124n11, 124n12,
  128n30, 128n31
Virgil   112, 116n23, 117
von Uexküll, Jakob   170–171

Wallace, R.J.   31, 36n10, 37, 43n22, 49
Warburg, Aby   112
Weiss, Helen   155n37, 167n63, 170–171, 176
Wieland, W.   150
Williams, Bernard   32–33
Woese, Carl   171–172

Xenocrates   91, 95–96
Xenophanes   111
Xenophon   81n19, 82, 82n25, 84, 84n36, 110,
  151, 151n29